W9-BJR-889

PROMOTING THE GENERAL WELFARE

GOVERNMENT AND THE ECONOMY

LLOYD D. MUSOLF
University of California, Davis

with an introduction by
GEORGE McGOVERN

SCOTT, FORESMAN AMERICAN GOVERNMENT SERIES
Joseph C. Palamountain, Jr., Editor

SCOTT, FORESMAN AND COMPANY
Chicago • Atlanta • Dallas • Palo Alto • Fair Lawn, N.J.

To Berdyne

Library of Congress Catalog Card No. 65-17727
Copyright © 1965 by Scott, Foresman and Company
All Rights Reserved
Printed in the United States of America

The American system of government strikes a balance between unity and diversity. There is a unity to our system, but it is a unity which tolerates—indeed, requires for its vigor and viability—a broad diversity of institutions, processes, and participants. By organizing the analysis of the sprawling complexity of the American system into smaller, coherent, but interlocking units, the Scott, Foresman American Government Series attempts to reflect this pluralistic balance.

This approach, we believe, has several important advantages over the usual one-volume presentation of analytical and descriptive material. By giving the reader more manageable units, and by introducing him to the underlying and unifying strands of those units, it puts him in a better position to comprehend both the whole and its components. It should enable him to avoid the not-uncommon circumstance of viewing the American system as a morass of interminable and unconnected facts and descriptions.

This approach certainly permits us to tap the expertise and experience of distinguished scholars in the fields of their special competence. Each writes about his specialties, and none is forced to deal with subjects remote from his ken or heart for the sake of "completeness." The unity of the series rests on the interlocking of the various volumes and, in the general emphasis on policy and policy-making, on the method of analysis as opposed to simple description. It does not rest on a unity of approach. The authors vary in their values, their accents, and the questions they ask. To have attempted to impose unity in these matters would have been to water down the series, for the diversity of approach reflects the diversity of the system, its participants, and its commentators. But the final value of this series and its ultimate balance between unity and diversity rest, of course, in the use to which it is put by the reader.

Lloyd Musolf's contribution to the series is a major one. He brings clarity and order to an area that too often seems to be impossibly confused, sprawling, and amorphous. He relates to principles public policies that are highly pragmatic, and he analyzes with dispassion policies whose making was accompanied by loud ideological strife and inescapable conflicts of interest.

Joseph C. Palamountain, Jr., *Editor*

INTRODUCTION

"We the People of the United States, in order to form a more perfect union, establish justice, insure domestic tranquility, provide for the common defense, promote the general welfare, and secure the blessings of liberty to ourselves and our posterity, do ordain and establish this Constitution for the United States of America."

With the brevity and aptness of language which was characteristic of the framers of our Constitution, one sentence served fully to express their hopes and objectives. No phrase in that preamble is more pregnant with meaning and broader in scope than the words "promote the general welfare."

In this volume, Professor Musolf explores in depth the economic activities of the federal government as it moves in different ways and on different levels to promote the general welfare. For those who still believe as Thomas Jefferson did, that the least government is the best government, this book may be a revelation of the extent of federal influence. For those who recognize, as Jefferson did, that the conditions of society change, calling for new institutional adjustments, this book is a useful guide to the growing range of federal activities.

Professor Musolf traces from the colonial period of our history the economic role that first the states and then more and more the federal government has assumed. As he points out, the greatest friction with the British government in the eighteenth century involved the economic policies of King George III. The mercantile system penalized the colonies in order to protect trading monopolies, industries, and shipbuilders of Britain.

Yet no sooner had the thirteen colonies achieved their independence than they too sought, by government action, to promote the economic development of the infant nation. In fact, Alexander Hamilton, as the first Secretary of the Treasury, recommended a number of measures including tariffs, establishment of standards and inspection, premiums, subsidies, and public works to expand the federal government's direct role in the economy.

Professor Musolf's book very cogently demonstrates that while the great theoretical debate over limited government versus big government has been going on ever since the eighteenth century—in fact, Adam Smith's *Inquiry into the Nature and Causes of the Wealth of Nations* appeared the same year as our own Declaration of Independence—in actual fact, our government has moved steadily to fill various specific economic needs as they became evident.

The real American philosophy in promoting the general welfare as in other demands on government has been pragmatism. American statesmen have always asked first, "Will it work?" The great majority of Americans have rejected the notion that government control may be good in itself. Instead it has usually been adopted as a last resort to achieve specific economic or social goals. On that practical basis, our federal government has moved, step by step, to accept responsibility for the economic health of the country.

In no field is this more evident than practical politics. Whereas a century ago candidates ran for President primarily on their regional backgrounds and their personal reputations, today the biggest issue in almost any campaign is the economy. The President, as a symbol of the whole national government, is blamed if unemployment is high and is credited if the economy is booming. This is becoming one of the most decisive factors in politics today. As a member of the Senate I am very much aware of the unremitting pressure on the federal government to provide effectively for the economic welfare of American citizens.

As one of our greatest statesmen, Woodrow Wilson, put it, "Government cannot take its hands off business. Government must regulate business because that is the foundation of every other relationship. It is futile, therefore, to have the politicians take their hands off. They may blunder at the business. But they cannot give it up." That is a statement few contemporary politicians of either party would deny today.

Professor Musolf has divided government actions into four specific roles. He describes the government as promoter, regulator, buyer, and manager. Some critics might question the possibility of making clear distinctions in many cases—for instance, how do you draw the line in the Department of Agriculture between promoting farm products, regulating production, buying surpluses, and managing public lands? But on the whole the division is reasonable and provides valuable insights into the very different kinds of operations that the government undertakes.

Historically speaking, promotion is probably the oldest of government actions in the field of economics, going back not merely to our own colonial days, but to policies of European powers for centuries preceding. Trade and tariff policies were very early recognized as a prime and proper method for government intervention in the national economy.

Under this general heading, Professor Musolf deals with farm programs; shipbuilding subsidies; tax benefits to specific groups; financing of highways, airports, and harbors; government information services like the Census; weather reports; crop estimates and scientific research; loans to farmers, small business, exporters, and homeowners; insurance policies; educational and public health services; and veterans programs—to mention only a few.

Promotion can include direct monetary favors, generally known as subsidies, or it can be limited to regulation of a nature likely to encourage certain conditions, as in the field of labor relations or consumer protection.

Perhaps with his tongue in cheek, Professor Musolf points out that recipients of government subsidies are very modest in their claims, either denying the existence of subsidies altogether or pointing to all the similar benefits received by others. Although in practice we have left the laissez-faire era behind, in theory many are still paying it lip service.

Regulation has in many areas developed as a necessary follow-up to promotion. The railroads, for instance, were provided with sizeable land grants from the federal government to encourage settlement in the West. They were so successful and became such powerful forces on the economic scene in the West and Midwest that the demand rose for their regulation. My own State, South Dakota, was one of many that tried to regulate the railroads independently, but finally, when the Supreme Court ruled that state commissions had no power to regulate interstate commerce, the federal government created the Interstate Commerce Commission, principally to ride herd on the railroads. Today, the issue has come full circle. The railroad spokesmen complain that railroads are over-regulated with the effect of unfairly promoting other forms of transportation.

To conflicts of this sort, there are, by their very nature, no final solutions, only a continuing process of trial and error and adjustment. Certainly the more complex the pattern of business and regulation, the more difficult it becomes for the government to withdraw.

Alexis de Tocqueville, in his *Democracy in America*, described this process of increasing government involvement in terms that are as valid today as they were a century ago:

> It frequently happens that the members of the community promote the influence of the central power without intending it. Democratic ages are periods of experiment, innovation, and adventure. At such times there are always a multitude of men engaged in difficult or novel undertakings, which they follow alone, without caring for their fellow men. Such persons may be ready to admit, as a general principle, that the public authority ought not to interfere in private concerns; but, by an exception to that rule, each of them craves for its assistance in the particular

concern on which he is engaged, and seeks to draw upon the influence of the government for his own benefit, though he would restrict it on all other occasions. If a large number of men apply this particular exception to a great variety of different purposes, the sphere of the central power extends insensibly in all directions, although each of them wishes it to be circumscribed. Thus a democratic power increases its power simply by the fact of its permanence. Time is on its side; every incident befriends it; the passions of individuals unconsciously promote it; and it may be asserted that the older a democratic community is, the more centralized will its government become.

Although the promotional and regulatory activities of our government began with the Constitution itself, more recently the government has come to exert even more direct influence through its own purchasing power. As a consumer of goods and services produced by the private sector of the economy, the federal government is undoubtedly one of the biggest spenders in the country. Approximately $41 billion out of nearly $100 billion was budgeted in fiscal 1966 for government purchases from private enterprise. Another $25 billion was allotted to pay civilian and military personnel for their services to the government.

The biggest impact of this buying was in the military and aerospace fields, which consume more than half of all federal expenditures. There is also a heavy impact on research facilities since the federal government today finances about three quarters of all research work. Businesses producing this kind of equipment or know-how, and communities where these firms are located, are heavily dependent on the federal government. Everyone from the grocery store owner to the real estate agent follows government procurement policies as closely as brokers follow the stock market.

At a time of declining defense budgets, I have been particularly concerned that the federal government play a responsible role wherever possible in the process of conversion from defense work to civilian jobs.

It is no immediate help to a shipyard worker with seniority and know-how in shipbuilding to offer increased federal aid to primary and secondary education. Expansion of mass transit does not offer any job prospects for a nuclear technician no longer needed in stockpiling warheads for missiles. And a reduction in excise taxes will not assist a community which has gone into debt financing schools, roads, and sewers for people who are transferred away.

Therefore, I would favor an extension of federal government responsibility to coordinate these shifts and produce maximum benefit for the public with minimum dislocation of jobholders and communities.

Basically, in my judgment, Americans recognized in the early 1930's that the government had a positive, as well as negative, role to play in the economy. President Franklin D. Roosevelt pointed out the shift in 1937 when he said: "A new idea has come to dominate thought about government—the idea that the resources of a nation can be made to produce a far higher standard of living for the masses if only government is intelligent and energetic in giving the right directions to economic life."

Certainly, the Great Depression, the policies of Franklin D. Roosevelt, and the impact of the Second World War brought the government from the point of merely reacting to economic problems to deliberate long-term planning toward desired economic goals.

Professor Musolf has mustered impressive evidence to document his story. While students will undoubtedly find his background material very useful, the general reader will probably be most interested and enlightened by his perceptive analyses of such current controversies as the creation of the Communications Satellite Corporation, the 1962 Trade Expansion Act, and the awarding of certain defense contracts.

Of particular interest to me in following the trends is the interplay between various branches of the government—the President, the Congress, and the judiciary. In the first years of the Republic it was primarily the Supreme Court that set the pace. Chief Justice Marshall's deep-rooted support for a strong, central government was the basis for such decisions as *Marbury* v. *Madison*, establishing the role of the Supreme Court in judicial review; *McCulloch* v. *Maryland*, upholding federal power to issue bank charters, and denying a state's right to tax institutions of the federal government; and *Gibbons* v. *Ogden*, broadly defining the federal power to regulate interstate commerce. Marshall literally charted the course which strong executives like Presidents Jefferson, Jackson, and later Abraham Lincoln, followed in creating one nation from a federation of sovereign states.

Not until the mid-1950's did the Supreme Court again play such an important role in pioneering constitutional concepts before either the President or the Congress took the lead.

During the intervening decades the Congress and the President have alternately acted to support economic programs. But in recent years the growing complexity of the economy has made it very difficult for the Congress to act without executive guidance. As a result, even constitutional prerogatives of the Congress, such as establishing tariffs on foreign imports, have been delegated to experts in the executive branch. Thus the Congress has gradually assumed the role of overseer and defender rather than initiator of most efforts to promote the general welfare today.

Finally, a fact which may seem self-evident to Americans but must surely seem surprising to most foreigners—even admitting the heavy responsibilities which the federal government today wields in the economy and the increased pressure for specific new programs— most Americans still regard the federal government with suspicion if not with downright hostility. Most Americans do not want the federal government to supersede local and state governments, to "control education," or to engage in great new industrial enterprises of its own. Unlike the attitude of Britishers toward their government, for instance, there is deep-seated resistance in the United States against the national government undertaking any programs without clear evidence that neither individuals, business, or local government will do the job. Whether it be medicare or ending water pollution, federal programs have not won wide support until it was established that locally based efforts had failed. The federal government is the last, not the first choice.

It is ironic that this attitude still persists, but the fact should be a warning to all those who serve or aspire to serve in our national government. American officials in Washington probably work under closer scrutiny and more critical eyes than government administrators anywhere else in the world.

For this reason, among others, fear of the so-called tyranny of centralized government has doubtless been overplayed. The American people have sharp eyes and can be expected to judge their national leaders and programs today, as they have in the past, pragmatically, on the basis of performance.

Americans regard their own national government with somewhat the same suspicion as was expressed by a visitor to our country a century ago, Thomas Huxley, who wrote: "I cannot say that I am in the slightest degree impressed by your bigness, your material resources, as such. Size is not grandeur, and territory does not make a nation. The great issue, about which hangs the terror of overhanging fate, is what are you going to do with all these things."

This book tells the story of what the federal government has done in promoting, regulating, using, and managing these resources. This story is an important part not only of government activities today but also of our great and dynamic heritage. It is well and accurately told in this volume.

Senator George McGovern

TABLE OF CONTENTS

Forging
a
Relationship

Generations of Americans have been impressed with the sentiment credited to Thomas Jefferson that the least government is the best government. Meanwhile, they have erected a huge governmental complex to meet the demands of the industrial society that the United States has become. For a pragmatic people—as Americans are commonly thought to be—the seeming paradox is intriguing.

Undoubtedly, much of the explanation derives from the inconsistency of thought and action normal in all human affairs. Many of the actions in both foreign and domestic affairs of Jefferson as President scarcely accorded with the views of Jefferson as political philosopher. Yet, granting this human frailty, the least-government theme has undoubtedly had great emotional impact for Americans. Not all Americans react to it in the same way. Some would apply it very literally as the only recourse to prevent the ship of state from being driven onto the rocks of socialism. Others, perhaps a majority—judging from the laws on the statute books—would argue that "least" must continually be redefined in terms of changing circumstances; these would admit the value of the theme as an anchor to windward but see no grave danger at present. Still others would assert that even the present governmental vessel is not large or sturdy enough to ride out the storms raised by the industrial age.

Though Americans differ in their social philosophies, all would agree that today government has many new functions and that old functions have been transformed in size and complexity. No longer is it accurate to compare the national government to a night watchman or to a policeman keeping order, but the order-keeping function retains its vitality. It has, in fact, become larger and more sophisticated because government today does much more than punish; it tries to *prevent* the conditions that may lead to the use of the night stick. For example, the unrestricted use of such products of the industrial age as airplanes, radio, and television would inevitably lead to chaos. Here, punishment must yield to licensing as the principal remedy. In a sense, then, many of the newer functions of government are merely different, more positive ways of handling old problems. Yet, in the aggregate, the impact of problems spawned by the industrial age is so vast that we tend to think of the governmental responses to these problems as unrelated to the past. So many new forms of property, new occupations and professions, and new types of working relationships have been created over the past century that the thread of novelty is bound to run through virtually all governmental approaches to economic situations.

In popular thought the notion of novelty is sometimes carried so far as to lead to the inference that the practice of laissez faire ruled American economic affairs until a sudden change occurred in fairly recent times. This is vastly oversimplified history. Laissez faire, the doctrine opposing governmental interference in economic affairs beyond the minimum necessary to maintain peace and property rights, was never consistently applied to the American economy. Its status as an ideology for the business-dominated American society of the late nineteenth and early twentieth century is a different matter. Nevertheless, business' strong reliance upon the protective tariff and other favorable government measures contrasted with its proclaimed belief in governmental passivity.

During the century and a half of British rule prior to independence, government's role in the economy was important, both at the level of the British raj and that of the colonies. Mercantilism, the dominant philosophy of the British, called for a high degree of governmental management of the Empire's economy to assure the delivery of colonial raw materials to the home country and the purchase of British goods by the colonies. Eventually the colonists took up arms to rid themselves of this system, and this is surely significant. Almost to the eve of the Revolution, however, the colonists exhibited some variety in their attitudes toward it. In the seventeenth century they strongly resented the British requirement that they sell and buy within the confines of the Empire. "As Great Britain became increasingly industrialized in the eighteenth century, the chorus of complaints in the colonies against high-priced British goods subsided, although the Southern planters remained un-reconciled to British monopoly."[1] Not until the passage of the Stamp Act in 1765 did the colonists finally begin the examination of their grievances that led, a decade later, to the Revolution. In their internal affairs, moreover, the colonists were not at all reluctant to assign a positive role to government. Price and wage controls were fairly common. Colonies defined standards of production for goods and granted charters to producers.

Nor did independence bring an immediate cessation of govern-mental activity in relation to the economy. In the half century after 1776 the Commonwealth of Massachusetts engaged in such activities as the following: the setting of manufacturing standards, inspection to guarantee these standards, the licensing of lotteries, the fixing of tolls to be charged by ferries and bridges licensed by the state, and the licensing of mill sites on condition that the millers use stand-ard weights and measures and accept limits on the charges for their services.[2] To take another example, the Commonwealth of Pennsyl-vania invested heavily in the stock of railroads, bridges, banks, and other enterprises, the total reaching over $6 million by 1843. Nor was governmental entrepreneurial activity limited to the topmost echelon. "Total municipal and county investments between 1840 and 1853 were estimated at fourteen million dollars—over twice the state investment at its 1843 peak."[3] Why were state and local governments often so active as partial owners of businesses? Sometimes, as in the case of banks, investments were made in the hope of public profit. Other state investments were made to promote the development of transportation facilities. Finally, stock ownership could serve as a means of guiding the activities of corporations that were developing the economy, though in Pennsylvania "the legislature persistently failed to provide in charters for a number of state directors pro-portionate to the size of state investment."[4]

Though the government of the newly independent nation was more cautious in its economic activities than the state and local governments, it too undertook positive steps. The next chapter reviews some of the early measures undertaken to promote a national econ-omy. The Constitution of 1787 opted for a government much stronger than that provided for by the Articles of Confederation, partly in order to get national, rather than state, supervision of the movement of goods in interstate and foreign commerce.

The governmental economic activity reviewed above, however, especially that occurring after 1765, took place under the banner of limited government. The frontier spirit of a new land, the regard for

individual rights to life, liberty, and property, and the eventual revulsion against the constrictive effects of mercantilism all played their
part in limiting the role of government in the economy.

As a doctrine, laissez faire varied in its influence on American
government. The eighteenth-century writings of the most vigorous
exponents of this economic philosophy—the physiocrats in France
and Adam Smith in England—were familiar to the framers of the
Constitution. The most vigorous espousal of laissez faire as a guide
to government's economic role came in the nineteenth century, however, both in Great Britain and in the United States. The attitude
of British officials during the Irish potato famine of 1845–1849 is a
classic case.

According to a well-documented account, one and one-half million persons perished, mostly from starvation, while the operation
of "natural" economic laws was closely observed. Grain was exported from the starving land by private entrepreneurs while government stood inactive. "Adherence to *laissez-faire* was carried to
such a length that in the midst of one of the major famines of history,
the government was perpetually nervous of being too good to Ireland
and of corrupting the Irish people by kindness, and so stifling the
virtues of self-reliance and industry."[5] A less spectacular example
was furnished by one of President Grover Cleveland's numerous
veto messages. In 1887, the very year in which the creation of the
Interstate Commerce Commission began a new era in the federal
government's economic activity, Cleveland was confronted with a
bill appropriating $10,000 to permit governmental distribution of
seeds to drought-stricken farmers in Texas. Strange as it sounds in
a day of massive help to farmers, the President stated that he was
vetoing the measure on the ground that "though the people support
the Government the Government should not support the people."[6]

Staunch believers in laissez faire felt that the harshness of the
industrial system, while regrettable, could not be mitigated for fear
of the consequences to industrial progress and to humanity itself.
One industrialist who articulated such views was Andrew Carnegie,
philosophically a disciple of Herbert Spencer, whose Social Darwinism had related industrialism to the inexorable laws of nature.
Writing in 1889, Carnegie acknowledged that "Under the law of
competition, the employer of thousands is forced into the strictest
economies, among which the rates paid to labor figure prominently,
and often there is friction between the employer and the employed,
between capital and labor, between rich and poor." Nevertheless,
"while the law may be sometimes hard for the individual, it is best
for the race, because it insures the survival of the fittest in every
department."[7] The corollary to a sublime faith in the workings
of the natural law of competition was a belief that any interference

by government in its operations was productive of harm. In actuality, Adam Smith had not gone this far; nineteenth-century laissez-faire economists such as Francis Bowen tended to overlook his support of a substantial sphere of action for government. Aside from protecting against violence and invasion, the sovereign, in Smith's view, was to try to protect "every member of the society from the injustice or oppression of every other member of it," and to erect and maintain "certain public works and certain public institutions, which it can never be for the interest of any individual, or small number of individuals, to erect and maintain."[8]

In an increasingly industrialized America, the laissez-faire ideology may have contained within itself the seeds of its own destruction. Just as the Magna Charta, though an agreement between King John and a handful of barons, ultimately provided a philosophical basis for the extension of political and civil rights to all Englishmen, so industrialization, by providing a basis for the improvement of the material conditions of some, made it difficult to deny the applicability of such benefits to all. Moreover, the advent of mass production implied a need for mass consumption, which in turn required mass purchasing power. For this reason—to say nothing of the egalitarianism manifest in the Populist and Progressive movements around the turn of the century—laissez faire faced a powerful challenge as the dominant ideology of what is sometimes called our business civilization. Long hours of labor for women and children, subsistence wages, and unsafe working conditions appeared increasingly anomalous in an economy growing in size, strength, and wealth.

The extent to which government, despite the doctrine of laissez faire, has aided in shaping the American economy is exemplified by the development of corporate enterprise in the United States. This illustration is particularly appropriate in view of the central place occupied by giant corporations in the economic development of this country. In the settlement of the New World, joint stock companies, operating under charter of the British Crown, had a prominent part. Their characteristics—permanent capital, limited liability, and legal personality—made them of use in sizable ventures. Both with the British and, later, with the Americans, the corporate device was closely tied to government. In the former case, corporations were regarded as arms of the state concerned with foreign exploration; in the latter, charters were granted to corporations by various American states as devices for economic development. The grant of a company charter for carrying on a business operation was regarded as a significant step in furthering the fortunes of a state.

A company that persuaded the legislature to grant it the privilege of operating a ferry, bridge, bank, or another essential business was naturally reluctant to see competitors awarded similar privileges.

Originally, the state legislatures often sympathized with this view, preoccupied as they were with getting a thriving economy established. Furthermore, charters were regarded at law as solemn contracts, an idea carried to the point where John Marshall's Supreme Court could decree in 1819 that even the charter granted to Dartmouth College by the English king was binding on the New Hampshire legislature.[9] Fortunately for the economic development of the young nation, the Supreme Court later limited the fullest application of this rule. In the *Charles River Bridge* case of 1837, it held that the contracts clause of the Constitution did not prevent a state legislature from granting a company a charter to build a bridge very near the point where another company, recipient of a charter in 1785, had profitably operated a toll bridge for many years.[10] Chief Justice Roger B. Taney argued that the opposite ruling would, for example, prevent a river valley from being used as a canal or railroad route because a turnpike company, long since defunct, had originally been given a right to use the route.

The quickening pace of technological development and industrial advance in the nineteenth century accorded well with the spirit of the Taney decision, but for the state legislatures it soon produced a challenge to the notion of guiding economic development through the granting of corporate charters. These, by the middle of the century, were handed out in perfunctory fashion. The relationship of corporations to government planning was abandoned. By contrast, business found increasing use for the entity that John Marshall had called "an artificial being, invisible, intangible, and existing only in contemplation of law."

In the post-Civil War period of great industrialization, the use of the corporate device accelerated even more, and leading corporations found their resources strained by the demands of the developing economy. The result was still another shift in the relationship between government and corporations. To enlarge their operations and to meet or restrict competition, industrialists strove to advance their fortunes by forming pools to control output and prices or by combining through "trusts." When these means proved inadequate, either because of the fragility of agreements that required competitors to follow certain courses of action or because of judicial frowns, a few states provided a safer way of combining by permitting the existence of holding companies. In effect, this step symbolized the coming of age of the corporation as an economic entity unconfined by state boundaries and the beginning of a period of competition among states to attract corporate headquarters to their own soil. The formation of holding companies and the increasing industrial concentration characteristic of the last two decades of the nineteenth century were immensely aided by the participation of investment bankers in the process. As a super-corporation owning part or all of other companies in order to control them, a holding company could serve as a much more effective tool of economic integration than the loosely united pools and trusts. Corporate giantism was made possible by the infusion of funds generated outside a given industry, thereby freeing corporations from dependence on their own resources alone.

At the very point in their history when corporations seemed to have everything going their way, the abuses perpetrated by some of them started a countertrend. It began most dramatically in the 1870's, in the Midwestern grain belt, an area influenced by frontier egalitarianism. Because the railroads furnished an economic lifeline for farmers and other small shippers, they could act monopolistically. The Granger movement began as a protest against the arbitrary price-setting practices of the railroads, and some Midwestern legislatures responded with attempts to regulate the railroads. In these states, corporations were increasingly viewed as plutocracies, violative of the rights of the people. The increasing involvement of financiers in the railroad companies further tarnished the corporate image and made Wall Street a term of opprobrium to agrarian radicals. As corporate giants in oil, steel, and other fields also perpetrated abuses, various legislatures besides those in the Midwestern grain states began to feel the pressure for action to restrain business giants.

The national government acted as the ultimate vehicle of restraint because action at the state level was frustrated by constitutional doctrine. The so-called Granger Cases struck down attempts by various Midwestern states to regulate the railroads on the ground that they were engaged in interstate commerce.[11] Similarly, state antitrust laws legally could not be applied to the interstate operations of corporations. The struggle over regulation was transferred to the national arena, and the Interstate Commerce Act of 1887 and the Sherman Antitrust Act of 1890 were the famous products of the reform effort.

As we have seen, those who felt themselves victimized by the economic power of corporate giants sought the help of government. In this process, repeated many times in the twentieth century, is a major clue to the current relationship between government and the economy. It is also testimony to the vigor of what is sometimes called "pressure-group democracy." The advance of technical knowledge produces new products and techniques, which in turn lead to a search for private capital and perhaps for favorable governmental actions. Meanwhile, those economic groups that feel threatened by the new development are not idle. Not only do they combat the newcomer in private economic channels, but they may seek to enlist government on their side. They may attempt to deny promotional aid by government to the new economic force, or they may back regulatory legislation that will restrict its actions. Right now, for example, the older forms of transportation are apprehensive of the competitive inroads that pipelines may make in the next generation, and they want the governmental rules under which the expanding pipelines operate to be at least broadly comparable.

Economic development has become so intertwined with the workings of democracy that chances for a passive role for government have become increasingly remote. Agriculture, business, and labor, or subdivisions of these broad economic interests, have a strong compulsion to recognize the relevance of what government does in relation to the economy. A group indifferent to the actions of government might find itself disadvantaged because of the alertness of a competing group. Governmental "actions" can take many forms. Some groups may seek governmental inaction in order to preserve perceived advantages or to allay uneasiness about what might emerge from the legislative or administrative mill once the machinery is set in motion.

Although government is broadly active in the shaping of today's economy, the transition from its more passive role of seventy-five years ago did not come smoothly or swiftly. Sometimes tragedy provided the impetus, as when the Triangle Waist Company fire claimed 146 lives on March 25, 1911, and inflamed public feelings about subhuman working conditions. When legislative bodies were aroused to action, they often encountered the firm opposition of the judiciary, which retained a laissez-faire outlook a generation longer than the other two branches of government.

The pace of change was also influenced by the tides of political fortune and, more deeply, by war and economic depression. Programs of social reform were characteristic of Woodrow Wilson's New Freedom and Franklin D. Roosevelt's New Deal. The mood of experimentation was greatly facilitated by the Great Depression of the early 1930's, which dealt a final, massive blow to the hands-off philosophy of government. Both world wars were instrumental in expanding the role of government in the economy. They immensely increased the industrial base of the nation and, in the case of World War II, ended an unemployment problem that all of Roosevelt's tinkering with the economy had failed to remedy. Governmental direction of the economy in order to win the war, minimize shortages, and keep inflation within bounds was found essential. Though many governmental agencies and programs did not survive the war or the depression that called them into existence, a number of them did. In addition, most Americans' notions of legitimate governmental concerns in relation to the economy were enlarged.

Since 1945, two new factors have helped to keep governmental economic activity from declining. The first is the cold war. Whereas the two world wars had called for extensive governmental efforts with the expectation that a more relaxed pace awaited the successful conclusion of the emergency, the cold war demanded an adjustment to the idea of dealing with a crisis that might last a generation or more. The complexity of modern weapons not only spawned entire new industries but required extensive governmental direction of research and development. The so-called "space-race" has accentuated this trend. The second equilibrating factor is the stabilizing role that government now plays in the economy. The lesson taught by the Great Depression is that government cannot sit idly by while an economic emergency develops. This concept has been expanded in practice to mean that the national government uses the various economic weapons at its command to attempt to raise or lower the level of economic activity as the times demand.

In the succeeding chapters, governmental economic activity is described under the four major headings of government as promoter, regulator, buyer, and manager. Government assists certain economic activities; it restricts others; it now buys an immense amount of goods and services; and it supervises the operation of certain natural resources, runs some business-like ventures, directs certain social services that provide economic security to individuals, and, increasingly, assures the stability and growth of the economy. What these diverse roles of government have in common is that they are all part of a response, democratically arrived at, to the demands of a vast and complex industrialized economy.

Government as Promoter

In the settlement and development of the New World, European governments were aggressive about undertaking policies which they assumed would contribute to the growth and prosperity of their nations. They emphasized strict government control of the economy to accumulate gold, achieve a favorable balance of trade, develop agriculture and manufacturing, and establish foreign trading monopolies.

ORIGINS AND SCOPE

Today it is generally agreed that the United States government is an active promoter of the economy. A matter of less complete agreement is how it assumed this role. Did it do so primarily as part of a twentieth-century movement toward the welfare state or through a logical extension of its earlier promotional inclinations? What makes the first answer superficially persuasive is the undoubted fact that the American colonists objected strenuously to British mercantilistic policies as they were applied to them. Thus, in the Declaration of Independence they censured the British king "For cutting off our trade with all parts of the world." A decade earlier, in 1765, the Stamp Act Congress had objected indignantly that the duties they were forced to pay were "extremely burthensome and grievous" and that "as the profits of the trade of these colonies ultimately center in Great-Britain, to pay for the manufactures which they are obliged to take from thence, they eventually contribute very largely to all supplies granted there to the crown."

Yet a fuller examination of early American attitudes toward promotional policies must go beyond the revolutionary documents. Independence was a sobering experience for a group of former British colonies scattered along a long coast on the edge of a huge continent. Despite the former colonists' revulsion against many features of mercantilism, they could scarcely afford to turn their backs on it altogether. In fact, promotionalism was a natural posture for government at all levels in the new nation. Scattered and disorganized as the nation was, the burden of responding constructively to the challenge of independence, of establishing economic credibility, fell first upon the state and local governments. Acutely aware of the need to establish flourishing economies, they tended to be far more concerned with this aim than with ideological niceties. While they were still colonies they had, in varying degrees, regulated the flow of commerce with other colonies, given tax exemptions to industries they wanted to encourage, granted monopolies and patents to stimulate new processes or assist entrepreneurs, offered land grants and loans, distributed bounties for the production of vital commodities, set standards of purity and measure for goods whose export they wanted to encourage, collected and disseminated economic information, instituted public training in vital production processes, and established government sawmills, warehouses, roads, and land banks. After independence many of the states intensified and expanded their efforts in these directions, though it must be recognized that there had always been considerable variation among the thirteen governmental units in the use of promotional devices.

Encouragement of the economy at the highest governmental level was forced to wait upon the demise of the weak national government (1781–1788) formed under the Articles of Confederation. In his first annual address to Congress in 1789, President George Washington justified a tariff on the grounds that "the safety and interests of the people require that they should promote such manufactures as tend to render them independent of others for essential, particularly military supplies." Better known is Alexander Hamilton's *Report on Manufactures*, one of a series of brilliant reports arguing for governmental promotionalism made by Washington's Secretary of the Treasury. It is testimony to Hamilton's persuasiveness that in a land overwhelmingly agrarian he succeeded in generating support for a national policy of promoting manufacturing. The *Report on Manufactures* argued at length against the then prevailing view "that agriculture is not only the most productive, but the only productive species of industry." In the *Report* Hamilton asserted that "The expediency of encouraging manufactures in the United States, which was not long since deemed very questionable, appears at this time to be pretty generally admitted." He attributed this change of sentiment to foreign restrictions on the sale of "the increasing surplus of our agricultural produce" and to signs of progress in American manufacturing. Finally, turning to the means by which to promote manufactures, Hamilton discussed ten devices employed by other countries. Among them were protective duties, "prohibitions of rival articles," "prohibitions of the exportation of the materials of manufactures," "the exemption of the materials of manufactures from duty," and inspection of manufactured commodities in order to prevent fraud and improve quality. He also viewed favorably certain other promotional measures of a more positive character. These included "bounties," which "are applicable to the whole quantity of an article produced, or manufactured, or exported," and "premiums," which "serve to reward some particular excellence or superiority, some extraordinary exertion or skill, and are dispensed only in a small number of cases." Additional promotional measures included "the encouragement of new inventions and discoveries at home, and of the introduction into the United States of such as may have been made in other countries; particularly, those which relate to machinery"; "the facilitating of pecuniary remittances from place to place"; and "the facilitating of the transportation of commodities." As to the last-named, he approved England's efforts at constructing roads and canals, not least for the effect better transport had upon breaking down local monopolies. Though Congress adopted only a small portion of the recommendations contained in the *Report on Manufactures,* it enacted significant measures proposed by Hamilton in various other reports made during his tenure as Washington's Secretary of the Treasury. His success in establishing a basis for governmental support of business is apparent when one considers that the infant government created a national bank, established a national currency, assumed previous national and state government debts, enacted a mildly protective tariff, and instituted policies for the sale of public land.

Without a doubt, Hamilton outdid his contemporaries in urging aggressive governmental actions to stimulate the economy of the new nation. Yet, the spirit of governmental promotionalism eventually infected even his arch rival and philosophical opposite, Thomas Jefferson. During the administration of the third President, such earlier promotional measures as the tariff and land sales piled up surplus revenue. In his first term, following the concept of "a wise and frugal Government" which he had endorsed in his inaugural address, Jefferson had simply sought to apply the surplus to the reduction of the national debt. In accordance with his aversion to taxes, Jefferson might have been expected to urge tariff reduction in anticipation of paying off the debt. Instead he proposed a major promotional scheme in his second inaugural address. He suggested a constitutional amendment permitting distribution of surplus revenue to the states so that it could be applied "*in time of peace,* to rivers, canals, roads, arts, manufactures, education, and other great objects within each state. *In time of war* . . . it may meet . . . the expense . . . without encroaching on the rights of future generations. . . . War will then be but a suspension of useful works, and a return to a state of peace, a return to the progress of improvement."

In point of fact, promotional activities by the national government were at first somewhat inhibited by scruples—at least on the part of Presidents Jefferson, Madison, and Monroe—about their constitutionality. Though these Presidents sometimes promoted isolated internal improvement measures, they believed that broader programs of this kind required the acquiescence of the states. As a consequence, the leaders of the major "underdeveloped nation" of its day tended to employ indirect means to promote its development. Because it appeared that the states had unquestioned constitutional powers to undertake promotional activities, the national government gave them enormous amounts of public land with the stipulation that revenue from the sale of the land be used to finance public improvements. Even after such decisions as *McCulloch* v. *Maryland* (1819)[1] had given Supreme Court sanction to a broad interpretation of federal power, the national government continued to rely mainly on indirect promotional efforts. These, however, were of immense significance for nation-building in the nineteenth century. Before 1871 the national government ceded about one eighth of the present area of the United States to states or private corporations to support the construction of railroads, canals, roads, bridges, and reservoirs, and for the support of education.[2] The value of this land when it was granted probably exceeded the amount spent by the national government between 1800 and 1850 on all other civil functions aside from the management and redemption of debt.[3]

Direct action by the national government to promote the economy had its advocates from the beginning. Henry Clay, taking up where Alexander Hamilton left off, sought to combine the promotion of Eastern manufacturing with programs appealing to the frontier. His "American System" offered public works to the latter while retaining Hamilton's emphasis on sound banking and protective tariffs. His 1818 "Address on Internal Improvements" made the following arguments in favor of public works:

> 1. ". . . in a new country, the condition of society may be ripe for public works long before there is, in the hands of individuals, the necessary accumulation to effect them. . . ."
> 2. ". . . there is generally, in such a country, not only a scarcity of capital, but such a multiplicity of profitable objects presenting themselves as to distract the judgment."
> 3. ". . . the aggregate benefit resulting to the whole society, from a public improvement, may be such as to amply justify the investment of capital in its execution, and yet that benefit may be so distributed among different and distant persons, that they can never be got to act in concert."
> 4. "Of all the modes in which a government can employ its surplus revenue, none is more permanently beneficial than that of internal improvement. . . . The first direct effect is on the agricultural community into whose pockets comes the difference in the expense of transportation between good and bad ways."
> 5. "But, putting aside all pecuniary considerations, there may be political motives sufficiently powerful alone to justify certain internal improvements."[4]

The passage of time and progressive economic development have outmoded the first two of these arguments, but it is amply apparent that twentieth-century promotional efforts at the national level employ the other three. Furthermore, promotionalism does not necessarily await the accumulation of "surplus revenue" but may be pursued even at the cost of an unbalanced national budget.

Nineteenth-century developments had a strong influence upon government's role as promoter. Henry Clay and the Whigs were generally unsuccessful in building promotional policies upon a base of Eastern business and Western farmers. They faced the opposition of the Democrats, who, under both Jefferson and Jackson, were suspicious of how the agrarian West would fare in a partnership centered on government promotionalism. The Civil War broke the deadlock. The Democratic party lost its influence in the North, and the newly born Republican party managed skillfully to appeal both to Eastern financial and manufacturing interests and to the settlers in the growing Midwest, who benefited from the Homestead Act of 1862 and from federally encouraged transportation facilities. The War Between the States had given so much impetus to industrialism, however, that the

TABLE I

Net Current Expenses for Aids and Special Services for Selected Years
(in millions of dollars)

Segments of the economy	Fiscal Year			
	1951	1959	1964	1965
Agriculture	905	3,484	5,488	4,458
Business	809	1,493	1,874	1,664
Labor	197	761	158	347
Homeowners and tenants	−160	−4	−50	7
	1,751	5,734	7,470	6,476

NOTE: Minus (−) indicates receipts exceeding expenditures. Figures for three other categories appearing in the budget—"veterans," "international," and "other"—have been omitted. Figures for 1964 and 1965 are estimates.

SOURCE: Budget of the United States Government for the fiscal years named.

former became the dominant partners. As a result, though business continued to benefit from high tariffs and gifts of land for transportation development, business was not inclined to extend promotionalism to other economic groups. Laissez faire was elevated to a principle of the highest moment in justification of governmental inactivity with respect to the interests of labor and, to a much lesser extent, of agriculture. Over the long run, this inconsistent stand undoubtedly intensified the determination of the latter groups to use the government for their own advancement. This they have largely achieved in the twentieth century, principally under Democratic auspices.

The extent and diversity of today's governmental promotionalism defy easy description and simple classification. In order to minimize duplication, efforts to promote the interests of labor and agriculture and certain business groups have been interwoven into the two succeeding chapters, which primarily deal with regulation. In the next section of the present chapter, various promotional programs will also be mentioned or discussed by way of illustrating points made about government's role as promoter. The remainder of this section, which so far has dealt with the origins of promotionalism, will be devoted to data showing its scope today.

One way of sensing the dimensions of the government's promotional activity is to consider the yearly governmental expenditures in aid of various economic groups. Table I, which reproduces figures from the annual budget of the national government, shows such data for selected years since 1951, when the analysis was first included in the budget. Though the expenditures have risen sharply, most of the increase is attributable to agriculture, principally because of the high cost of the price-support program. Agricultural expenditures would be higher still if the costs of net additions to the major commodity inventories had been included. They were omitted because the possibility exists that they may be sold at prices which will recover all or part of the costs of acquisition. At the opposite extreme from agriculture, programs for homeowners and tenants have not entailed a large net expense.

For what purposes are the expenditures in aid of the listed economic groups made? The following explanation is taken from a recent congressional document:

> Current aids to agriculture consist chiefly of costs and losses stemming from the price-support program, the sale of surplus commodities for foreign currencies, and the payments under the soil bank program. Major items in current aids to business consist of aids to air and sea navigation and for maritime operating subsidies. Current aids to labor consist primarily of unemployment insurance and expenses of public employment offices. For homeowners and tenants, current aids consist chiefly of (1) annual contributions to local authorities for low-rent public housing projects; (2) grants for the capital losses of slum clearance and urban-renewal projects; and (3) net administrative expenses for all housing programs. The actual current expenses for homeowners and tenants are now offset by receipts from the insurance of mortgages and savings and loan share accounts and the net earnings from holdings of mortgages and other housing loans.[5]

The variety of promotional programs is staggering. In 1960 the Joint Economic Committee of the two houses of Congress attempted to compile a list of "subsidy and subsidylike programs of the U.S. Government." As the Committee admitted, the problem of deciding whether or not a particular program falls into the subsidy category is often a matter of dispute. The list below represents the fruits of the Committee's labors, and includes "the various Federal programs, past and present, which, by one criterion or another, might be considered to partake of or involve an element of subsidy regardless of original intent of any particular program."[6]

I. Grants to business firms and corporations to carry out specific objectives.

Shipbuilding differential subsidy.*

Ship-operating differential subsidy.

Subsidies to wartime producers of various raw materials and consumer items to stimulate production without violating price ceilings.

Land grants and cash contributions for railroad construction.

Government subscriptions to railroad securities.

Subsidies to shipping and air lines for carrying mail.

Partial financing of plants to generate electricity from atomic fuels.

II. Farm subsidy programs.

Commodity price-support program, which maintains a floor under the price of certain agricultural commodities by guaranteeing such prices through nonrecourse loans (i.e., no recourse against the producer if he chooses to repay the loan through forfeiting the crop) to farmers.

Surplus disposal programs, in which the government purchases farm surpluses at higher prices than the market level.

Conservation and soil bank payments, the latter made in return for taking land out of production on a longer-range basis than in the case of the former.

International Wheat Agreement, under which the price of wheat to American farmers is maintained at levels above those on the world market.

Sugar Act payments, a subsidy to domestic sugar growers who meet certain conditions of employment, production, and marketing.

Irrigation and flood control.

Grazing rights in national forests and other public lands at fee levels well below charges on private lands.

Agricultural extension services.

III. Tax benefits to specific economic groups.

Depletion allowances to minerals producers and other extractive industries.

---

*This subsidy is supplemented by (1) governmental assumption of the full cost of defense features built into a ship; (2) generous trade-in allowances on old vessels; (3) easy-payment plans for vessel purchases; (4) government loans of up to 75 per cent of a vessel's purchase price; and (5) exemption of profits of subsidized shipping companies from the corporate income tax, when placed in reserves for new construction.

Accelerated amortization of defense facilities for holders of certificates of necessity.

Specific concessions to small business under the Technical Amendments Act of 1958.

Authorized deductions on income tax computations, of particular assistance to particular groups of individuals such as borrowers (including home mortgagors), the elderly, the blind, and the sick.

Tax reductions, which have the inevitable effect of benefiting certain individuals and firms more than others.

IV. Indirect assistance to specific economic groups.

Financing of highway construction, costs of which may be borne unequally, resulting, some critics maintain, in a subsidy to truckers.

Financing of airport construction.

Construction of air navigation aids—traffic control equipment, weather reporting facilities, radio beams, instrument landing systems.

Improvements to harbors, dredging of rivers, construction of canals, and assistance in financing construction of canals.

Protective tariffs.

Government purchase restrictions under the Buy American Act.

Reserving trade between American ports to American-flag shipping.

Cargo preference, e.g., requiring goods purchased for the Army and Navy, exports financed by government loans, and half of foreign aid shipments to be transported in American-flag vessels.

V. Government economic programs with incidental economic effects similar to those of subsidies.

Letting of government contracts for supplies, research, and development, etc.

Special provisions favoring (1) small businesses and (2) depressed areas in awarding of government contracts.

Disposal of surplus property (e.g., manufacturing plants, ships, and many other items) at less than market value.

Stockpiling of minerals and other strategic materials.

Silver purchasing.

VI. Free or below-cost services (other than loans or insurance).

Statistical information of importance to business, industry, and labor.

Maps, charts, and aids to navigation by the Coast and Geodetic Survey and the Geological Survey.

Crop estimates by the Crop Reporting Service.

Weather forecasts by the Weather Bureau.

Scientific and industrial research by such agencies as the National Bureau of Standards, Geological Survey, Bureau of Mines, Forest Service, Fish and Wildlife Service, Tennessee Valley Authority, Bureau of Public Roads, Department of Agriculture, Food and Drug Administration, and the Atomic Energy Commission.

Certain postal services provided free and various others provided below cost, such as second- and third-class mail and rural free delivery.

Management and technical assistance to small business.

Counseling assistance to small business on government contract procedure.

Protection against forest fires.

Homestead grants and land sales to farmers.

Construction and assistance in maintaining farm-to-market roads.

VII. Lending and loan guarantee programs of federal agencies in effect in fiscal year 1960.

A. Direct loan programs.

Housing and Home Finance Agency:

Federal National Mortgage Association: Purchase of government-insured mortgages on homes to provide a degree of liquidity for mortgage investments.

Urban Renewal Administration: Loans to local public agencies for slum clearance and urban renewal projects.

Community Facilities Administration: Construction loans to colleges and universities.

Public Housing Administration: Loans to local authorities for construction of low-rent public housing.

Veterans Administration: Direct housing loans in rural areas and small towns.

Department of Agriculture:

Rural Electrification Administration: Loans, chiefly to cooperatives, to provide electric power and telephone service to farms.

Farmers Home Administration: Loans to farmers to "strengthen the family-type farm and encourage better farming methods."

Commodity Credit Corporation: Loans to farmers with commodities as collateral.

Department of Commerce, Maritime Administration: Direct loans for vessel construction; no new commitments made since 1956.

Department of Health, Education, and Welfare, Office of Education: Loan funds for student financial aid, construction, and acquisition of teaching equipment.

Department of State:

International Cooperation Administration: Loans under Agricultural Trade Development and Assistance Act to promote multilateral trade and economic development.

Development Loan Fund: Loans to governments of underdeveloped nations or organizations and persons therein.

Export-Import Bank: Loans to finance exports and imports and to promote economic development in lesser-developed countries.

Small Business Administration:

Business loans to small business.

Disaster loans to small business.

Purchases of debentures of and loans to small business investment companies.

Loans to state and local development companies.

Expansion of defense production: Authorization for the Treasury Department (domestic loans) and the Export-Import Bank (foreign loans) to make direct loans for expansion of industrial capacity, development of technological processes, or production of essential materials.

B. Loan guarantee and insurance programs.*

Housing and Home Finance Agency, Federal Housing Administration: Insures wide range of real estate loans.

Veterans Administration: Guarantees housing, business, and farm loans to veterans.

Farmers Home Administration: Insures farm ownership and soil and water conservation loans.

Commodity Credit Corporation: Guarantees private loans on commodities.

Maritime Administration: Guarantees private construction loans and mortgages on passenger and cargo-carrying vessels.

---

*Several of these programs do not now involve net losses to the federal government. Insurance and loan guarantee programs involve federal commitments which could result in losses to the government at some future time. These programs are in the nature of subsidies in the sense of providing insurance or loan guarantee services not available or available only at higher cost from private enterprise.

Civil Aeronautics Board: Guarantees loans for aircraft purchases by local air services and other small airlines.

Interstate Commerce Commission: Guarantees loans to railroads under Transportation Act of 1958.

Defense Production Act (Sec. 301): Authorizes guarantees by various agencies on loans to defense contractors and subcontractors.

Development Loan Fund: Guarantees loans to governments of underdeveloped nations, their organizations, and citizens.

Small Business Administration: Encourages private lending to business by participating in loans with private lenders.

VIII. Insurance programs undertaken by the federal government.*

Agricultural crop insurance—Federal Crop Insurance Corporation.

Bank deposit insurance—Federal Deposit Insurance Corporation.

Savings and loan association deposit insurance—Federal Savings and Loan Insurance Corporation.

Federal employees' group life insurance, retirement insurance, and health insurance—Civil Service Commission.

U.S. Government life insurance, national service life insurance, veterans' special term life insurance, and service-disabled veterans' insurance—Veterans Administration.

Old-age and survivors insurance and disability insurance—Bureau of Old-Age and Survivors Insurance.

Unemployment insurance (jointly with the states)—Bureau of Employment Security.

Railroad unemployment and sickness insurance—Railroad Retirement Board.

Maritime war risk insurance—Maritime Administration.

Aviation war risk insurance—Department of Commerce.

Flood insurance—Federal Flood Indemnity Administration.

IX. Federal-aid payments to states and local units.†

Department of Agriculture:

Agricultural experiment stations.

Cooperative agricultural extension work.

School lunch program.

National forests fund—shared revenues.

Submarginal land program—shared revenues.

Cooperative projects in marketing.

---

*See preceding note.
†As reported in the 1959 Report of the Secretary of the Treasury.

State and private forestry cooperation.
Watershed protection and flood prevention.
Commodity Credit Corporation—donations of commodities and special school milk program.
Removal of surplus agricultural commodities.
Department of Commerce:
 Bureau of Public Roads—construction—Federal-aid highways (trust fund) and other.
 State marine schools.
Department of Defense, Army: Lease of flood-control lands—shared revenues.
Executive Office of the President, Office of Civil and Defense Mobilization: Federal contributions and research and development.
Department of Health, Education, and Welfare:
 American Printing House for the Blind.
 Office of Education:
  Colleges for agriculture and mechanical arts.
  Cooperative vocational education.
  School construction and survey.
  Maintenance and operation of schools.
  Library services.
  Defense educational activities.
 Public Health Service:
  Venereal disease control.
  Tuberculosis control.
  General health assistance.
  Mental health activities.
  Cancer control.
  Heart disease control.
  Sanitary engineering activities.
  Construction of hospital and medical facilities.
  Construction of waste treatment works.
  Construction of health research facilities.
  Polio vaccination assistance program.
 Social Security Administration:
  Maternal and child welfare services.
  Old-age assistance.
  Aid to dependent children.
  Aid to permanently and totally disabled.
  Aid to the blind.
 Office of Vocational Rehabilitation.
Department of the Interior:
 Federal aid to wildlife restoration and fish restoration and management.

Migratory Bird Conservation Act and Alaska game law—shared revenues.

Payments from receipts under Mineral Leasing Act—shared revenues.

Payments under certain special funds—shared revenues.

Bureau of Indian Affairs.

Department of Labor: Unemployment Compensation and Employment Service Administration.

Federal Power Commission: Payments to states under Federal Power Act—shared revenues.

Housing and Home Finance Agency:
Defense community facilities and services.
Urban renewal program.
Urban planning assistance.
Public Housing Administration—annual contributions.

Federal Aviation Agency—federal airport program.

Tennessee Valley Authority—fertilizer distribution for research and education.

Veterans Administration:
State and territorial homes for disabled soldiers and sailors.
State supervision of schools and training establishments.

X. Federal-aid payments to individuals within states.*
Department of Agriculture:
Agricultural conservation program.
Administration of Sugar Act program.
Great Plains conservation program.
Commodity Credit Corporation—soil bank program.

Department of Commerce: State marine schools (subsistence of cadets).

Department of Defense:
Air Force National Guard.
Army National Guard.

Department of Health, Education, and Welfare:
National Institutes of Health.
Office of Education—defense educational activities.
Office of Vocational Rehabilitation—grants for special projects, training, and traineeships.

Department of Labor:
Unemployment compensation for veterans and federal employees.
Temporary unemployment compensation.

---

*As reported in the 1959 Report of the Secretary of the Treasury.

Atomic Energy Commission: Fellowships and assistance to
schools.
National Science Foundation:
Research grants awarded.
Fellowship awards.
Veterans Administration:
Automobiles, etc., for disabled veterans.
Readjustment benefits and vocational rehabilitation.

ATTRIBUTES OF PROMOTIONALISM

In order to understand the meaning of "government as promoter," one must go beyond a catalog of expenditures and programs.
Though such a summary has value as a guide to the promotional
labyrinth, it needs to be supplemented with a description of the kind
of climate one finds there. This section attempts such a characterization, generalizing from specific examples.[7]

1. *Over a period of time governmental policy toward some segments of the
economy has veered drastically between promotion and regulation.* The railroads
offer a good example. For the first forty years of the railroads' existence, both state and federal governments were eager to push their
development as a means of settling new lands and developing the economy. But after 1870, when a good deal of consolidation had occurred
among railroad companies, governments in the United States were
pressured to curb the economic power and abuses of what had once
been a truly "infant industry." After the advent of competing means
of transportation, however, and particularly since World War II, the
railroads have once again become the object of governmental solicitude. State and local governments have provided some tax relief, and
the national government has considered providing subsidies to the
railroads for commuter traffic and freeing the railroads from some of
the regulatory shackles that the railroads believe are hampering them
in competing with road, air, and water carriers.

2. *At any given moment, governmental policy toward a specific segment
of the economy may include a mélange of promotion and regulation.* Ever since
New Deal days, farm policy has been oriented toward promoting the
welfare of farmers through measures that regulate their actions.
Production quotas, marketing quotas, retirement of farm land for conservation purposes—all these have had as a principal goal the improvement of agricultural conditions. To take an entirely different
example, governmental policy toward atomic energy has striven to
meet two partly conflicting objectives: (1) to promote the development
of atomic reactors for the generation of electricity and (2) to require
the satisfaction of extremely high safety standards before permitting
the construction and operation of such reactors.

3. *Promotionalism, broadly considered, is not limited to monetary favors to specific groups but often includes other kinds of favorable legislation.* Examples drawn from protective legislation for workers and consumers illustrate the point, as well as demonstrating further the mixture of promotion and regulation. State laws forbidding child labor and establishing maximum hours and minimum wages preceded those of the national government, though they often failed the constitutional test before courts that gave a high priority to "freedom of contract" between employer and employee. The increasingly interstate character of the economy in the closing decades of the nineteenth century and the reluctance of states to drive industry from their borders made federal protection of labor ever more necessary. Not until the Great Depression and the New Deal's drive for social justice, however, did the attitude of the Supreme Court toward protective legislation become favorable. The Fair Labor Standards Act of 1938 signaled the advent of an era in which the national government was able to extend protection of working conditions not merely to children and women but to all workers. Workmen's compensation laws also fought an uphill battle until the judiciary abandoned common-law doctrines hostile to the concept and acknowledged the constitutionality of statutes that compensated injured employees through insurance funds built up out of employers' premiums. After stormy years of industrial strife over the issue, the National Labor Relations Act of 1935 protected the right of workers to join unions and bargain collectively.

The twentieth century has also seen broad activity by the national government to protect the consumer. One of the accomplishments of the muckrakers was to alarm the public about the methods of production employed in certain food and drug industries. The Pure Food and Drug Act of 1906 attempted to prevent adulteration and misbranding; the Food, Drug, and Cosmetic Act of 1938 further strengthened the government's arsenal for protection of the consumer. Both acts were the products of public indignation following notable scandals, and the pattern was repeated after the well-publicized thalidomide tragedy of 1962. As before, Congress, which had listened rather indifferently to testimony about the risks to health associated with some new life-saving drugs, was galvanized into action and strengthened the hand of the Food and Drug Administration. Agitation over danger from insecticides provides another example of an area where future protective legislation for consumers is likely.

4. *Successful promotion of the interests of one economic group tends to constitute a precedent for others in the same broad area of the economy.* The promotional benefits that the railroads obtained tended to constitute the standard preferred by more recent commercial carriers. Just as the railroads were heavily subsidized in their infancy, so the twentieth-century motor and air carriers expected to receive federal aid of

one kind or another. This the railroads, heavily regulated and no longer receiving governmental largesse, opposed. They argued that railroads must provide both their own roadbeds, unlike trucks and buses, and their own terminals, unlike airlines. Furthermore, the preferential rates at which the land-grant railroads hauled government personnel and property until 1946 meant that the government recouped much of the value of the subsidies previously granted the railroads. When it is considered that still other competitors of the railroads, the inland water carriers, are almost completely dependent upon governmental efforts to construct and maintain the water routes used, the irony becomes even greater. Railroad magnates must sometimes yearn to turn back the clock and reconsider the wisdom of accepting subsidies.

5. *Promotionalism tends to produce great reticence among its beneficiaries.* It is no accident that the word "subsidies" rarely appears in statutes. It is used in no statutes authorizing promotional activities, and it appears in only one appropriation title and in the language of one other appropriation, both associated with maritime activities.[8] "To promote" usually means "to aid identifiable individuals or groups in the economy," and the natural tendency of the recipients is to minimize the aid or even to deny its existence. Thus, newspaper and magazine publishers, who receive subsidies in the form of below-cost postal rates for their publications, usually assert that it is the reader who is the prime beneficiary. Another favorite tactic of subsidy recipients is to marshal data designed to show that subsidies are as numerous on the American scene as fleas on a dog. Probably because of the immense publicity about farm subsidies in the postwar period, agricultural pressure groups in particular have made use of this device. The opposite tactic seems to have been characteristic of business groups in the nineteenth century and the early decades of the present century. As the preceding section noted, at the very time that business was receiving the benefit of the protective tariff and various public aids to transportation, its spokesmen were trumpeting a philosophy of laissez faire and campaigning in its name against subsidies for other economic groups.

6. *The case for a specific promotional program is strengthened in proportion to the extent to which it can be associated with high national purposes, the list of which appears to be increasing.* The most obvious claim of high national purpose centers around national defense. When war and peace were easily distinguishable—as before the era of the Cold War, "police actions," and guerrilla warfare—subsidies were perhaps both more straightforward and more temporary. During World War II, for example, the Reconstruction Finance Corporation undertook a massive program to stimulate production of materials and supplies considered essential to the war effort.[9] Another huge sum was spent by the RFC and the Commodity Credit Corporation to compensate dairy, wheat,

sugar, and soybean producers for delivering their goods at prices too low to provide an incentive.[10] Even wartime subsidies have not always been free from peacetime implications. As its price for supporting rather liberal price ceilings on farm products, the farm bloc succeeded in obtaining statutory guarantees for a high, fixed price-support level for farm products for a period extending two years beyond the official end of hostilities.

National defense inevitably becomes a rather ambiguous concept in the twilight zone of the constant threat of total war along with actual involvement in less major actions. Some subsidy programs begun during World War II have been renewed since that time, and others have been instituted as a result of lessons learned during that war. Accelerated, and hence tax-reducing, amortization of defense facilities in the amount of $7.3 billion was granted private firms during World War II; the program was renewed after the outbreak of hostilities in Korea and was continued until the end of 1959, resulting in almost $4 billion more for which certificates of necessity were granted.[11]

As a result of Congress' desire to avoid a repetition of the shortage of essential minerals experienced during World War II, some elements of the mining industry have been granted incentives to keep them operating in peacetime. It would, of course, be inaccurate to imply that subsidies in peacetime for purposes related in some manner to national defense are an entirely new development. Assistance to the mining industry was stepped up after World War II, but Western "silver senators" were instrumental in instituting a governmental purchase program for silver as far back as 1878. From the early days of this century the Bureau of Mines has developed new mining devices and aided the industry in other ways. A recent example of governmental assistance to mining is the Geologic Survey's discovery in Alaska in 1962 of new deposits of beryllium, a scarce and valuable metal used in defense facilities, which started a rush of prospectors to the area.[12]

Historically, the maritime shipping industry is among the oldest of industries with a successful claim to national defense assistance, for the first tariff statute, passed in 1789, reduced customs duties for goods imported in American vessels and levied a tonnage tax in favor of American shipping.[13] During the nineteenth century mail subsidies were paid. In the present century construction-differential subsidies up to 50 per cent of the cost of the vessel have been paid, as well as subsidies designed to make up the difference between the cost of operating American ships and that of operating foreign vessels, whose operating costs are lower. About three fourths of the operating subsidies go for the wages of seamen. These subsidies illustrate the difficulty sometimes encountered in keeping the goal of aiding national defense in peacetime above the suspicion that enrichment of recipients is the major end in view. So virulent was the controversy over the lobbying activities of one of the shipping companies during the Grant administration that in 1874 all existing subsidy contracts were terminated, though the program was resumed in 1891.[14] The more recent subsidies, though free from major scandal, have not escaped the criticism that inefficiency is being protected or competition blunted. Some taxpayers have objected to the high cost of superliners, for which the 50 per cent limitation was waived. Shipping companies have sometimes quarreled. For example, in 1963 one American shipping company operating in the Far East complained to the Federal Maritime Commission and to the Maritime Subsidy Board that two groups of subsidized shipping lines had engaged in rate cutting and various other discriminatory practices in an attempt to drive the complainant out of business, thereby violating a provision in the Merchant Marine Act of 1936 that forbids the use of federal subsidies as a weapon against competitors.[15] Divisions in the ranks were less typical than laments about the inadequacy of subsidies, however. Thus, the American Maritime Association charged that the federal maritime budget of $36,402,000 for 1964 was "totally inadequate" because it did not subsidize "tramp and domestic shipping and the Great Lakes fleet."[16]

The Kennedy administration's drive to stimulate economic growth typified the broadening of the list of national goals. By permitting industry to depreciate equipment more rapidly and by granting it a tax credit of 7 per cent for investment in new machinery, Congress and the President hoped to stimulate business activity. In 1962 corporations reaped a cash benefit of $2.3 billion from these two subsidies.[17]

One of the older national goals that still possesses considerable emotional capital is the familiar American aversion to monopoly and giantism. Two areas of the economy that have benefited heavily from this sentiment are agriculture and small business. The promotion of agriculture goes back to the origins of the Republic and, ranging to the present day, has become ever broader and more complex. From the beginnings in a land policy that opened up the frontier for culti= vation there have gradually come to be elaborate information services, government credit facilities, soil conservation, rural electrification, and, above all, price supports. Agricultural representatives have been remarkably successful in invoking the image of the "family farm" struggling against encroachment by giant corporations that would turn a cherished way of life into a mere business operation. Similarly, the four-million-odd small businesses in this country have found staunch defenders in the halls of Congress. To help small businesses survive in an era of corporate giants, the Small Business Administration was created in 1953 and authorized to provide various helpful services, including granting loans, licensing and assisting small business investment companies to make loans that small businesses cannot get elsewhere, increasing small business' share of government contracts, improving management practices, and acting as a clearing house for information sought by small businessmen. Though the SBA's interest rates often compare with commercial rates, it can lend at much lower rates in depressed areas.

7. *The costs and benefits of promotionalism are often difficult to assess.* Several factors contributing to confusion should be noted. First, promotionalism often has a "rippling" effect. Obviously, it is not only publishers and advertisers who benefit from low second-class postage but all Americans who can read—a result that Jefferson would have heartily endorsed. (Whether the recipients of "junk" mail addressed to "occupant" would agree that they are being subsidized to their benefit is more debatable.) The beneficiaries of many of the government's housing programs range from owners to renters, from contractors to financial institutions. Multipurpose river valley projects can be said to benefit whole regions of the country, though presumably not to the same degree for every inhabitant of a given area. In any case, so broad are the effects of promotionalism that one economist has said, "Nearly every government action which impinges on the private economy (and nearly every one does) is likely to have what have been termed subsidy effects."[18] As a consequence, according to the House of Representatives' Committee on Agriculture, "virtually all the population would seem to be in a subsidy recipient posture and, moreover, almost all are participating in the payment of costs."[19]

A second element that confuses the picture is that accurate cost calculations may have to await the passage of time. A loan made or guaranteed by the national government may, under the terms of the loan, not be paid off for years. The principal that was loaned becomes a "cost" only if it is not repaid. The interest paid by the government on funds provided for lending purposes is a "cost" to the extent that it is not compensated for by the interest paid by the borrower; but the cost to the government of borrowing money will change during the years that the loan is being repaid. Calculating the cost of agricultural price-support programs may be even more dependent upon twists of fate. A famine in another part of the world or the outbreak of a major war can have a significant effect on the "cost" of the price-support program. For a starving Europe after World War II, American wheat provided a basis for beginning the task of reconstruction under favorable political circumstances. So vital was European political stability considered to be that one may wonder whether, if surplus grain had not been available, the United States would not have been willing to pay dearly for foodstuffs with which to supply

Europe. In 1963 the poor grain harvest in the Soviet Union raised the question of whether to reduce the stupendous costs of the price-support program by selling grain for gold.

Thirdly, the calculation of benefits in relation to cost is often in dispute. Multipurpose dams provide a ready example. Because such dams are often designed to benefit flood control, irrigation, navigation, and electric power generation, disagreements over the formulas used to assign portions of the total cost are inevitable. Each interested party—including, of course, the relevant government agencies—seeks to maximize the benefits and minimize the costs of the specific purpose of dam construction with which it is concerned. At the same time, agencies and groups seeking congressional authorization and appropriations for a dam tend to overstate the total benefits and understate the total costs in an effort to arrive at the magical one-to-one ratio between costs and benefits that Congress has favored. The chronic postal deficit provides another example of the difficulty of balancing costs and benefits among users of a government-provided service. The Post Office Department's own calculations indicate that all mail but first-class mail is carried at a loss, but these calculations do not take into account the preferential treatment given first-class mail. Should this benefit be considered? In addition, publishers of periodicals sometimes make the point that they go to considerable expense to package and deliver their product to the post office and minimize postal costs in other ways, while users of first-class mail are catered to by the postal service.

Finally, cost and benefit calculations are confused by the difficulty, if not the impossibility, of evaluating the social costs of failing to undertake a promotional action. In this category are such questions as the relationship of slums to juvenile delinquency, of low farm income to eroded land, of a low level of education to technological unemployment, and so on. Should one attempt to measure the cost of improving housing, education, and living conditions for underprivileged groups against the cost to society of not doing so? If one attempts such a calculation, whom shall one consider the beneficiaries, and to what extent?

THE FUTURE OF PROMOTIONALISM

Promotionalism as a national government policy seems in little danger of eclipse. Not only can its origins be traced back to the nation's beginnings, but its scope and variety have steadily increased over the years. Each extension of promotionalism has been a warrant for a further extension, each grant to one economic group the ground for a demand by its rival. This is not to say, of course, that promotional measures are customarily enacted with a disregard for the locus of political power. On the contrary, Congress and the White House have constituted the arenas where decisions on promotionalism have been fought out. At present, for example, congressional representatives of a declining agricultural population battle to retain the benefits agriculture has obtained, meanwhile resisting the efforts of urban-based legislators to divert more governmental resources to promote the solution of city problems.

Important as interest group activity is in expanding governmental promotionalism, a new and perhaps even more powerful element has emerged in the last generation: America's world responsibilities. This country's efforts to develop new weapons, provide military and economic aid to other nations, and assert world leadership have had remarkable repercussions upon the economy. For example, in 1953 private industry expended $4.3 billion for research and development, of which 60 per cent was derived from corporate funds. A decade later industry's annual outlays for research and development totaled $13 billion, of which 60 per cent was derived from the government.[20] The immense impact of this type of governmental promotionalism has

> enabled the U.S. to snatch leadership in research from Europe and to produce 80% of the world's current research. Almost all the nation's breakthrough products of recent years—from jet planes to fertilizers to aerosol bombs—have been largely bankrolled by Washington. The only important basic products that business has devised wholly on its own are Bell Laboratories' transistors and the picture-in-seconds cameras of Polaroid.[21]

There is no doubt that business and the entire economy have benefited enormously from governmental activity of this type and magnitude. The structure of industry can hardly remain unaffected. Over four fifths of the government's expenditures in 1961 for research and development by industry was accounted for by the aircraft and missiles industry together with the electrical equipment and communications industry.[22] Businessmen thus have grounds for worry that this form of governmental promotionalism is overly skewed toward the defense-related industries, with unfavorable consequences for the availability of scientific and technological manpower and funds for the more purely commercial areas of business. Government spokesmen in turn are concerned that the big increases in science funds have not led to corresponding increases in the rate of growth of the economy. While the adverse effects can be overemphasized—business in general eventually benefits from defense-related scientific progress, and total private expenditures for research and development have doubled in the last decade—there is no doubt that new and perplexing problems have been raised for government in its role as promoter.

Given the scope of governmental promotionalism, it is not surprising to find internal contradictions aplenty. The simultaneous attempts of the Department of Agriculture to improve the yield per acre of all types of crops and to dispose of crop surpluses or to remove them from the market are often cited. Less well known is the plight of industries caught in the toils of United States shipping policy. One aspect of this problem is the requirement, imposed by the Jones Act of 1920, that all commerce between American ports must travel in American ships. As a result of the consequently higher costs to shippers, the Pacific Northwest lumber industry has steadily lost out to Canadian timber interests in supplying the East Coast. So desperate did the plight of American lumber companies become that in 1962 Congress amended the Jones Act to permit foreign ships to carry lumber from the Northwest to Puerto Rico; in December 1963 the Senate passed a bill authorizing a two-year extension of the amendment. The passage of the 1962 statute was the signal for cries of alarm from American shipowners, who saw this action as the first ominous crack in their protective dam. Yet, even with the Jones Act safeguarding the coastwise shipping industry from foreign competition, the number of dry-cargo ships plying between United States ports is today only slightly more than one fourth the number twenty-five years ago. The Act's requirement that ships used in the coastwise trade be built in American shipyards, where costs are high, and secondly, the inroads on the coastwise shipping business made by competing forms of transportation account for the decline. To review the situation, shipyards in the United States benefit from the Jones Act, but their high costs limit the number of ships built and therefore limit the benefits from the subsidy. American shipping lines engaged in coastwise commerce are aided by the exclusion of foreign shipping lines but would prefer to cut costs by having their ships constructed in foreign shipyards. Shippers find the Jones Act restrictive and, where alternative domestic means of shipment are not particularly feasible, have an incentive to agitate for exemption from the Act's requirements, as the Northwest's lumber industry has done. Direct operating subsidies, now used in ocean shipping and justified for national defense purposes, have been proposed for coastwise shipping. Probably they would increase the chances for the survival of American coastwise shipping companies but reduce the business of domestic competitors in the transportation industry; they would also increase the taxpayers' bills. An improvement of the situation may be foreshadowed by an upswing in coastal traffic noted in 1964 and traced to an energetic attempt by shipping lines and port cities to get more business; by the rapid development of Puerto Rico, Hawaii, and Alaska; by rising costs of overland transport in some cases; and by increasing highway congestion.

Just as generals are sometimes said to prepare for the last war, so some promotional policies appear to be designed to preserve outdated economic arrangements rather than to facilitate an adjustment to new trends. Politically speaking, this phenomenon is, of course, not surprising, for established economic groups tend to carry much political weight. The public policy consequences of ignoring the long-term trend away from agricultural and extractive industries and toward complicated manufacturing and new service industries can be severe, however. What has happened is that manpower in declining agricultural and mining areas or in one-industry towns has actually been encouraged, by promotional policies that protect outdated economic arrangements, to stay where it is. Protective devices include high tariffs, price supports, production subsidies, deficiency payments, and import quotas. Producers that have benefited from one or more of these devices include producers of wheat, cotton, sugar, wool, dairy products, petroleum, lead, zinc, and some other minerals. One measure of the impact on the national economy of such devices is that "the value of primary production in lines where domestic prices are held substantially above world prices now amounts to between $15 and $20 billion yearly."[23] Further consequences are higher prices for consumers, checks on the mobility of labor, barriers to export trade, and resentment abroad when protected goods are "dumped" overseas.

In recent years a few signs of progress in adjusting promotionalism to changing economic conditions have appeared. On a small scale, at least, there have been attempts to retrain workers, assist businesses and communities in adjusting to new types of economic endeavor, and encourage farmers to take land out of production and place it in a conservation reserve. The problems are immense, and the new emphasis has not had all the success that was hoped for. There are also limits on what can be done quickly, aside from the limits imposed by politics. Many Americans would want relatively inefficient industries kept on a stand-by basis if such a policy helped to keep the country ready for an international emergency. Some are also persuaded that because of the world-wide population explosion the present agricultural surpluses are a hedge against starvation. Sentiments such as these militate against drastic revisions in government's promotional function.

Government
as
Regulator: I

In the United States regulation has tended to appear as a later form of governmental activity than promotion. This is to be expected, as youthful economic entities, whether in business, agriculture, or labor, usually need encouragement and, in any case, rarely have enough power to constitute a threat to the welfare of other economic units or of the community as a whole. The separability of promotion and regulation, both in point of time and in terms of governmental philosophy, can be overemphasized. Though railroad regulation began a half century after an era of governmental promotion of the railroads, in the familiar sequence, the latter has again gained strength at a time when regulation remains an important fact of life. And, in different ways, a mixture of promotional and regulatory measures has been applied to both agriculture and labor. Particularly for the former, it is difficult to decide whether the main thrust of such measures as those dealing with the conservation of farm land is promotional or regulatory.

Regulation is a form of governmental activity that has firm roots in American society. Economically and politically, it is based upon at least three kinds of motivation. The first and most elemental is the desire to curb the abuses of an economic group that has gained significant power over others. The second, less punitive and more constructive, is the desire to shape the economy along lines considered compatible with the spirit of democracy. Thus, government has been concerned with such matters as the relationship of employer to employee, the relationship of the labor union to its members, and the economic power wielded by big business and big labor. Finally, regulation, particularly at the state level, has sometimes had the purpose of protecting an established occupation or profession through restrictions on entry and standards of performance—the "guild" effect.

In constitutional and legal terms, regulation appears as a powerful governmental activity because of the expansive interpretation it has been given by the courts. Early in our history the Supreme Court under Chief Justice John Marshall interpreted the national government's constitutional authority "To regulate commerce . . . among the several States" broadly, with the consequence that the stage was set for the kind of governmental regulatory power that twentieth-century conditions demand. Thus, even though the conservative Supreme Court of the half century before 1937 viewed the commerce clause more narrowly than had Marshall, the national authority to regulate was only temporarily restricted. Today it is once again probably adequate for the numerous and intricate challenges faced by the government. By bringing within the national regulatory authority not merely interstate commerce itself but also first those actions having a "direct effect" and later those having a "close and intimate" effect on interstate commerce, the Supreme Court found grounds for supporting federal restrictions even upon wheat grown and consumed on a single farm and upon building employees who service corporations in interstate commerce. Just as Marshall had interpreted the word *regulate* broadly to mean "to prescribe the extent of," so today's Court has interpreted it to include promotion, protection, restriction, and prohibition, thereby giving Congress a wider choice of weapons in dealing with the problems of an industrial society. In addition, because the Supreme Court has also endorsed uses of the taxing power for other than purely revenue purposes, Congress often has a choice between the commerce clause and the taxing and spending clause when it decides to regulate. By way of illustration, Congress chose, in 1951, to require gamblers to register and pay an annual license fee as a way of seeking some control over their activities.

In ideological terms, regulation has drawn strength from the general belief that it is a halfway house between laissez faire and socialism. If the former became increasingly inappropriate as the Industrial

Revolution continued, the latter appeared equally inappropriate in an economy largely based on vigorous private enterprise. Certainly regulation lacks the ideological appeal of the other two, but America has generally not been fertile soil for elaborate ideologies. Regulation permits, and even invites, the piecemeal, pragmatic approach to specific public policy problems that seems to fit the American temperament.

So massive is the pile of existing regulatory legislation that it would be foolhardy to attempt to review it comprehensively in the space of this chapter and the next. Rather than describe the measures that pertain to each regulatory area, it seems more appropriate to characterize the approach developed for each, for if any generalization can be made it is that diversity has ruled the day. Not only has Congress dealt with regulatory problems on a particularized basis, but successive Presidents and Congresses have often had sharply contrasting views of the proper scope and emphasis of specific regulatory programs. Furthermore, the various regulatory agencies have followed different approaches, the courts have often significantly molded thinking about regulation, and interest groups have added their influence to the shape of events. In this and the succeeding chapter the major regulatory areas will be painted with a broad brush.

COMPETITION AND TRADE PRACTICES

No other area demonstrates so well the meandering course of government as regulator as does that of competition and trade practices. The interpretation of the Sherman Antitrust Act of 1890, the basic and best-known federal statute, certainly has meandered widely. The language of Section 1 seems plain enough: "Every contract, combination in the form of trust or otherwise, or conspiracy, in restraint of trade or commerce among the several states, or with foreign nations, is hereby declared to be illegal." Yet the debates in Congress provided relatively little guidance to the courts in interpreting the clause. Clearly, Congress was responding to a popular concern over "trusts" and "monopolies," but it was not at all clear what, if anything, Congress regarded as being "in restraint of trade." Further confusion was provided by the strong inclination of Richard Olney, President William McKinley's Attorney General, to prosecute labor unions under the statute rather than the business combinations in restraint of trade against which the statute was presumably directed. Furthermore, the courts tended to see the Sherman Act as a warrant for continuing the old common-law doctrine that regarded monopolies as illegal and contracts in restraint of trade as against public policy and unenforceable. Lacking vigorous prosecution of the act, baffled as to whether new forms of combination fit into the old common-law categories, and, in general, disinclined to interfere with giant corporations, the courts provided little guidance and no leadership in the task of establishing regulatory guidelines.

In the late 1890's, after the Supreme Court acted to outlaw pools and similar forms of loose combinations of independent firms, business turned to tighter forms of "combination," i.e., mergers and holding companies. Under Theodore Roosevelt a giant railroad holding company was successfully prosecuted,[1] but Roosevelt, for all his trust-busting reputation, left office with no major industrial trust dissolved. The less spectacular William Howard Taft instituted more antitrust actions than the total begun after 1890 under his four predecessors.

Two cases initiated under Roosevelt and fought to a conclusion under Taft provided important interpretations of the Sherman Act and set the stage for further congressional action. In 1911 the Supreme Court ruled that both the Standard Oil Company of New Jersey and the American Tobacco Company had engaged in a variety of predatory practices against their respective competitors.[2] These included temporarily lowering prices to drive out competition, buying up plants and closing them, obtaining rebates and other favors from railroads, cornering available sources of raw materials, and bribing employees of other corporations to obtain commercially useful information. The Court ordered the dissolution of both combinations. Nevertheless, these were limited victories. As the stockholders were few in number and closely associated, the main effect of dissolution was to give the same individuals a controlling interest in many companies instead of a few. More far-reaching was the distinction between "good" and "bad" trusts that emerged from the decisions— what Chief Justice White in the majority opinion called "the rule of reason." Contrary to the statutory wording, only those combinations in restraint of trade that demonstrated an intent to monopolize an industry were to be illegal. The enunciation of the rule of reason created uncertainty in the business community as to what practices would be considered illegal, and it created dismay among backers of the Sherman Act, who feared its judicial emasculation.

The desire to achieve greater precision in antitrust law and to lessen the influence of a conservative judiciary led Congress to pass two significant statutes in 1914 under Woodrow Wilson's leadership. The Federal Trade Commission Act established an independent regulatory commission with authority to investigate complaints and issue cease and desist orders that are appealable to the Courts of Appeals; the act also declared "unfair methods of competition in commerce" unlawful. The Clayton Act specified prohibited practices and placed enforcement responsibility primarily upon the Federal Trade Commission and the Department of Justice. The act outlawed price discrimination, tying contracts (forcing a buyer to accept a second product to get the one he wants), exclusive dealing arrangements, and inter-corporate stock acquisitions whenever their effect was "to substantially lessen competition or tend to create a monopoly in any line of commerce."

Though Congress had sought to provide for administrative interpretation and elaboration, judicial construction of the statutes was to prove decisive for many years in shaping regulatory action. Whether competition is substantially lessened or the likelihood of monopoly increased might have been treated as a question of economic fact within the Federal Trade Commission's jurisdiction. Instead, the courts tended to treat it as a question of law. The Commission was strongly affected not only by discouragement over reversals in court but also by the striking contrast in attitudes toward the Clayton and FTC Acts held by the Wilson and Coolidge administrations. The latter took the position that vigorous regulation of business practices could only inhibit business activity.

During the 1930's several events worked toward instilling greater vigor into public policy on competition and trade practices, a vigor that carried over to more recent times. Though Franklin D. Roosevelt's first term had seen the suspension of antitrust activity in favor of industrial codes generated under the National Recovery Administration (NRA), a strong revival of antitrust policy was a feature of his second term. Under Thurman Arnold the Antitrust Division of the Department of Justice linked enforcement of the Sherman Act to a drive to end economic stagnation. An enlarged staff placed greater emphasis than in the past upon the collection of economic data and the selection of economically significant cases for prosecution. Congress authorized a full-scale study of the economy by the Temporary National Economic Committee (TNEC), whose reports provided more comprehensive information about the economy than had hitherto been available. In 1938 Congress also passed the Wheeler-Lea Act, which strengthened the Federal Trade Commission Act. By forbidding "unfair or deceptive acts or practices in commerce" the new statute relieved the FTC of having to prove injury to competitors when it sought to prevent "unfair methods of competition in commerce." The decade of the 1930's also witnessed a change in the direction of greater acceptance of the findings of regulatory agencies by reviewing courts.

Apparent in even a brief summary of public policy toward competition in trade practices are pervasive ambiguities toward large-scale business. All governmental institutions, including the courts, tend to reflect an ambivalence in our society on this point. While admiring big business for its contributions to an affluent society in the form of goods, services, and jobs, Americans usually display a sympathy for the underdog sufficient to prevent the economic power of big business from having completely free rein. Examples of sympathetic action abound at various governmental levels. In the 1930's many states responded to pressure from independent retailers by passing laws taxing chain stores on the basis of the number of outlets they had; often the taxes were on a graduated basis. "Fair trade" laws also began to achieve popularity with state legislatures in the "depression decade." By not permitting trademarked goods to be retailed at prices below the levels fixed by manufacturers, these laws have favored small retailers in their competition with large stores and discount houses. At the federal level, the Robinson-Patman Act of 1936 was passed in order to prevent chain stores and other large purchasers of manufactured goods from receiving quantity discounts in excess of the cost differences in selling to them as compared with selling to smaller purchasers. The statute represented an attempt to tighten up the Clayton Act's prohibition of price discrimination.

It is perhaps symbolic of American ambiguity about big business that measures designed to protect the little fellow have not always had such protection as their major, or at least exclusive, effect. For example, though the Robinson-Patman Act placed the burden on huge grocery chains to justify the quantity discounts they received, small retailers were disconcerted to find that the chains could prove that the costs of selling to them were sometimes even less than the discounts had indicated. What the act had accomplished was to place large firms under surveillance in transactions of this kind and to place the burden of proof on them to justify the price concessions they were able to obtain. To give another example, resale price maintenance ("fair trade") laws protect small retailers against price competition from chain stores, discount houses, and department stores, but they also have the ardent backing of various large manufacturers who are eager to see their products sold at fixed prices despite traditional ideas about free competition in the market place. Such state statutes, authorizing price-fixing agreements violating the Sherman Act, could not be applied to goods moving in interstate commerce until that act had been amended to exempt from its coverage price agreements authorized by state laws, a step taken in the Miller-Tydings Act of 1937. After the Supreme Court decided in 1951 that this exemption did not apply to retailers who had not actually signed a resale price maintenance agreement with a manufacturer, Congress passed the McGuire-Keough Fair Trade Enabling Act of 1952, which amended Section 5 of the Federal Trade Commission Act. Not only did it in effect force non-signing retailers to abide by minimum prices set by manufacturers, when authorized by state legislation, but it extended the power of manufacturers by permitting them to fix exact rather than minimum prices and by legalizing contracts that required whole-

salers to bind retailers to observe the retail prices fixed by manufacturers. Though the courts sanctioned this statutory arrangement,
related developments prevented it from being widely effective. In the
eleven years after the McGuire-Keough Act was passed, the non-
signer clause was invalidated by state courts or legislatures in twenty-
two states, in five of which the entire fair trade law was eliminated.[3]
As a consequence, fair trade proponents have redoubled efforts to
obtain federal enforcement of resale price maintenance, as opposed to
federal authorization of state enforcement.

The most clearly defined rules for competition deal with overtly
abusive practices, as might be expected. Predatory actions were the
downfall of Standard Oil and American Tobacco in the very cases
that produced the softened interpretation of the Sherman Act known
as the "rule of reason." Though these decisions undoubtedly curbed
the most obviously predatory practices, the courts have had occasion
in more recent times to reaffirm their view on blatantly anticompetitive practices. Both in 1959 and 1961 federal district courts found companies and certain of their officials guilty of making price-fixing agreements with their competitors.[4] In both instances, short jail terms
were imposed on officials, marking the first such punishment for corporate executives since the passage of the first federal antitrust law
in 1890. The 1961 group of cases received widespread publicity because they involved General Electric, Westinghouse, and other well-
known electrical equipment manufacturers. It is significant that the
judicial treatment of these companies and their officials received
widespread approval in editorial columns.

When overt abuses are lacking and the question is one of size
alone, public policy and attitudes have been much more ambiguous.
The Supreme Court has often been sharply divided. A landmark case
was *United States* v. *U.S. Steel Corporation* in 1920.[5] Formed in 1901,
the giant corporation controlled directly about half of the steel industry when the case came to trial and through its price leadership
strongly influenced the remainder. By a four-to-three vote, the Court
decided that it was not an illegal combination or a monopoly and
decided against dissolution of the company. The majority believed
that U.S. Steel's timely abandonment of price-fixing agreements
and of the famous "Gary dinners" at which steel industry decisions had been made meant that abusive practices were not involved. As to giantism and its economic effects, the majority stated
that "the law does not make mere size an offense or the existence
of unexerted power an offense." A generation later, in 1948, the
Supreme Court once more upheld, again by a one-vote margin, the
doctrine that the mere existence of great economic power is no reason
to dissolve it. Columbia Steel Company, a subsidiary of U.S. Steel,
was permitted to acquire the largest independent steel fabricator on

the West Coast.[6] The merger was approved despite the fact that it would exclude all other steel manufacturers from the business of supplying rolled steel to this fabricator and that competition between the latter and U.S. Steel in the sale of structural fabricated products and pipe would be eliminated. No attempt to monopolize was involved, in the opinion of the majority, because U.S. Steel's action reflected a "normal business purpose" rather than an "unreasonable restraint" of trade. The two decisions involving U.S. Steel, coming as they did a generation apart, seemed to foreclose attacks on bigness unless abusive practices were involved.

Yet, as a mark of the fluidity of antitrust policy, it should be noted that events since 1948 have pointed in the opposite direction. Two important developments may be singled out for special attention. The first was Congress' strengthening, in 1950, of the antimerger provision in the Clayton Act. The second relates to the emergence of a broader judicial view toward antitrust statutes.

Though Section 7 of the Clayton Act of 1914 had forbidden intercorporate stock acquisitions that substantially lessen competition or tend to create a monopoly of any line of commerce, judicial interpretation rendered the provision virtually ineffective. In 1926 the Supreme Court, in a five-to-four vote, decided that the statute did not cover the acquisition of one firm's assets by another, even if the action had been based upon an illegal acquisition of voting stock.[7] From 1926 onward, the Federal Trade Commission vainly urged Congress to plug the loophole through which anticompetitive mergers could be effectuated by the purchase of assets. In 1950 Congress finally acted. The legislative history of the Celler-Kefauver Act made plain that the amended Section 7 was to be applied to all types of mergers—horizontal (between competitors), vertical (between a supplier and a customer), and conglomerate (between makers of different products). What course of action would the Supreme Court follow this time? Judicial attitudes had changed, but the surprise was in how much they had changed.

Not only the 1950 amendment but also the original Section 7 have been given a scope by the judiciary that makes this provision of the Clayton Act a powerful proclamation of public policy on competition. The evidence for this statement is found in decisions of the Supreme Court in 1957 and 1962. The first involved a suit by the Department of Justice against Du Pont de Nemours for its World War I acquisition of 23 per cent of the stock of General Motors Corporation.[8] The suit was brought mainly under the Sherman Act, with violation of Section 7 cited almost as an afterthought. It was the Clayton Act provision—the same one so thoroughly emasculated by an earlier Court—on which the Court relied to find that Du Pont's controlling stock ownership in General Motors gave an illegal edge over other suppliers of automotive finishes and fabrics in competition for sales to General Motors. The decision was doubly significant. It meant that any mergers made subsequent to the enactment in 1914 of Section 7 could be judged in the light of their current "reasonable likelihood" of producing a lessening of competition or a tendency toward monopoly. Secondly, it meant that Section 7 could be applied to vertical acquisitions (Du Pont's relationship of supplier to General Motors) as well as to its more traditional category of horizontal mergers (among competitors). Because the *Du Pont* decision had been decided by an unusual four-to-two vote, the first interpretation of the 1950 amendment by a full Court was awaited with special eagerness. This interpretation came in 1962 when the Supreme Court unanimously declared illegal the Brown Shoe Company's acquisition of the G. R. Kinney Company.[9] Because both companies distributed as well as manufactured shoes, the merger tested the 1950 amendment's application to conglomerate (both horizontal and vertical) mergers. Since neither shoe manufacturing nor shoe distribution is an oligopolistic industry and since both companies were tiny by comparison with Du Pont and General Motors, the case provided a good test of the meaning of the 1950 amendment. Placing heavy stress on its belief that Congress intended to halt monopoly in its "incipiency," the Supreme Court voided the merger. The existence of numerous companies in shoe manufacturing and distribution, the Court implied, permitted mergers of modest-sized firms to affect competition strongly. Though Kinney manufactured less than one half of one per cent and retailed less than 2 per cent of the shoes in the nation, its acquisition by Brown not only permitted the latter to become the third largest American shoe manufacturer but also lessened competition for the supplying of shoes to Kinney, the country's largest independent shoe chain.

The government is now fully empowered to use the control over mergers given it by the Celler-Kefauver Act in far more forceful ways than in the past. Furthermore, a statement of the majority in a case subsequent to the *Brown Shoe Company* case indicates that the tasks of trustbusters may be simplified. "Where a merger is of such a size as to be inherently suspect," said the Supreme Court in 1964, "elaborate proof of market structure, market behavior and probable anticompetitive effects may be dispensed with in view of Section 7's design to prevent undue concentration."[10] Since the passage of the 1950 amendment, the Antitrust Division, which shares jurisdiction with the Federal Trade Commission in enforcement of the Clayton Act, has been alert to the more favorable conditions for the prevention of mergers. The greater facility with which mergers may now be stopped in their incipiency, however, raises a major policy question. What should be the attitude toward oligopolistic structures created *before* the means for preventing them were made relatively easy?

Although the Clayton Act has thus become a potent weapon against mergers, a second development of significance is that the Sherman Act has also been vastly strengthened and sharpened as an instrument of policy. The change began with a case decided in 1945, three years before the *Columbia Steel* case, by the Court of Appeals of the Second Circuit. It acted as a court of last resort since so many Supreme Court justices had disqualified themselves because of prior connections with the prosecution of the case that the Supreme Court could not muster a quorum of six to hear the appeal. Judge Learned Hand's opinion in the case, *United States* v. *Aluminum Co. of America,* introduced a test for monopoly not related to abusive actions but to the power to control prices.[11] Only those firms "who do not seek, but cannot avoid, the control of a market" can escape being branded illegal monopolies under Section 2 of the Sherman Act. Because Alcoa had consistently expanded its capacity in order to meet the needs of a rapidly growing market, commanding 90 per cent of the virgin ingot market, it could not come under this exception, according to Judge Hand. Whether Alcoa had actually charged "unfair" prices was not the point: ". . . it must sell at some price and the only price at which it could sell is a price which it itself fixed." This power to fix prices he declared to be a test of illegal monopoly. A year after Hand's widely noticed opinion, the Supreme Court specifically endorsed his approach in a case involving monopolization by the three leading cigaret producers, though in later cases it qualified the Alcoa doctrine.[12]

The emphasis in the *Alcoa* case upon market control has tended to supplant "intent" as a basis for judging whether the Sherman Act has been violated. Instead of judicial mind reading as to the purpose of a merger, courts are now more inclined to ask whether a crucial percentage of the relevant market will be seriously affected. As noted above, the latter line of thought has also been pursued in Clayton Act cases.

In deciding whether there is market control, the definition of the relevant market is crucial. Judge Hand calculated Alcoa's control of the market at 90 per cent on the basis of using virgin ingots as the market. When the *Alcoa* case was remanded to a district court, it took into consideration not only scrap aluminum but also other metals that compete with aluminum.[13] Similarly, the Supreme Court declared in 1956, in a case involving Du Pont's monopoly of cellophane, that the relevant market was flexible wrapping materials and that therefore Du Pont was not guilty of monopolization.[14] Nevertheless, the very next year, in the Du Pont-General Motors case noted previously, the Supreme Court adopted a radically narrower definition of the relevant market, defining it as fabrics and finishes for automobiles rather than for all uses. In general, the increasing diversification of industry and increasing substitutability of materials and products have made the determination of a relevant market much more difficult.

It is plain that the Supreme Court will make no blanket definitions of a market or of a disqualifying percentage of market control but will concentrate upon an analysis of the economic situation in each case before it. Ever since a 1954 case involving the United Shoe Machinery Corporation, it has also been clear that the Supreme Court will require higher standards of behavior of firms with substantial market power than in instances where numerous firms are competing with relatively equal chances for forging ahead of their competitors.[15] The approach of the Supreme Court indicates that firms need not be national giants in order to fall afoul of the Sherman Act. In April 1964, for example, the Court invalidated the merger of two banks in Lexington, Kentucky, on the ground that after their combination into one firm they had more than half of the commercial banking business in the county (the relevant market).[16] This was, however, a five-to-four decision.

Public policy toward competition and trade practices has a difficult task in dealing with a huge and complex economy. It faces such questions as the following, some of which have been touched on here: Is size itself a threat to competition or to other values? Shall market power be the criterion for monopoly, and, if so, what is the relevant market? Does the increasing diversification of industry promote competition by pitting firms in one industry against those in another, or does it discourage competition and the establishment of new firms by putting an even greater premium on size and mergers? Shall resale price maintenance laws be encouraged to protect small retailers or discouraged to assist the consumer's budget?

The American economy is in a period of considerable ferment, and considerable flexibility is required of antitrust agencies if they are to deal rapidly and discerningly with difficult questions. There are indications that these agencies are actively trying to meet this challenge. During the first half of 1964, almost 700 mergers were announced, and every one underwent at least preliminary scrutiny by the Antitrust Division. During the same year the Division streamlined its procedures for issuing advance opinions on mergers and extended the scope of the opinions to activities in foreign commerce. The Federal Trade Commission, which has often been criticized for pursuing minor offenders while overlooking major ones, announced in 1964 a new policy of undertaking studies of competition in specific industries and issuing broad rules stating whether it would prosecute certain mergers. Though advance rulings have not always proved practicable in the past, the efforts of the two agencies portend alertness in dealing with a great upsurge of mergers in the 1960's. A provision of the original Sherman Act, providing that firms injured by a price-fixing conspiracy are entitled to sue for triple damages, has achieved a new significance since the twenty-nine manufacturers of electrical equipment were convicted of price fixing in 1961. Within a few months, more than 1500 damage suits were filed, most of which were later settled out of court. When eight steel concerns were indicted for a similar offense in 1964, the triple-damages provision again loomed in the background in the event of conviction.

TRANSPORTATION

In a dynamic society that has seen modes of transportation rise and fall and intense rivalry develop among them, regulatory arrangements are, as might be expected, somewhat chaotic. For each form of domestic transportation to which national regulatory policy has been applied, different emphases can be discerned. Even the splitting up of transportation regulation among governmental agencies is not symmetrical. Rail and motor carriers have been regulated by the same agency, but air transportation is divided between two; water carriers, meanwhile, have been shunted among several agencies.

GROUND AND WATER TRANSPORT

Railroad regulation, the pioneer among national efforts, illustrates the difficulty of applying the right regulatory remedy at the right time. Although 1887 is conventionally considered the date when the Interstate Commerce Commission began to regulate railroads, a more realistic date is 1906. If abuses by railroads meant that the nation was eminently ready for vigorous railroad regulation at the earlier date, the combination of a weak statute, an unsympathetic judiciary, and a powerful railroad lobby combined to prevent effective action. For twenty years the ICC marked time by collecting information, making reports, issuing protests, and repeatedly asking Congress for more authority. Finally, in the Hepburn Act of 1906, it was explicitly given the power to set maximum rates. During the decade that followed, the scope of railroad regulation was increased further, as Congress authorized the ICC to determine rates more rationally through valuing railroad property, to suspend rate increases until they could be investigated, and to prevent lower rates for "long hauls" as compared with "short hauls." This time the story of judicial emasculation was not repeated, for the courts began to defer to the Commission as an expert body enforcing legislation passed by the representatives of the people.

Railroad regulation, nevertheless, still lacked a coordinated approach to problems affecting the carriers, the shippers, and the public. Though the ICC could now establish maximum rates, it had been given no criteria for determining what rates were reasonable. It had no jurisdiction over the financial structure of railroads and was therefore handicapped in ascertaining the value of the investments from which the rates were to be calculated. Considered as a whole, the country's railroads suffered from considerable duplication of effort, nonproductive competition, and smallness of scale. World War I brought matters to a head by placing unprecedented demands upon railroad service, demands so great that government operation of the railroads was undertaken in 1917 in an effort to speed the movement of items necessary for the war effort.

The wartime experience in the operation of the railroads as a national system, coupled with a widespread awareness of the deficiencies in existing regulatory measures, led to passage of the Transportation Act of 1920. In brief, this comprehensive statute broadened the Commission's rate-making power to include minimum rates, extended its jurisdiction to railroad finances, encouraged the consolidation of railroads under Commission supervision with the proviso that competition would not be unduly restricted, and authorized the Commission to require safe and adequate service from the railroads—the latter including control over abandonment of existing lines and the construction of new ones.

Ironically, just when regulatory policy had finally become sufficiently comprehensive not only to prevent major abuses but to provide a positive emphasis, time ran out. The structure of regulation that had been painfully constructed was, unfortunately, suited to an era that was about to end—the era of railroad dominance in transportation. Had the ICC been given the statutory means in 1920 to shape motor carrier and domestic water carrier industries, it is conceivable that it might have been able to cope with the swiftly changing picture. The absence of such authority increasingly faced the Commission with the dilemma of whether to consider railroad regulation as a closed system, as the 1920 statute had seemed to consider it, or whether to recommend a new regulatory approach that would recognize the emergence of other forms of transportation. Because the atmosphere of the 1920's was not friendly to regulation, the ICC did not tackle this dilemma boldly. It tended to wait for pressures to develop before adjusting the rate structure. As a result, the ICC found itself importuned by the railroads to lower rates in areas where competition with other forms of transportation was acute, pressured by congressmen to prevent favoritism to certain regions of the country, and assailed by shippers in areas where the railroads were trying to maintain rates sufficiently high to offset rates lowered in competitive areas. On top of all this, the Great Depression dealt a body blow to railroad revenues and increased the ICC's feeling of protectiveness for the industry.

Between 1935 and 1940, Congress gave the Interstate Commerce Commission authority to regulate motor carriers and broadened its jurisdiction over water carriers. The increasingly interstate character of bus and truck traffic on the nation's developing highway system led to demands for federal regulation after about 1925. The long genesis of the Motor Carrier Act of 1935 may be attributed to the complexity of regulating an industry with innumerable small operators employing various kinds of arrangements with shippers. Not only was the industry structure much more chaotic than that of the railroads, but considerable opposition developed from farmers, who feared interference with use of trucks in marketing, and from portions of the motor carrier industry, which feared regulatory restrictions. Federal action was sought, on the other hand, by some of the bigger bus and truck operators, who desired more stability in competition; by many small shippers, who objected to prices for service charged by the larger carriers; and by the railroads, who naturally wished to see their competitors brought under regulation. The 1935 statute, though representing the triumph of those who favored federal regulation, recognized the character of the motor carrier industry. The Interstate Commerce Commission was not permitted to regulate intrastate rates as a part of the control over interstate rates, as it had been authorized to do for railroads; state regulation remains important in the motor carrier industry. Among the various exceptions listed in the Motor Carrier Act is one for farmers' trucks. Unlike the railroads, which are uniformly classed as common carriers, the motor carrier industry is dominated by contract carriers and private carriers, though common carriers also have an important role to play. While all three types of carriers were made subject to safety rules, the act differentiated among them as to economic regulation. The common carriers were most fully regulated, the contract carriers less so, and the private carriers not at all. Common carriers, which are for hire by all, require a certificate of convenience and necessity and are subject to ICC regulation of rates, fares, service, financial matters, combinations, and consolidations. Contract carriers, which limit their services to specific shippers with whom they contract for a definite period of time, require only a permit to operate. Their minimum rates are set by the ICC, but only in order that some protection be afforded to the common carriers.

Federal regulation of water carriers was spotty and confused before 1940. Regulation was divided between the Interstate Commerce Commission and the United States Shipping Board, created in 1916, or its successor, the Maritime Commission, established in 1936. The ICC's jurisdiction was limited to water carriers controlled by railroads. Regulation by the Shipping Board and its successor was limited to ocean transport and transport on the Great Lakes and in interstate coastwise traffic. Traffic plying from one coast to another and on inland waterways other than the Great Lakes was excluded, together with contract and private carriers. Both the Shipping Board and the Maritime Commission tended to concentrate on subsidy programs rather than on regulation. The Transportation Act of 1940 made several changes in water carrier regulation. It transferred jurisdiction over domestic water transportation to the ICC. Regulation was made analogous to motor carrier regulation, including the differences between regulation of common carriers and contract carriers. The amount of tonnage actually being regulated was vastly decreased, however, by exemptions for private carriers, for contract carriers not competing "substantially" with other types of transport, and, in general, for common carriers of bulk goods.

After 1940 the ICC could face its regulatory dilemma more squarely, though the task of regulation was rendered yet more complex. The Transportation Act of 1940 contained a statement of "national transportation policy" that directed the ICC "to recognize and preserve the inherent advantages of each [mode of transportation]." In general, the ICC interpreted this directive along the lines of a live-and-let-live policy. It encouraged reductions by rail or motor carriers in order to bring about an equality of rates between rivals from the two camps, but it was much less inclined to permit any reduction once equality was achieved. Thus, in the absence of a comprehensive national transportation policy, a conservative regulatory agency found it expedient to present peacemaking as a policy. The railroads, in particular, objected to the ICC approach because it prevented rate cutting as a weapon for countering commercial truckers' inroads into the business of hauling high-value freight. The Transportation Act of 1958 helped the railroads by declaring that the "rates of a carrier shall not be held up to a particular level to protect the traffic of any other mode of transportation." In an effort to win grain traffic from barge lines, four Southern railroads cut some of their rates 600 per cent and more in 1961. Though barge lines in the area protested that these cuts were selective and made with the intent of driving them out of business, they were unsuccessful in persuading the courts to interfere. In 1963 the Supreme Court ruled (six-to-three) that Congress did not intend federal courts to have authority to delay railroad rate changes by injunctions.[17] The dissenters noted disapprovingly that the railroads did not lower rates for the connecting rail links that the barge lines must use when transporting cargo between St. Louis and Birmingham, for example. Such selective rate cutting, according to the Court's minority, left the water carriers in a precarious financial condition. Undoubtedly the ICC, in dealing with intermodal competition, frequently must consider whether consenting to rate cuts made by one regulated carrier will result in the bankruptcy of another regulated carrier.

The ICC's difficulties in regulating several modes of transportation under a variety of statutory directives reflect a lack of national consensus on policy and, more specifically, a lack of agreement as to the proper mixture of promotion and regulation for each mode of transportation. Rival interest groups have pushed their points of view with great vigor. In the postwar years the railroads have gained considerable sympathy for their argument that they should be permitted greater freedom in competing. By the Transportation Act of 1958 the ICC was empowered to guarantee up to $500 million in private loans to railroads and, more importantly, to permit the discontinuance of interstate train or ferry service that is unprofitable. Since 1958 the railroads have requested further loosening of the regulatory shackles. Truckers have countered that the railroads' financial power and bargaining leverage would enable them to drive truckers out of business and then raise rates. Truckers themselves have been accused of not paying an adequate amount for their use of the public highways, a complaint met with the retort that trucks constitute about 16 per cent of the vehicles using the highways but pay about 37 per cent of the special highway users' taxes. Still another interested party is the Inland Waterways Common Carriers Association, which admits to free use of publicly financed waterways by its members; it has based its defense upon the proposition that, unlike the railroads, barge lines have not raised rates for many years. Communities and industries benefiting from the low rates naturally have fought user charges for barge lines.

The basic question raised by such conflicting viewpoints is whether it is both feasible and desirable to seek uniformity of governmental treatment of each mode of transportation. The variation in regulatory conditions among all forms of transportation is so great and so seemingly capricious that there is a need for careful reëxamination of the reasons for diversity. Some idea of the degree of variation was conveyed in President Kennedy's message to Congress on transportation policy in April 1962:

> Some carriers are required to provide, at a loss, services for which there is little demand. Some carriers are required to charge rates which are high in relation to cost in order to shelter competing carriers. Some carriers are prevented from

making full use of their capacity by restrictions on freedom to solicit business or adjust rates. Restraints on cost-reducing rivalry in rate-making often cause competition to take the form of cost-increasing rivalry—such as excessive promotion and traffic solicitation, or excessive frequency of service. Some carriers are subject to rate regulation on the transportation of particular commodities while other carriers, competing for the same traffic, are exempt. Some carriers benefit from public facilities provided for their use, while others do not; and of those enjoying the use of public facilities, some bear a large part of the cost, while others bear little or none.[18]

Some of these policies are more difficult to render uniform than others; each would have to be examined on its merits. For example, it would seem that in adjusting rates the railroads are seriously disadvantaged by having to give thirty days' notice of a change and perhaps fight the proposal before the ICC and the courts for months or years, whereas barge companies can change their rates at will on 90 per cent of what they carry and trucking companies on two thirds of their cargoes. But how much consideration should be given to the structure of competing industries, i.e., the predominance of railroad giants as contrasted with the existence of numerous small contract carriers and private carriers in motor and water transport? Are stricter rules justified for modes of transportation that have more powerful competitors? It can be argued that a lack of uniformity in regulation is implicit in Congress' declaration that "the inherent advantages" of each mode are to be preserved. While this argument carries much weight, it has its limits. Many of the differences in regulatory rules appear to be as much the product of historical accident as of design, and there is far from a perfect correlation between size and regulatory restrictions. Some would also question whether intermodal competition is as important as it is sometimes asserted to be. Trucks, it is argued, were regulated to prevent them from destroying each other through cutthroat competition rather than to curb rivalry with the railroads. More to the point, for a seven-month period in 1960, motor carriers filed 647 protests against the tariffs of other motor carriers, whereas they filed only 297 against rail tariffs and eight against water tariffs.[19] These data are far from conclusive, and it is significant that one third of the cases cited involved the question of intermodal competition.

The problems of air carrier regulation differ significantly from those of railroads, motor carriers, and water carriers. Aside from passenger traffic, there is little direct competition between the airlines and other forms of transportation. Also, until recently, rate regulation has not been nearly so prominent for airlines as for land carriers; government's primary concern has been promotional. This is not to say that the railroads, in particular, have not cast envious glances at the bounties airlines receive in the form of government-supplied air terminals, when the railroads not only must supply their own terminals but pay taxes on them. Historical factors again provide the explanation: in the air age an airport is the mark of a community that has arrived; the airlines can claim that the railroads received an equivalent subsidy in the extensive public lands they were given in their own early years.

AIR TRANSPORT

Air transport regulation may be said to have gone through three stages in its relatively brief history. The first stage, lasting to 1938, involved considerable reliance upon regular departments of the national government. Despite the efforts of the Wright brothers and other pioneers, commercial air transportation became a reality only after the great impetus given to the airplane by the First World War. It was not until 1926 that federal regulation became a reality, and then it concerned only safety rules. The Department of Commerce was authorized to administer safety regulations and to carry on promotional activities. Curiously, it was the Postmaster General who first had economic regulatory power over airlines. Though he possessed the authority to contract for the carrying of airmail from 1925 onward, it was not until 1930 that he was empowered to select, consolidate, or extend routes for mail transport, prescribe financial accounting methods and personnel requirements, and specify the nature of passenger service by mail planes. The key to the growth of the air transport industry were the payments for carrying the mail. Initially not conceived of as subsidies—being limited to four fifths of the airmail revenue—the payments were made more generous by Congress in 1930 to encourage passenger traffic; airlines found them a lucrative financial base for route expansion.

By the middle 1930's air transport had become an important industry, and government's relationship to it had become complex. The Department of Commerce administered safety regulations and some promotional activities; the Interstate Commerce Commission, by the terms of the Air Mail Act of 1934, fixed rates for the carrying of mail; and the Postmaster General regulated service, accounting, and intercorporate relations. Unified regulation under the ICC was sought unsuccessfully by President Roosevelt in 1937. In the following year, however, the Civil Aeronautics Act was passed. It provided for two new agencies to take over the regulatory and promotional tasks. The Civil Aeronautics Administration, under the supervision of the Secretary of Commerce, was given the job of handling promotional activities associated with airports and air navigational facilities as well as the task of administering safety rules. The Civil Aeronautics Board, an independent regulatory commission, was given the authority to issue certificates of convenience and necessity to air carriers; to approve rates, airmail payments, and subsidies; and to make air safety rules. Rate making had a strong subsidy component because the 1938 statute charged the CAB with setting airmail payments at a level consistent with the continued growth of an airline industry. The Civil Aeronautics Act thus continued and expanded the principle of promotional regulation of air transport.

The third phase of air transport regulation, which began in the 1950's, has witnessed two important shifts. First, the promotional element in regulation has been more sharply differentiated and has been administered with greater discrimination as to need. Prior to 1953 subsidy payments to air carriers were not segregated from total governmental payments to them. Under President Eisenhower's Reorganization Plan No. 10 of 1953, amounts paid for carrying airmail were segregated in accounting from amounts paid for promotional purposes. This arrangement was incorporated into the Federal Aviation Act of 1958. During the 1950's, as domestic trunk lines and international carriers became stronger, subsidy payments to them were gradually eliminated. Simultaneously, however, subsidy payments were made in ever increasing amounts to local service carriers, as this element of air transport became of greater consequence. The second development in air carrier regulation has involved changes in regulatory responsibility. Vastly increased air traffic and the use of fast jet planes made previous safety rules obsolete in the 1950's. In 1958 the Federal Aviation Agency was created to take over the making of safety rules from the Civil Aeronautics Board and their administration from the Civil Aeronautics Administration, which was abolished. The FAA was also given the responsibility of coordinating the use of air lanes by military, as well as civilian, pilots. The revocation and suspension of certificates held by airlines or pilots may be appealed from the FAA to the CAB and from there to the courts. The CAB retained its responsibility for the economic aspects of air transport, including rates, routes, and subsidies.

Regulation of air transportation has posed knotty questions about the proper balance between freedom of action for the carriers and restrictive rules on them. The dilemma applies to questions of safety as well as of economics. Recognizing the need to acquire and retain public confidence, commercial airlines have been cooperative about grounding their planes pending the investigation and correction of hazards. Nevertheless, the administration of safety regulations, particularly in their application to pilots, has often been controversial. The first administrator of the Federal Aviation Agency complained vigorously in print about the "sustained, highly organized pressure campaigns . . . encountered at every turn."[20] From his point of view, associations of private and commercial airline pilots, as well as the commercial carriers themselves, "had grown used to a situation in which the regulator was regulating with an eye more to the wishes of the regulated than to the needs of the public." As an example of his belief that safety regulations are far from being too stringent, Administrator E. R. Quesada cited the case of a commercial pilot whose pilot rating the FAA had revoked after a hearing in which it was determined that he had violated regulations. Yet the pilot was able to continue flying pending disposition of his case on appeal to the Civil Aeronautics Board; several months after the FAA cited him, he and twenty-two passengers lost their lives in the crash of a chartered plane.

Economic regulation of air carriers has revolved mainly around the question of right of entry. Viewed against the possibility of having numerous competing carriers flying many routes, the CAB policy appears restrictive. Considered against the other extreme— the possibility of allowing established carriers to combine freely—the CAB policy appears much less conservative. No new trunk lines have been added since 1938, when the CAB was established, but existing lines have been allowed to extend their routes and. add new ones. On the one hand, this policy has been hard on the non-certificated carriers—the "non-skeds"—which have only been permitted chartered flights. On the other hand, the certificated carriers have complained that the CAB has allowed so much competition among them on certain routes that operations have become unattractive and even unprofitable. Recently, the CAB has given indications that it is listening sympathetically to the complaints from both groups of carriers and their spokesmen in Congress, while holding to a middle course. In 1964 the Board proposed that more cargo business be shifted from the certificated carriers to the "non-skeds" and that the latter be given a larger percentage of the transatlantic military mail. During the previous year a CAB decision met the certificated carrier's criticism of overcompetition on routes. The decision was to revoke a temporary certificate granted to Northeast Airlines in 1956 to fly the lucrative New York-Miami route already served by Eastern Airlines and National Airlines. Although the carrying out of the decision was delayed by Northeast's appeal to the courts, it was reaffirmed by the Board in 1964 after a court-directed reëxamination of the evidence. It may well be that this decision was taken to offset the CAB's refusal, also in 1963, to permit Eastern, a money-loser since 1961, to merge with American Airlines. The merger would have created the nation's largest airline, one handling over one third of domestic air transportation. This refusal, a three-to-two party line vote, probably also reflected the stand of the Department of Justice, which said that the proposed merger would result in a monopoly.

The desire to promote competition in regulated transportation industries, where many merger applications have been filed in recent years, may have prompted President Kennedy in 1962 to establish an Interagency Committee on Transport Mergers with the mandate to "formulate general Administration merger policies and to arrive at a Government position as to each pending transportation merger of significance."[21] Such mergers fall under the aegis of the independent regulatory commissions, and hence the Interagency Committee, composed of representatives from regular departments, has only the power of persuasion. In 1963 the head of the Antitrust Division of the Department of Justice, representing the Committee, appeared at a hearing held before an ICC examiner on the question of merging the two Eastern railroad giants, the Pennsylvania Railroad and the New York Central. He represented the government's position as one of opposing this merger of giants while recognizing the need for consolidating smaller Eastern railroads in order to improve transportation facilities.

UTILITIES, COMMUNICATIONS, AND SECURITIES

These important areas of regulation—utilities, communications, and securities—overlap somewhat. "Public utilities" is a nineteenth-century term that originally pertained to any business "clothed with a public interest." The extension of the frontier of regulation rendered this definition virtually meaningless. In 1934 the Supreme Court declared that "It is clear that there is no closed class or category of businesses affected with a public interest" and that "The phrase 'affected with a public interest' can, in the nature of things, mean no more than that an industry, for adequate reason, is subject to control for the public good."[22] Terms have a way of living on, however, and electrical and natural gas "utilities" are found throughout the length and breadth of the land, although, as we shall see, these two industries are markedly different. Two forms of communications —telephone and telegraph—often are labeled "utilities," although two more modern communications media—radio and television— usually are not. "Securities" are discussed at this point because they are interwoven with the other areas, as well as with transportation.

For transport and for public utilities, which are the subject of the next section, rate making is important, and it is well to understand how rate making fits into our constitutional scheme. For government to fix the price of goods sold by entrepreneurs was at first considered by some of the affected businesses as the taking of property without due process of law in violation of the Fifth and Fourteenth Amendments. Under the guidance of the courts, the fixing of rates for certain property dedicated to public use or "clothed with a public interest" was fitted into the constitutional structure. In brief, the courts legitimized rate making by establishing safeguards on the way it could be employed by government agencies. A balance was sought between the interests of the consumer and of the investor. As businesses labeled "public utilities" often had a monopoly, governmental surveillance over rates was adjudged reasonable. Yet, because the property was privately owned, it was assumed by the courts that the rates charged by the business in question should be adequate to cover not only operating expenses but also the capital costs of the business. The latter include depreciation of the plant and a return on the capital investment. It is out of the second of these that interest can be paid on the debt and dividends on the stock. The matter of the proper *rate* of return for the owners of the business has been questioned within a relatively narrow range. In general, it has been assumed that the risks of doing business as a protected monopoly are not so great as for unregulated businesses. Over the years, a rule-of-thumb figure of 5 to 8 per cent as a rate has come into general favor. The rate base (i.e., the figure upon which the return is calculated) has been more controversial. Three methods of determining property value have been especially prominent: the "reproduction cost" method involves finding the cost of reproducing the property at present prices; "original cost," the actual cost to the utility of the present property; and "prudent investment," original cost less those expenditures that would not have been made by a competent and prudent businessman. The task of regulatory bodies in rate making was endlessly complicated by the Supreme Court's decision in 1898 that "fair value" could be ascertained from a long list of criteria, some contradictory, which were "to be given such weight as may be just and right in each case."[23] Regulatory agencies found it difficult to decide which method of calculating property value would meet the approval of a specific court at a specific time, and various state commissions virtually abandoned formal rate proceedings in order to avoid protracted and expensive litigation. The confusion persisted until the 1940's, when the Supreme Court decided to restrict judicial participation in rate making. In 1942 it stated that "The Constitution does not bind rate-making bodies to the service of any single formula or combination of formulas," and that "the courts cannot intervene in the absence of a clear showing that the limits of due process have been overstepped."[24] Two years later, it specifically overruled the 1898 case, emphasizing that "the total effect of the rate order" was the crucial question.[25] The relaxation of judicial restrictions on the methods employed by rate-making bodies does not, of course, prevent the courts from striking down confiscatory rates, for example, as a violation of constitutional due process.

The differences between the electrical and natural gas industries have affected their regulation by government. These differences rest largely upon the extent to which electricity and natural gas flow in interstate commerce. Typically, electric utilities are integrated businesses that generate, transmit, and distribute their product. Though increasing numbers of such power systems are interconnected, less than 10 per cent of the electricity produced by the private companies is sold at wholesale in interstate commerce to distributors for resale. Federal supervision of these transactions is important, but the direct impact of federal regulation falls on a far smaller segment of the total business of the electric power industry than of the natural gas industry. The concentration of natural gas deposits, largely on the western side of the Gulf of Mexico, has necessitated a strong emphasis upon the interstate flow of natural gas, a phenomenon which in turn has vastly complicated industry structure and federal regulation. Natural gas producers, which include virtually the entire petroleum industry, are not subject to federal regulation as such, but because they sell their product largely in interstate commerce they come under federal regulation at that point. The second segment of the natural gas industry consists of a relatively small number of huge transmission pipeline companies whose operations are directly under federal regulation. Finally, there are the thousands of gas distributors who are under state regulation but depend upon the Federal Power Commission for protection in dealing with the pipeline companies. The Commission has no authority over the securities of natural gas companies, but it has limited authority over those issued by electric companies operating in interstate commerce when the state commissions do not exercise a security review jurisdiction.

Though a larger segment of the railroad industry than of the electrical utilities falls under federal regulation, a resemblance to the history of railroad regulation may be noted. As with the railroads, electrical utilities were first encouraged by local and state governments, later regulated by state governments, and finally regulated by the national government, but the chronology differed. The electricity industry was only beginning when the shortcomings of state railroad regulation were becoming apparent in the 1880's. Effective state regulation in the electricity field began in 1907, a year after the Hepburn Act vitalized the national regulation of railroads. Effective national regulation of electric utilities dates from the New

Deal. Yet despite the time differences, the regulation of both industries suffered from a too-little, too-late complex; governmental efforts
came as a result of citizen complaints and not in anticipation of
abuses or of future industry patterns. Government, it must be said,
faced difficulties in staying abreast of the developments in electricity
generation, transmission, distribution, and utilization. Technological
advances were rapid, and what was once a local industry quickly
became interstate. The spectacular growth of the industry in the
1920's coincided with the advent of the small investor who was ready
to "take a fling" on promising stock issues, the proliferation of
holding companies, and a rash of mergers. Because the courts undertook to pass on rates themselves, rate regulation in the states almost
ground to a halt while the commissions sought to follow the bewil-
dering court edicts about the "fair value" upon which to base rates.

The 1930's marked the turning point in electrical utilities regulation. As noted above, just after the close of the decade the Supreme
Court discouraged further judicial efforts to force regulatory commissions to use a particular method of valuation for rate-making
purposes, thereby encouraging broader administrative initiative and
setting the stage for fruitful national-state collaboration in electrical
utilities regulation. Even more significantly, the political arms of the
national government moved to remedy the conditions that had encouraged excesses of a nature and on a scale impossible to deal with
at a lower jurisdictional level. Probably no other industry soared
so high in the heady atmosphere of the 1920's nor plunged so low
after the stock market crash of 1929.

The substance of national regulatory policy can be set forth
briefly. The Federal Water Power Act of 1920 requires federal licenses
for hydroelectric power development on government lands or on
navigable waters of the United States. The Federal Power Commission, created in 1920 as a weak agency headed by three cabinet
officials acting ex officio, was made an independent regulatory body
of five members in 1930 and given broader duties under the Federal
Power Act of 1935. The Commission's range of authority was enlarged to include fixing wholesale rates and charges for interstate
transmission and overseeing mergers, records, and accounts of utilities engaged in interstate commerce. The same statute, nevertheless,
made clear Congress' strong reliance upon state regulation of electrical utilities. Federal regulation was to extend only to those matters
not subject to regulation by the states; the FPC was not given jurisdiction over interstate *retail* rates; it was empowered to create joint
boards of state and federal commissioners and to delegate matters
to them for decision; it was authorized to hold joint hearings with
state commissions on matters under FPC jurisdiction in which states
have an interest; and it was directed to make available to state

commissions not only information and reports but also members of its staff.

Another facet of national regulatory policy has been an attempt to encourage financial underpinnings more solid and less devastating to the small investor than intricately pyramided holding companies such as the Samuel Insull "empire," whose collapse, it is estimated, cost investors $4 billion. During the 1920's vast holding companies had been formed, not to provide better service but to control immense financial resources with modest stock investments. The Public Utility Holding Company Act of 1935, one of the most stringent regulatory measures in American history, in essence forbade holding companies except to the extent that they could be justified as providing more efficient electricity operations. Quick, unresisting compliance with so drastic an edict of corporate reorganization was not forthcoming. A series of Supreme Court decisions between 1938 and 1946 upholding sections of the act gradually allayed fears of unconstitutionality, and the patient work of the Securities and Exchange Commission in inviting the submission of reorganization plans and permitting flexibility in divestment eventually not only inspired confidence but considerably enhanced the financial stability of the remaining holding company systems.

In the 1930's public utility regulation was affected not only by the statutes reviewed above but also by the national government's development of hydroelectric power facilities, represented by the Tennessee Valley Authority and multipurpose dams in the West. Sponsors of these projects hoped that governmental competition would stimulate rate reduction and increase electricity use.

Although regulation of the electricity industry has achieved much greater effectiveness since the 1920's, old problems constantly arise in new guises. During the inflationary years after World War II, the companies often complained that increased costs were eating into the rate of return permitted by regulatory bodies. By contrast, in 1961 the two hundred leading utilities earned almost half a billion dollars above the figure that a 6 per cent return would have brought. The question of a proper rate of return on investment is partially affected by the money market; if non-regulated businesses are receiving annual returns considerably higher than regulated utilities, the latter, it is argued, may have difficulty attracting capital. In rebuttal, it is pointed out that the protection against competition and against confiscatory rates attracts capital to utilities even when rates of return are lower than for unregulated private enterprise. In any event, the private utilities, a growth industry in the postwar era, have financed their tremendous expansion of facilities with ease.

Another controversy revolves around technological advances in the industry and the FPC's limited power to deal with their consequences. The recent development of extra-high-voltage lines and much larger generating plants has made it feasible and economic to transmit electricity over greater distances than in the past and to consider the pooling of electric power and the integration of power systems. Though the industry has been making great strides toward capitalizing on these changes, the Commission has expressed doubts as to whether full benefits, in terms of cost reduction and lower rates for the consumer, will be realized. At present, the FPC merely has authority to encourage "the voluntary interconnection and co-ordination of facilities for the generation, transmission, and sale of electric energy." It does not have the authority to license power sites other than hydroelectric nor to require certificates of conven-ience and necessity for the construction and operation of extra-high-voltage lines. Nor can the Commission require the private power systems to include publicly-owned power, represented chiefly by about a thousand rural electric cooperatives and about two thousand municipal systems, in the integrated systems. The increasing obsoles-cence of small power plants and the availability of economically generated electric power in large private systems has accentuated the problem of deciding who will benefit from technological advances. At least a partial answer was provided in a unanimous Supreme Court opinion in March 1964. The Court decided that the FPC properly asserted jurisdiction of a California utility's sale of electric power to a municipality in that state, since part of the power had been generated out of state. The Court interpreted the Federal Power Act as granting the FPC ". . . jurisdiction of all sales of electric energy at wholesale in interstate commerce not expressly exempted by the Act itself. . . ."[26] The decision means that local power dis-tributors, many of whom are publicly owned, can purchase power at interstate wholesale rates if the utility with which it deals obtains some of its power from sources outside the state.

The complex natural gas industry has posed challenging regu-latory problems. State and local regulation of gas utilities was com-mon in the early decades of this century, but the gas was manu-factured from coal or oil by local companies. With the development in the 1920's of pipelines capable of carrying natural gas, regulation became much more complicated. In the 1930's producing states took steps to limit the withdrawal of gas in order to conserve it and to protect the property rights of all the producers. When the utilities that had been manufacturing gas began to purchase natural gas from interstate pipeline companies, state and local regulators lost control over an essential ingredient of the local utilities' costs. The rates charged to an intrastate utility by an interstate pipeline company could be regulated only by a national instrument, and in 1938 the Federal Power Commission was given this authority as well as ancillary powers similar to those it holds over the electricity industry.

The limits to the analogy with electricity regulation have been neatly stated as follows: "The policy problem was more than one of utility regulation because gas is a scarce resource, because its interstate transmission can raise conflicts of interest between producing and consuming states, and because the impact of gas on other fuels presents questions of national energy resource policy."[27] One advantage accruing to the FPC in dealing with a regulatory problem with so many facets was that, unlike most other national regulatory experiments, the national government moved to regulate natural gas while the industry was in its infancy.

Has the early arrival of national regulation been able to offset the immense complexity of the regulatory problem for natural gas? The answer is mixed. Regulatory action has helped to avoid the pattern of exploitation that characterized industries where national regulation arrived on the scene long after economic power had been concentrated. Nevertheless, ever since the passage of the Natural Gas Act in 1938 there has been intense controversy over a problem that is important to producers, retailers, and users of natural gas: the value of the gas as it comes from the field and enters the pipeline.

The Natural Gas Act furnished only ambiguities: "the production and gathering of natural gas" was exempted from it, but at the same time the courts had made plain that any sale to an interstate pipeline was a sale in interstate commerce. Because of the immense financial stakes involved, Congress has been the scene of bitter controversies between representatives of gas-producing states (backed by independent gas producers—the oil companies) and representatives of large gas-consuming states. Twice Congress has passed bills exempting natural gas producers from the act, only to have Presidents Truman and Eisenhower veto them (the latter because of the publicity given to a crude attempt to influence the vote of one senator through a sudden campaign contribution by an oil company). Though the Federal Power Commission was reluctant to regulate natural gas producers on the basis of the 1938 statute, in 1954 the Supreme Court ruled that the Commission had been too restrictive in its interpretation of the act.[28]

Ever since the Supreme Court's 1954 decision the Federal Power Commission has struggled to find a suitable formula by which to regulate producers. For pipeline companies, as for other utilities, there is a reasonably predictable relationship between the amount of expenditures of the regulated company and the amount of service provided. Calculations of the rates charged and the rate of return to the utility can roughly be based on the cost of service. For producers of natural gas, however, there is no such relationship between amount of investment and amount of gas produced. The dilemma was well stated by Justice Robert H. Jackson:

> Does anybody imagine that Roe can get or ought to get for his gas five times as much as Doe because he has spent five times as much? The service one renders to society in the gas business is measured by what he gets out of the ground, not by what he puts into it, and there is little more relation between the investment and the results than in a game of poker.[29]

In response to the FPC's call for suggestions, producers argued for a current market-price standard and representatives of gas-consuming states for a cost-of-service approach, neither of which the FPC deemed suitable. In 1960 the Commission finally announced a broad program for regulating producer rates on an area-price basis. Though the method for determining prices in each of twenty-three producing areas was deliberately left vague, the Commission's objective, according to its general counsel, was to "set prices adequate to maintain gas supplies needed for the nation's consumers, but at prices no higher than necessary to accomplish that purpose."[30] Two prices, a higher one for new wells because of rising costs and a lower one for older wells, were established in each area. In 1963 the Supreme Court upheld the area-price plan by a five-to-four vote.[31] The dissenters echoed the view of public utilities commissions in gas-consuming states that a failure to regulate prices individually on a cost-of-service basis would disadvantage consumers. Actually, enforcement of price ceilings by the FPC brought an end to the steady rise in wellhead gas prices between 1954 and 1960, a period in which the FPC's backlog of cases grew rapidly while the Commission was virtually immobilized by its inability to establish a regulatory formula to apply to producers.

COMMUNICATIONS

Turning to the regulation of communications, one is struck by the diversity of approaches required of the Federal Communications Commission in dealing with the telegraph and telephone industries, on the one hand, and with radio and television, on the other. While the former fit the utility regulation formulas, radio and television regulation requires a more subtle, unconventional approach. To prevent chaos on the airwaves, the number of radio and television stations must be limited and the stations carefully assigned frequencies or channels, restrictions that do not affect the other great mass medium, the press. But in supervising radio and television, government must avoid trampling on the freedom of communications that is prized in a democracy. To add to the dilemma, a television channel, in particular, is exceedingly lucrative, and the pressures that descend upon the heads of Federal Communications commissioners are, as a consequence, unparalleled.

The regulation of the two older forms of communication finds few parallels in other lands, where those media are usually run by the government. In this country both the telegraph and telephone industries have operated under a rather tolerant form of regulation. Though the telegraph was a marvel of the mid-nineteenth century, it has long been in decline. The situation led the FCC to promote the merger of Postal Telegraph with Western Union in 1943, to grant substantial rate increases, and to authorize the closing of offices and reduction of hours of service. By contrast, the telephone industry has steadily flourished, to the point where today American Telephone and Telegraph (the Bell system) is the world's largest corporation, with assets of $28 billion, a yearly budget of over $3 billion, a labor force greater than the population of Boston, 2¼ million stockholders, and annual revenues that in 1963 exceeded the combined incomes of thirty state governments.

How has the Bell system achieved its position of dominance? Partly by being aggressively expansionist, technologically alert, and, from its early days, lavish in its public relations campaigns; partly by its favorable regulatory situation. In general, regulation of telephone rates by states—which affects 75 per cent of Bell's business—has not been vigorous. State regulation has had to contend with the technological complexity of telephone regulation, the interstate character of the Bell system, the predominance of numerous small and unorganized customers of the company, and the favorable community image cultivated by AT&T. Federal regulation—which covers Bell's interstate and overseas business—is more adequate in concept and in execution, but it has had difficulty in reaching to the heart of the Bell system—the intrasystem transactions among Western Electric, Bell Laboratories, and AT&T. "Mother Bell" is not only both an operating and a holding company, but she also owns subsidiaries which develop and sell equipment to her local operating companies. Consequently, many opportunities have existed for transactions within the vast system to be made at prices permitting large profits to the subsidiaries but resulting in increased costs to the consumers. Through the leverage of an investigation authorized by Congress in the 1930's, the Federal Communications Commission was able to negotiate some reduction of AT&T rates, both intrastate and interstate. More significantly, the range of governmental information about the vast corporation was extended. Information on the net book value of assets, depreciation charges, and profit rates of subsidiary companies has aided the FCC and the state commissions in determining rate charges. The high profit rates of Western Electric, the equipment manufacturing subsidiary, have been the particular concern of joint state-federal investigation from time to time. Price reductions in Western Electric sales to Bell operating companies have been negotiated as a result of these investigations and have produced substantial customer savings. Another governmental avenue of approach to Western Electric involved an antitrust suit in the 1950's that resulted in a consent decree permitting the company to remain within the Bell system but making its patents available to other manufacturers and requiring it to make its costs public.

Though success has been far from total, regulation of the telephone industry thus appears to have shown improvement. Good use has been made of available regulatory powers to form a better, though still incomplete, picture of AT&T's costs and charges. The possibility of more drastic regulatory action has restrained Bell or forced it to turn back from efforts at greater domination. Thus, early in the twentieth century Bell acquired control of Western Union but shortly thereafter was persuaded by the threat of antitrust action to disgorge the telegraph company, agree not to buy up competing telephone companies, and agree to make long-distance connections for telephone calls among independent companies. In recent years, despite Bell's immense size and remarkable growth rate, the 2850 independent telephone companies managed to increase their operating revenues 213 per cent between 1951 and 1963 and to operate 50 per cent more telephones in 1963 than in 1955. Of the more than 81 million telephones in the country, the Bell system has 85 per cent. General Telephone and Electronics, the giant of the independent companies, has one third of the remainder.

Developments in 1964 indicated considerable alertness on the part of government agencies in preserving competition. The Antitrust Division filed a suit to prevent General Telephone and Electronics from adding three good-sized companies to the thirty operating companies it now has. The primary purpose of the suit, brought under Section 7 of the Clayton Act, was to avoid the effects of merger upon vertical competition, i.e., the elimination of equipment purchases on the open market by an arrangement for the three companies to purchase only from General Telephone and Electronics. A decade earlier the Division had consented—permanently, as a consent order was employed—to let the Bell system continue to purchase exclusively from Western Electric, its subsidiary, with much greater consequences for competition among equipment manufacturers. By its 1964 suit, the Division served notice that a similar arrangement was undesirable for a newer, increasingly powerful company. During 1964 another government agency, the Federal Communications Commission, acted to restrain the Bell system in several ways. Though these actions involved both raising and lowering rates, they were not at cross-purposes because goals attuned to the respective situations were sought. The FCC required Bell to reduce charges on long-distance calls so as to let subscribers benefit from the substantial growth in the number of telephones in service and from the company's efficiency and to bring its rate of return down 7.9 per cent to a level nearer the 7.25 per cent it recommended in 1963 (parenthetically it may be noted that Bell's rate of return has hovered around the former figure despite FCC reductions in interstate rates in 1959 and 1960). On the other hand, the Commission required Bell to raise its monthly rental charges for Telpak, a combined communications service, because it found evidence that the charges had not been based upon cost of service but had been set abnormally low in order to attract big users, primarily in industry. A desire to prevent Bell's domination of a new field also accounted for the FCC's decision to restrict Bell to voice communications in transatlantic service. Having in mind that Bell already owned three transatlantic cables capable of carrying both voice and record data, the Commission decided to require Bell to share ownership of a fourth cable with three large firms in the teletype business and to limit its operations to the telephone side.

Regulation of wireless communications involves far-reaching questions touching on the very essence of life in a democracy. The influence of radio and television on the lives of people in modern society is demonstrably great, even greater, perhaps, than that of the press, whose right to free expression has been zealously guarded under our constitutional system. Limitations on the number of radio frequencies and television channels foreclose complete freedom of expression in wireless communications. Even without the necessary restriction on freedom of entry, it is doubtful that public policy would wish to sanction complete freedom for radio and television. These media have an unrivalled immediacy, because they reach into every home and find an audience of widely varying ages and tastes. Their influence on politics is potentially so great that political parties are assured "equal time" by law. Their impact on public opinion is theoretically so immense that restrictions on editorializing are demanded. In view of all this, establishing a universally acceptable interpretation of a broadcaster's responsibilities is probably impossible. This, then, is the shape of the regulatory dilemma.

In meeting it, neither the Federal Communications Commission nor its predecessor, the Federal Radio Commission (1927–1934), has had the benefit of much statutory guidance, nor would one expect it in the circumstances. From the necessary scarcity of broadcast outlets Congress correctly inferred that licensing of broadcasters should be the chief regulatory tool. The statutory criterion for awarding a license is whether an award is in the "public interest, convenience, or necessity," a notably vague standard but perhaps unavoidably so. The other statutory guidelines also complicate the regulatory problem. One imposes a flat prohibition on the FCC in censoring program content; the other charges the regulatory agency with promoting competition.

How shall the "public interest, convenience, or necessity" be balanced against the "censorship" provision of the Communications Act so that no violence is done to either? If the former is to mean anything, the FCC must evaluate proposed programing before granting new licenses and past programing before renewing licenses. Still, program content is not to be censored. The FCC has been extremely cautious in using its life-or-death power over broadcasters. In its "Blue Book" for radio broadcasters, based on a study made in 1946, the FCC noted the extreme commercialization of radio but stated that the prime responsibility for improvement rests with the stations and the networks. On very rare occasions the FCC has denied a license renewal. In 1964 a radio station owned by two individuals who had been involved in rigged television quiz shows was refused a license renewal on the ground that the owners lacked the proper character qualifications.[32] For television, as for radio, the Commission has relied strongly on appeals for self-improvement. In the early 1960's one FCC chairman received wide publicity for his characterization of television as a "wasteland," and his successor made a public appeal to broadcasters to curb the frequency of commercial announcements.

The Commission has been unable to devise a regulatory tool falling between the ineffective one of exhortations to improve and license revocation, which it has thought too harsh. Thus, economic imperatives continue to rule the situation. Broadcasters, like other businessmen, seek to increase profits; as the amount of time in a broadcasting day is fixed, attempts to increase profits mean the insertion of more and more commercials. Should there be limits on the profit motive in a medium with public service responsibilities? In some countries radio and television have been viewed in such exclusively public service terms that the government has been charged with their operation and "commercials" have been prohibited or sharply restricted. Most, if not all, observers would agree that government operation is unsuitable in the huge and diversified United States; the burden of finding a solution will most likely continue to rest with a regulatory commission.

The difficulties in the way of the Federal Communications Commission should not be underrated. If it seeks diversity in programing, it is confronted with reports from listener rating services that persuade broadcasters to drop programs failing to win large audiences and commercial sponsorship. Unlike most other regulatory agencies, it awards rich prizes in the form of stations and channels, a process that brings a tremendous concentration of pressure upon it. Perhaps most significantly, the FCC has had frequent evidence of congressional solicitude for the broadcasting industry. When the Commission proposed that television stations be bound by the restrictions on advertising in the industry code, which is voluntary and therefore ignored by many stations, the industry strongly protested. The FCC then dropped the proposal, well aware that an industry-backed bill to prevent the FCC from limiting "commercials" had been approved by the House Committee on Interstate and Foreign Commerce. As the FCC, in dropping the proposal, had nevertheless declared that it had the authority to limit commercials, the bill was pushed through the House and received an overwhelming (317-to-43) vote of approval in early 1964. Some members of Congress own television channels or radio stations, a larger number enjoy the benefits of having channels or stations in their home areas absorb the costs of taped and filmed programs featuring themselves, and all congressmen naturally hope for favorable treatment in news programs. All this does not excuse shortcomings in the FCC's performance. Investigation by the House Subcommittee on Legislative Oversight between 1958 and 1960 revealed a considerable acceptance of favors by some Commission members.[33] In the opinion of many observers, the Commission has failed to set forth meaningful standards for the granting and denying of licenses or to apply standards consistently. As to the latter, it has applied erratically its policy of "diversification"; i.e., if two applicants are equal in other respects, the applicant who is not affiliated with other communications media will be preferred. With reference to the numerous applicants owning newspapers, the actions of the Commission have ranged from a refusal to consider diversification in one case to making it the controlling consideration in another.

In discharging its responsibility to promote competition in broadcasting, the FCC has faced a more traditional regulatory responsibility. The ranks of the regulated have been split, and the Commission has sought to aid the weaker party. Both radio and television stations have found the economic power of the networks overwhelming because of the popular appeal of network programs. As regulatory power over the networks was not dealt with by statute, the FCC has employed the device of asserting control over the contracts that its licensee stations sign with the networks. Its aim has been to acquire for the local outlets more freedom in broadcasting. Another facet of maintaining competition involves the ownership of stations. Substantial multiple ownership has developed despite the FCC's limitations on the number of licenses issued to a single broadcaster (seven) and the prohibition on issuance of more than one license in the same medium in the same service area. The effectiveness of promoting competition has also been limited by the FCC's inconsistent attitude toward intermedia ownership, as noted above, and by the FCC's ineffective policies concerning FM (frequency modulation) radio stations and UHF (ultra-high-frequency) television channels when these first became possible. In view of the provision in the Communications Act of 1934 charging the FCC with promoting experimental uses of frequencies, its lack of success in stimulating the development of FM after 1940 and UHF after 1952 led to harsh criticism from some quarters. In both instances, the Commission failed to anticipate the faint possibilities of survival for the new type of broadcasters when existing receivers were not equipped to receive the broadcasts and programs could therefore not find sponsors. This deficiency was remedied for television when Congress passed a statute in 1962 requiring that television sets manufactured after May 1, 1964, be equipped with UHF channels (numbered 14 to 83).

The effects of this action on competition as well as on the improvement and diversity of programing remain to be seen. There have been suggestions that the FCC employ the threat of shifting to UHF selectively. Statistics tend to show that the size of the total television audience does not change significantly when more stations are added. Thus, it is suggested that in a city where two stations are making large profits while choosing to carry only the more mediocre network programs, the FCC might use the threat of increased competition from the larger number of outlets available under UHF to persuade the existing stations to improve their choice of network programs.[34]

SECURITIES

The American economic system depends heavily upon the confidence of investors, and that confidence in turn depends heavily upon integrity in the selling of stocks. That seventeen million persons owned shares in American corporations only thirty years after the low mark of the Great Depression in 1932 is testimony both to the prosperity of the nation and to confidence in the regulated stock-selling system.

A movement to mass stock ownership began in the 1920's, but it received a serious setback in the 1929 stock market collapse. Congressional investigations in the early 1930's publicized grave abuses in the sale of securities, the operation of security markets, and in financial reporting. Commercial and investment bankers colluded to speculate in bank stock and to manipulate securities prices. Certain large investors received the benefit of preferential prices in stock purchases, and market "insiders" made fortunes at the expense of the small investors. The public, lured by soaring securities prices and glowing descriptions of securities issues, freely purchased stocks on margin. When the speculative bubble burst, it became obvious to the more responsible members of the securities industry that reform would have to be a prerequisite to the reëntry of the small investor into the stock market.

The regulatory structure erected in the years after 1933 formed the basis for the return of investor confidence. For the preceding twenty years state governments had made some attempt at regulation through the so-called "blue sky" laws, and these statutes, widely varying in effectiveness, provided some record of experience for national regulation. The model adopted in the Securities Act of 1933, however, was the British Companies Act of 1844, which had stressed the principle of full disclosure. Though not attempting to guarantee the worth of a stock investment, as is sometimes mistakenly assumed, the Securities Act of 1933 required the issuers of new securities to furnish a registration statement to the regulatory body and a digest of the statement called a "prospectus" to the public twenty days before the stock could be sold. Sanctions were imposed for false statements; in practice, the Securities and Exchange Commission permits the issuing company to alter a registration statement that it finds inadequate. As a result of the laws, the American investor has more information available about a company in which he is investing than do most investors in European companies. The Securities and Exchange Act of 1934, besides creating the Securities and Exchange Commission as a policing body, extended the registration requirements to all stock issues and required securities exchanges to register information about their structure and finances. In addition, the act forbade various manipulative practices, authorized the Federal Reserve Board to set margin requirements, and gave the SEC authority to restrict borrowing by those engaged in the sale of securities. Subsequent statutes extended regulation by the SEC to public utility holding companies, over-the-counter markets, corporate reorganizations, trust indentures, investment trusts, and investment advisors.

Though powerful statutes back up the SEC, it has relied to a large extent upon self-regulation by securities exchanges. What SEC spokesmen have called "cooperative regulation" is the key to regulatory policy in this important area. From time to time the SEC has become dissatisfied with the extent of self-policing by the securities exchanges and has moved on its own administratively or asked for further legislation. Through persuasion the SEC induced the New York Stock Exchange in the mid–1930's to adopt trading rules designed to assure fair practices, but the Commission soon became dissatisfied with the mild punishments meted out by the Exchange for rules violations. The arrest in 1938 of a former Exchange president for grand larceny undercut opposition to firmer policing, assured reorganization of the Exchange to give greater representation to commission brokers and others having dealings with the public, and induced the Exchange to work with the SEC in developing more comprehensive rules for the protection of customers' funds and securities.

The next great test of cooperative regulation came in the 1960's. Between 1945 and 1961, the number of investors had tripled and the value of listed stock had increased 400 per cent. The immense volume of business and the eagerness and inexperience of many of the small investors put strains on trading rules and tempted some securities dealers to engage in misrepresentation and manipulation. The SEC began to stir in 1961 when reports of stock rigging on the American Stock Exchange began to circulate and in May 1962 when stock prices throughout the nation dropped sharply. The Commission set up a special study group that undertook hundreds of interviews and sent out thousands of questionnaires to individuals and firms directly or indirectly involved in securities trading. The study group's three-part report in 1963 shook the securities industry, though few could dispute the array of abuses and shortcomings uncovered by the investigators. These included high-pressure sales by some mutual funds, irresponsible and misleading statements by investment advisors, inadequate information by companies trading on over-the-counter markets, misleading statements by public relations representatives or corporations planning to float securities, and highly inadequate training for securities salesmen. The most severe criticism was reserved for the market "insiders": *floor traders*, who were thought to be trading for their own profit and benefiting from inside information; *over-the-counter traders*, some of whom were accused of "indifference, incompetence, and venality" in trading unlisted stocks; *stock specialists*, who were found to be more interested in their own profits than in their assigned function of attempting to stabilize the market by going against its trends; and *odd-lot traders*, who were accused of setting higher charges for odd-lot transactions (i.e., less than one hundred shares) than necessary.

Though the 175 recommendations in the special report had not specifically mentioned statutory enlargement of the SEC's powers, the Commission was able to induce Congress to pass the Securities Acts Amendments of 1964. The statute required widely held companies of substantial size to make public reports of their financial condition and to disclose other information already required of companies whose stock is traded on the securities exchanges rather than in the over-the-counter market. About 2500 companies were affected. The statute also empowered the SEC to establish minimum standards of character and competence for individuals entering the securities industry and to impose minimum financial requirements on securities firms. In order to extend the self-policing principle, the statute also required everyone in the securities industry to belong to some organization with authority to discipline its own members. This provision was primarily intended to encourage the National Association of Securities Dealers to undertake more extensive self-policing action along the lines developed by the New York Stock Exchange.

Cooperative regulation has been justified by a former SEC chairman on the ground that "we are dealing with business practices—the spectrum of ways in which day-to-day financial transactions are being conducted—and with evolving standards."[35] The Commission has consciously avoided any attempt to treat the securities industry as a closely regulated, profit-controlled public utility, though it has emphasized that investor protection cannot be sacrificed to provide profits for the industry. The industry itself naturally has favored a maximum of self-policing. It has argued that an abundance of detailed governmental rules would tie up in red tape the sensitive process of marketing securities. In the past, some investment houses have complained vigorously about SEC-imposed delays in approving registration statements. A second reason that most of the securities industry favors self-policing is that it permits the industry to discipline unethical individuals or groups without attracting as much unfavorable publicity as when a government agency undertakes discipline. Finally, the industry has hoped to gain and retain public confidence through its willingness to operate under self-imposed rules.

Cooperative regulation carries with it two risks, namely, that it may violate the antitrust laws and that the regulatory agency will become a pawn of the regulated industry. As to the first, the 1963 decision of the Supreme Court in *Silver* v. *New York Stock Exchange* is of significance.[36] By a seven-to-two vote, the Court found the Exchange in violation of the Sherman Act because it had directed its members to cut off all telephone connections with an over-the-counter securities dealer in Texas. The Court acknowledged that the act's provisions would have to be weighed against the Exchange's self-policing responsibilities, but it held that if the Exchange took action that would ordinarily violate the antitrust laws and could not justify that action in terms of its regulatory function, then it must pay the penalty. The Court implied, but did not explicitly state, that the Exchange might have escaped being found in violation of the Sherman Act if it had permitted Silver to present arguments against severing the wire connections and if its actions had been reviewed by the SEC. The decision is likely to convince both the SEC and the securities industry (because of the possibility of triple-damage suits) that more direct supervision of self-policing is necessary.

Despite the *Silver* case, there are indications that the SEC, while perhaps overly patient with its clientele, stands ready to correct inadequacies in self-regulation in the securities industry. An example of alert action was its issuance of rules in 1964 restricting floor traders. The Commission found that the Exchange's own laxly enforced rules had resulted in a conflict of interest whereby trading in stocks was manipulated to the floor traders' advantage. In expressing its dissatisfaction with the Exchange's "ineffectual" record, which "has seen cycles of regulation followed by erosions of exchange rules," the Commission insisted that the supervision of floor traders would have to be under its control.[37] A further indication of the SEC's attitude was afforded by an official's statement in 1963; realizing that compromises with the industry were not going to be reached on the entire range of recommendations made by its special study group, he was quoted as saying:

> There is going to come a point where we are just going to have to put some rule in by ukase. We are willing to take that step if we have to—if we still feel, after listening fully to the industry's point of view, that what we want and they object to is necessary. We may have to prove that we are willing to take that step—to put something in by ukase—to avoid being pushed back and back.[38]

With cooperative regulation continuing as the basic SEC approach, however, a difference of opinion with the Antitrust Division of the Department of Justice developed in the wake of the *Silver* case.[39] Though the Commission agreed with the Division that the securities industry should not be made completely exempt from the antitrust laws, it argued that some type of special treatment is necessary if the method by which the industry has been regulated is to be preserved. Seeking a strengthening of cooperative regulation, the Commission proposed that self-regulatory actions it has reviewed and approved be exempt from antitrust prosecution. The Antitrust Division has opposed this proposal on the ground that some of the other regulatory agencies have displayed pro-industry viewpoints and that the future membership of the SEC might also not be independent-minded. If the Division's viewpoint prevails, as seems likely, cooperative regulation under the SEC will be put to even greater tests in the future.

CHAPTER FOUR

Government
as
Regulator: II

As applied to agriculture, labor, and the protection of consumers, regulation has followed highly diverse patterns. Public policy toward agriculture has comprehended both promotion and regulation, as it has for many business fields. The major difference is that most regulatory action in agriculture has not had the aim of curbing abuses but of restricting the actions of individual producers to promote their interests as a whole. Another difference is that these regulatory efforts have often been made more palatable by the use of democratic devices to assure producer assent and administrative support. Regulation has been employed in two principal ways in the labor field. First, the welfare of workers has been promoted by the imposition of restrictions upon employers in their use of labor. Second, governmental regulation of labor-management relations has strongly affected both the coming to power of labor unions and their subsequent relationship with management. Public policy toward consumers has involved still another perspective on regulation. Though consumers have been unorganized and weak, government has increasingly taken upon itself the task of protecting them; regulation has thus restricted sellers of goods and services in their dealings with consumers.

AGRICULTURE

To an extent rarely paralleled elsewhere in the American economy, the regulation of agriculture is regulation in the service of promotionalism. It is true that the regulation of business and labor often has the effect of protecting the status of those within a restricted field, and so the status of the regulated group often has been promoted. This is a far cry, however, from the range and scope of the effort made to promote agriculture by restricting farmers.[1]

It was not always thus. Until the 1920's public policy in agriculture was almost purely promotional. Farmers, of course, were affected by and interested in the regulation of other groups. Indeed, complaints by farmers were central to the grass-roots Granger movement that led to state and federal regulation of the railroads and to state regulation of such facilities as grain elevators in the 1870's and 1880's. But the 1920's saw two changes of emphasis. First, regulation was extended beyond the carriers of agricultural produce to cover as well the commodity markets in which farmers sell their goods. Second— and far more important—policy-makers began to search for ways to impose regulation on farmers themselves in the interest of stabilizing the market for farm goods and assuring farm prosperity.

Though rail transport of farm goods had come under federal government surveillance in the late nineteenth century, livestock and grain markets were still open to farmer criticism. In the 1920's Congress passed laws aimed at curbing monopolistic actions. The Packers and Stockyards Act of 1921 regulated the rates and charges for services of meat packers. This action followed a well-publicized Federal Trade Commission investigation in 1917–1918 of discriminatory practices among the "Big Five" meat packers. Abuses among speculators trading in "futures" (buying or selling commodities at a fixed price, with delivery to be made in the future) led to further congressional action. Trading in futures performs useful functions. It tends to stabilize prices, to offer a wide and continuous market, and to equalize national and international prices. In some futures markets, however, traders engage in such practices as juggling prices, circulating false crop reports, and cornering the market. After years of agitation by farm organizations, a regulatory statute based on the taxing power was passed in 1921. Declared unconstitutional, it was replaced by the Grain Futures Act of 1922, which was based on Congress' power over interstate commerce. The limited regulatory authority it granted, centering on advising and fact finding, soon proved inadequate. After more years of agitation by farm groups, a stronger statute was passed in 1936. The Commodity Exchange Act of that year made price manipulation and market cornering criminal offenses, and it outlawed certain trading operations that had been subject to abuses. The

Commodity Exchange Authority, as the Department of Agriculture's enforcement agency under the act is now called, has the power to review applications of exchanges to trade in regulated commodities, to register floor brokers for trading privileges, to audit brokerage firms to see that customers' funds are properly segregated, to spot check on trading practices, and to supervise daily transactions. The 1936 statute extended controls, formerly applied only to grains, to cotton, butter, eggs, and potatoes. In subsequent years other commodities were added, although the coverage is far from complete. Onions, once included, were later removed. Because of wild trading in sugar futures, the Department of Agriculture unsuccessfully sought legislation in 1963 to place sugar under the statute. The low margin requirements in futures trading on regulated markets—as little as five cents on each dollar pledged—as contrasted with seventy cents in the stock market—have drawn criticism.[2] They have been defended on the basis that in futures trading margin is considered a performance bond, not a down payment. Instead of acquiring shares, the trader is making a contract to buy or sell six to twelve months in the future; a 70 per cent margin requirement, it is argued, would tie up an immense amount of money and therefore drive up commodity prices. So far, this reasoning has prevailed. Aside from commodity market regulation, the Department of Agriculture is responsible for protective programs dealing with such matters as the licensing of warehouses, the importation of potentially infectious plants or animals, and the labeling of seeds.

An understanding of agricultural regulation may be furthered by a brief review of the basis for the trend away from purely promotional measures to a mixture of promotion and regulation. A century ago, a sharp controversy over whether the public lands should be sold at a goodly price or given away in the interest of promoting the westward movement of settlers was resolved in favor of the latter solution. The Homestead Act of 1862 permitted a settler to acquire 160 acres in return for his occupancy of the land for five years. Later, as the arable land was exhausted, a further promotional measure was placed on the statute books. The Reclamation Act of 1902 authorized a reclamation fund designed to make the farming of 160-acre plots in the dry West feasible through irrigation. The fund was to be financed from the sale of public lands, royalties from oil leases on public lands, and receipts from water rights on completed irrigation projects.

Other kinds of promotional aids were also given to agriculture. The Department of Agriculture became notable for its elaborate research programs dealing with the betterment of farm animals and plants in the interest of raising farm income. The results of research were made available through the land-grant colleges established under the Morrill Act of 1862 and through an extensive agricultural extension system operating largely through county agents and reaching into every phase of farming and farm living. When the mechanization of farming increased the farmer's requirement for capital, he was able to rely upon the government credit agencies. The Federal Farm Loan Act of 1916 established a dozen federal land banks. As these banks made only long-term loans, Congress set up intermediate credit banks in 1923 to supplement the original scheme. When these two devices needed bolstering during the Great Depression, other steps were taken. The Emergency Farm Mortgage Act of 1933 permitted moratoriums on mortgages and reduced interest rates; the Farm Credit Act of 1933 set up banks to serve cooperatives engaged in marketing farm products and purchasing farm supplies; and the Rural Electrification Administration was created to bring electrical power from rural electric cooperatives to farms, a venture that privately-owned electrical utilities had previously found financially unattractive. Still other promotional measures over the years partially exempted farmer cooperatives from the antitrust laws and subsidized the export of agricultural commodities.

Aided by substantial government support, agricultural productivity outstripped population growth and engendered efforts to cope with overproduction and its effects. World War I and its aftermath brought on the beginning of this policy change. As agricultural producers had vastly expanded their output to meet wartime demands, the contraction of the overseas market when European producers came back into the picture was all the more severe. As a result, an agricultural depression of severe dimensions antedated the industrial depression that began with the collapse of the stock market in 1929. During the 1920's various schemes for supporting farm prices were debated, and one major farm measure, the McNary-Haugen Bill of 1927, was passed by Congress twice, only to meet with vetoes by President Coolidge. Under President Hoover, the Agricultural Marketing Act of 1929 was enacted into law. It created a revolving fund of a half-billion dollars for the use of the Federal Farm Board in stimulating cooperative marketing and purchasing agricultural commodities with a view to stabilizing their prices. Unfortunately, the onset of the general depression engulfed the efforts of the Farm Board to directly influence prices. This first direct intervention of government in the markets for farm products thus antedated the New Deal by almost four years. Prior to 1929 public policy in agriculture had had the aim of helping the farmer adjust to a free market economy. That the change to active government intervention in the market was accomplished under a Republican administration is further evidence that ideology is secondary to pragmatism in the American setting.

Under the stimulus of ever worsening farm conditions, the New Deal added other elements to Hoover's formula. The lesson learned from the Federal Farm Board experience was that production controls should be added to attempts to stabilize the market through loan and purchase operations. Under the Agricultural Adjustment Act of 1933 farmers who agreed to reduce acreage or marketing of corn and hogs, wheat, cotton, tobacco, and rice were paid sums deriving from a tax on processors of farm products. After the Supreme Court declared this statute an unconstitutional exercise of the taxing power in 1935,[3] Congress in 1938 passed another statute with the same name based on the power to regulate interstate commerce. This time the Supreme Court approved.[4] The 1938 statute, like that of 1929, emphasized price stabilization. Though the precise formula has varied in the statutes passed since 1938, the general procedure for organizing the market for the intended benefit of the farmer has involved a *quid pro quo* whereby the farmer agrees to limit his production or his marketing in exchange for a guaranteed minimum price for his crop. An important medium for arranging this exchange has been the Commodity Credit Corporation (CCC) of the Department of Agriculture. It has offered loans to farmers for certain crops at a support price calculated as a percentage of "parity," a figure in turn originally based upon a formula for restoring farm purchasing power to the 1909–1914 level but adjusted since then. The loans made by the CCC were labeled "non-recourse" loans because the Corporation has no recourse against the producer if the market price for his crop turns out to be less than the amount of the loan made to him. Obviously, this means that the farmer is assured of a minimum price for his crops. A similar guaranty was sought for producers of milk and fruit by passage of the Agricultural Marketing Agreement Act of 1937. Under this statute marketing orders are issued that fix the minimum price paid to producers.

When the government began supporting prices of farm products, the level of support was bound to become a controversial issue. Until 1938 the Secretary of Agriculture had complete discretion as to whether to make loans and at what price levels. The 1938 statute made CCC loans mandatory on corn, wheat, and cotton within the range of 52 to 75 per cent of parity and fixed attention upon the percentage. Aided by the need to stimulate farm production during World War II, the farm bloc succeeded in getting mandatory price supports of 90 per cent of parity written into the law; this protection was extended into the immediate postwar era. When farm prices began to decline in 1952, the price supports for the specified crops became effective and the CCC began acquiring large holdings. In an effort to reduce the cost to the government, the Eisenhower administration succeeded in getting a bill through Congress in 1954 establishing flexible price supports on cotton, corn, wheat, rice, and peanuts, though tobacco, the other "basic" commodity, retained the 90 per cent level. Despite the setting of price support levels as low as 75 per cent and the imposition of marketing quotas, the holdings of the CCC continued to increase. This result, plus a decline in the ability of the farm bloc to obtain high fixed price supports, has somewhat shifted attention away from price-support formulas in recent years.

Soil conservation regulations, ostensibly designed for the well-being of future generations, have contained features aimed at increasing immediate income and stabilizing production and prices. Thus, they are also a part of the scheme of promotional regulation. Though the Soil Conservation Act of 1935 provided only for governmental assistance to farmers in preparing detailed work plans for preventing erosion, the Soil Conservation and Domestic Allotment Act of 1936 authorized payments to farmers for shifting from soil-depleting cotton, tobacco, and grain crops to soil-conserving legumes and grasses. The Agricultural Act of 1956 established the concept of the "soil bank." This consisted of a temporary program, lasting until 1959, to pay farmers not to grow crops in the basic commodity category and a longer-range program that authorized the Secretary of Agriculture to contract with farmers to take land out of production for five or ten years. The farmers were compensated by financial assistance for establishing conservation practices on the land and by annual rental payments for keeping the land out of production. Even with more than 28 million acres withdrawn from production in 1960, however, crop output continued to increase, largely because of the continuing technological explosion in agriculture. Since 1961 a feed grain acreage diversion has served as a kind of soil bank.

The extensive regulatory scheme involved in promoting the interests of farmers has been made more palatable by the use of techniques emphasizing bureaucratic responsiveness and farmer-centered democracy. County agents stationed throughout the country provide the Department of Agriculture's Extension Service with eyes and ears attuned to local needs. Departmental officials use field surveys to sample farmers' opinions. Before marketing quotas and acreage allotments are applied to cotton, wheat, tobacco, rice, and peanuts, two thirds of the producers of each crop must vote for the arrangement in a referendum conducted by the Department. If approval is gained, farmer-elected county committees administer the program under the supervision of the Department's Agricultural Stabilization and Conservation Service. One soil-conservation program is administered by these committees and another by similar committees associated with the Department's Soil Conservation Service. Under the latter program, by 1963 farmers had organized and were directing almost three thousand soil conservation districts that covered 96 per cent of the nation's farms.

Farmers used their political power to get an elaborate plan of promotional regulation on the statute books so that they might avoid the harsh consequences of a free market—freer, on the whole, than that for producers of manufactured goods. Several factors made farmers more vulnerable than industrialists to the workings of a competitive system. There were great numbers of small, widely scattered producers who lacked a knowledge of demand or supply for their products. Often farmers were dependent upon a single crop for their income. The produce of each farmer came to the market at roughly the same time. Production occurred over a considerable period of time, requiring farmers to anticipate market conditions months ahead. The weather, crop diseases, insect infestation, and other factors over which farmers had little or no control drastically affected production. A relatively inelastic demand for farm products meant that the more farmers produced, the less they received for each unit.

In this setting farmers became hypersensitive in their dealings with less chaotic segments of the economy, such as railroads, millers, farm machinery producers, and bankers. The change to promotional regulation was facilitated by rural overrepresentation in state and national legislatures and by the image from the Jeffersonian past of agriculture as the heart and soul of America. By the same token, promotional regulation is bound to be affected by continuing urbanization and by legislative reapportionment along population lines.

Promotional regulation, though it ended market chaos, has had only mixed success. Its accomplishments, while considerable, differ markedly from those used to justify the system. One hope was that farmers' incomes would rise when production was controlled. On this point, it has been observed that

> if the objectives of all the federal farm programs of the last quarter century had been to increase farm production, raise farm efficiency, lower food costs for consumers, make available great reserves of grain for protection against drought or war, one could say that they had been highly successful. But since the objectives were to reduce output and raise farm income, government intervention has not, from the farmer's viewpoint, been a howling success. Today per capita farm income—including the money value of house rent and of food and fuel consumed on the farm—is still about half of per capita non-farm income, the same as in the mid-1930's.[5]

A second, related justification for the system was that it would eliminate rural poverty. Though the objective was and is worthy, promotional regulation has been an inefficient instrument for achieving it. The relatively small output of the needy farmer means that his benefits from price supports and soil-conservation measures are too limited to be meaningful. By contrast, the large commercial farmers, who employ expensive and intricate farm machines and commercial fertilizers, have prospered under a system of guaranteed markets and prices. In 1959 the families that lived on the 800,000 farms selling more than $10,000 of farm products annually had an average family income of almost $10,000, but the families living on the 2.3 million farms selling less than $5,000 of farm products annually had an average income of $3,750.[6] Price supports and soil-conservation payments, meager as they are for the poorer farmers, have undoubtedly slowed the migration from farm to city, but because of worrisome urban unemployment rates a case can be made for such a delay. Another kind of adjustment, a change to the growing of crops that the free market might value more highly, has also been delayed by the system of selective price supports, and this delay appears less defensible.

Because of the mounting irritation of the public at the costs of farm subsidies and some dissatisfaction among farmers themselves at the controls to which they are subject, agricultural spokesmen have increasingly considered some freeing of the market. On this point a division of opinion has, in any case, existed among the leading farm groups in the postwar era. The American Farm Bureau Federation and the National Grange, representing chiefly relatively prosperous farmers from areas with sufficient rainfall to take some of the gamble out of farming, have favored decreased governmental controls. The chief support for extensive government controls has come from the National Farmers Union, an organization with its chief base of support in the marginal lands of the western half of the country. Recently it has urged direct payments to farmers to bolster income. A sudden return to a free market, it is generally recognized, would work hardships on marginal farmers, and, therefore, less drastic remedies have usually been suggested. One involves setting a maximum on the price-support payments that any single producer can receive. While requiring close supervision to prevent the employment of dummy producers, the effect should be to reduce the incentive for large producers to produce more and more for government storage units and to increase the incentive for a partial shifting to non-surplus crops. This suggestion is resisted by those who point to the undeniable production accomplishments of American agriculture. Efforts to re-train marginal producers for other employment have also been proposed. Other ideas that have been circulated include offering incentives to farmers to turn crop land into grassland available for cattle·raising (a suggestion opposed by cattlemen, who are already concerned about prices for cattle), gradually decreasing the subsidies to farmers over a five-year period of transition to a free market, and liberalizing agricultural trade. In any event, it is well to remember that promotional regulation of agriculture, for all its shortcomings, has given America plenty in the midst of world hunger, a population explosion that is outrunning the increase in world food production, and the notorious agricultural difficulties of the two leading Communist powers.

As in certain business fields, public policy toward labor has followed the familiar cycle of promotion-abuses-regulation. There are two outstanding differences, however. In the first place, efforts to promote the interests of labor have encountered formidable obstacles and heartbreaking delay, particularly in the courts. Secondly, much labor legislation deals with industrial relations and, since this involves business as well as labor, its analysis is not truly comparable with that tracing the regulation of a single economic group.

Until well into the present century, labor fought an uphill battle both to gain protective legislation over working conditions and to earn the right to organize and bargain collectively. Generally speaking, battles won in the legislative arena were lost in the courts. At a time of business hegemony, common-law treatment of labor evolved only slowly from a handicraft mentality. Whatever the basic reason, the judiciary found it difficult to reconcile statutory measures in the labor field with constitutional provisions and even with the common law.

Protective legislation dealing with the labor of women and children, hours and wages, and industrial injuries all proved difficult of acceptance. So swift has been the transformation of society in the twentieth century that the toleration of child labor and its widespread use before World War I now seem incredible. True, child labor legislation slowly advanced from the pioneer Massachusetts statute of 1842 that forbade children under twelve from working more than ten hours a day to the most advanced laws of seventy years later that prohibited the employment of children under sixteen in manufacturing, mining, and merchandising. Even today, however, state child labor laws vary widely in the degree of protection they offer as to type of occupation and permissible hours of work. At the federal level, the Supreme Court twice struck down congressional efforts to prohibit the interstate transmission of goods made by child labor. A majority of the Court decreed that neither the interstate commerce clause nor the taxing and spending clause provided authorization.[7] A proposed constitutional amendment to abolish child labor failed to gain the approval of two thirds of the states between 1924 and 1941, when the question was finally resolved in another way. In 1938 the Fair Labor Standards Act again outlawed child labor for goods sent through interstate commerce, and this time a majority of the Supreme Court agreed to the constitutionality of the step in the 1941 case of *United States* v. *Darby Lumber Co.*[8]

Federal and state limitations on the number of hours worked and on minimum wages ran a similar gauntlet. The presentation of a typical "Brandeis brief"—a marshaling of statistics on the economic and social effects of prevailing industrial practices—finally convinced the Supreme Court in 1908 to uphold state efforts to restrict hours for women for the protection of their health.[9] Similar legislation for men met a hostile reception for a longer period. Ironically, the two political branches of the federal government had pioneered in this field in the mid-nineteenth century by limiting the working hours of federal government employees. Early in the twentieth century Congress restricted the work week in certain occupations, especially in transportation where it could be argued that the safety of travelers was endangered by long working hours for employees. Even so, it was not until the Supreme Court's approval of the Fair Labor Standards Act in 1941, in the *Darby* case previously cited, that federal and state governments were given an unqualified green light for legislation fixing maximum hours of labor.

Minimum wage legislation made even slower headway in the courts. A 1923 Supreme Court decision made it plain to the states that minimum wage statutes would be considered a violation of what the Court considered the freedom of contract required by the due process clause.[10] As recently as 1936 the Supreme Court reaffirmed this view,[11] but in 1937, in a dramatic reversal not unrelated to FDR's court-packing efforts, it finally endorsed Oregon's minimum wage law,[12] opening the way for the endorsement, in the *Darby* case, of similar provisions in the federal Fair Labor Standards Act of 1938.

On the question of responsibility for injuries suffered at work, common-law rules developed by the judiciary in the first half of the nineteenth century presented huge obstacles. An injured factory worker faced the difficult prospect of financing a lawsuit in which he had to show that he had not been negligent in any way (the "contributory negligence" rule), that another employee's negligence had not contributed to his injury (the "fellow-servant" rule), and that he had not been aware of the risks of injury in the particular occupation he had entered (the "assumption of risk" rule). If, in spite of these hurdles, the worker won his case, his employer could always appeal and count on the worker's savings to be exhausted before the case was finally settled.

This harsh system was displaced in two stages. As early as the 1880's some states began to deprive the employer of his common-law defense. Second, when it was found that judicial processes did not easily lend themselves to settlement of industrial injury claims, the European idea of having employers insure themselves against injury claims was widely adopted. Compulsory workmen's compensation laws met constitutional obstacles for a time, but in the second decade of the twentieth century the Supreme Court finally settled the issue in a series of decisions. Though such laws are now on the statute books of all states, they differ widely in terms of coverage, extent of protection, and form of administration. The insurance may be carried in a state or a private fund, and the rates are usually based on an employer's accident and disease record, thereby providing a strong incentive for safety programs. Because of various exemptions, only about two thirds of all workers are covered. Compensation benefits usually cover death, disability, medical care, and, increasingly, rehabilitation; there has been much controversy as to the adequacy of each, as well as litigation over whether particular injuries are job-related. Workmen's compensation referees usually handle the awards, but the immense and growing complexity of cases has prevented full realization of the expeditious handling hoped for by transfer of cases from the courts. Despite the many problems, the system constitutes a great advance in dealing with the fifteen to twenty thousand deaths and the two million injuries of workers that occur annually.

The evolution of public policy toward labor-management relations bears many similarities to the history of protective labor legislation. The differences are mainly those that a continuing tug-of-war between the powerful business and labor groups can bring.

Labor-management relations in the United States were first governed by common-law rules that virtually foreclosed effective joint action among laborers as a weapon against employers. Both strikes and boycotts were difficult for the courts to tolerate because the common-law image of industrial relations was one in which the individual employer dealt with the individual employee. Before 1842 unions were in fact regarded by the courts as illegal conspiracies regardless of their objectives or behavior. Even thereafter, vigorous union action was precluded by judicial views that government must provide businesses with the assurance of free access to labor, raw materials, and customers. Given the greater economic power of employers, this meant that law enforcement agencies often became the allies of business in economic warfare. While picketers and strikers were harassed, the use of company unions and strikebreakers was facilitated. One of the most powerful, court-endorsed weapons was the "yellow-dog" contract. These agreements required employees not to join unions or participate in their activities; governmental backing came in the form of court decisions upsetting state laws that declared the agreements illegal and of judicial injunctions forbidding labor leaders from organizing employees bound by them. Until the New Deal days the courts also nullified federal efforts to increase labor's power in industrial relations disputes. The Sherman

Antitrust Act of 1890, aimed at business trusts, became the vehicle for destruction of the Danbury hatter's union in 1908.[13] Though the Clayton Act of 1914 foreclosed further use of antitrust statutes to dissolve unions, courts so interpreted the act as to permit the continued use of injunctions against picketing and secondary boycotts.

The decade of the 1930's gave labor its charter to organize effectively and to become a powerful bargainer with business in industrial relations. The Norris-LaGuardia Act of 1932 removed labor unions from the constant threat of injunctive action by making "yellow-dog" contracts unenforceable and by outlawing injunctions that forced employees to cease a strike or that prevented them from joining a union, picketing, or boycotting. The New Deal quickly produced other industrial relations legislation. The National Industrial Recovery Act of 1933, though later declared unconstitutional, encouraged the growth of unionism by protecting labor's right to organize and bargain collectively. This right the National Labor Relations (Wagner) Act of 1935 reaffirmed and enlarged. The statute established a National Labor Relations Board with authority to hold elections in plants to determine the employees' collective bargaining representatives and with further authority to prevent specified "unfair labor practices" by employers. The forbidden practices included interfering with employees or their unions, discriminating against employees for union activities, and refusing to bargain in good faith.

Thus was born one of the most controversial and difficult regulatory assignments ever attempted. Not only did powerful business leaders bitterly resent government supervision of their industrial relations practices, but labor, far from being united through government support of its objectives, engaged in bitter internecine warfare over the question of the form of unionism. Because of its greater flexibility and aggressiveness, the industrial union form of organization espoused by John L. Lewis' newly formed Committee for Industrial Organization (later renamed the Congress of Industrial Organizations) gained most from the new statute, although the American Federation of Labor, organized on the basis of craft rather than plant affiliation, fought back vigorously. Neither the AFL nor the CIO found complete satisfaction with the administration of the act by the five-man Board, but the Board itself finally gained clear legal status, even in the eyes of industrialists, when the Supreme Court declared the National Labor Relations Act constitutional in 1937.[14]

After World War II industrial relations regulation took a turn that recognized labor's change in status from weakness to strength. During the war the immense productivity demanded of industry and the no-strike pledges given by labor subdued industrial strife, but the difficulties of peacetime adjustment reopened old wounds. A rash of strikes, various abuses by labor of its new-found economic power, and the advent of a conservative Congress combined to produce the Labor-Management Relations (Taft-Hartley) Act of 1947. Its philosophy was one of providing more restraints upon the actions of labor unions. In providing checks upon unfair labor practices by unions, it implicitly recognized the role of government in restraining private action that exceeds the bounds of propriety. Though regulatory statutes had similarly checked business behavior, the speed with which government action shifted from promotion to restriction of labor was much greater.

The Taft-Hartley Act put the new philosophy into effect by weakening the Wagner Act's restraints on industry and by adding a new list of unfair labor practices—this time practices forbidden to unions. The proscribed practices included coercing employees or employers, engaging in secondary boycotts or strikes to force an employer to deal with a union other than the one recognized by an election held by the National Labor Relations Board, and refusing to bargain in good faith. The Board itself was deprived of its former authority to issue complaints in unfair labor practice cases and was reduced to deciding cases brought by its general counsel, who was separated from the Board in all possible ways. The reorganized agency became much more protective of the rights of business in industrial relations disputes, to the distaste of labor. Not only was the Board operating under a legislative mandate which was less one-sidedly pro-labor, but the Eisenhower appointees in the 1950's were less sympathetic to unions. After a Democratic administration came to power in 1961, it was once again the turn of businessmen to criticize the NLRB. The closeness with which both business and labor scrutinize the background of appointees and prospective appointees to the Board, as well as its decisions, testifies to the importance both attach to the administration of industrial relations statutes.

The continuing concern of Congress with the activities of unions led to the Labor-Management Reporting and Disclosure Act of 1959. Its coverage extends to workers covered by the Railway Labor Act as well as those under the Taft-Hartley Act. The 1959 statute established a "Bill of Rights of Members of Labor Organizations" and provided for enforcement of these rights in federal district courts. The rights include the freedom to nominate officers, vote in elections, express views, assemble, communicate with legislators, and voice opinions on proposed increases in dues, fees, and assessments. Unions are required to file annual fiscal reports and reports on internal organization with the Secretary of Labor, as well as to make the information in these reports available to their members. Union officers and non-clerical employees must file annual reports with the Secretary as to financial transactions with employers with whom they deal in their official capacity. Employers are also required to file reports on such financial transactions. The act also provides that a trusteeship (control by a parent labor organization over a subordinate union whose normal independence has been suspended) can be established only to correct corruption or financial misdeeds, to make sure that the union's duties as a bargaining representative are fulfilled, to restore democratic procedures, to make sure that union contracts are followed, or to carry out the legitimate objects of the labor organization. Rules for democratic union elections are also specified. The best-known provision concerns the limitation upon members of the Communist party holding union office.

In the postwar period unions have been dismayed at their lack of growth relative to a sharp growth in the size of the labor force. Membership in unions totaled 17,490,000 in 1956, which constituted 24.8 per cent of the labor force. By 1961 the respective figures had declined to 16,303,000 and 22 per cent. Though a slight rise was recorded in 1962, the last year for which figures are available, it is evident that labor unions have failed to extend their influence through the sustained growth of which they could boast before World War II. Automation has cut into prospective membership ranks, but more significant is the failure of unions to organize white-collar labor. The unions had 2,463,000 white-collar members in 1956 and almost 200,000 fewer white-collar members in 1962.

Another barometer of the relative influence possessed by business and labor, as well as an important focus of their conflicts, is the form of union-security agreement permitted by industrial relations statutes as interpreted by the NLRB and the courts. The Wagner Act did not deal with the content of collective bargaining agreements. Therefore, it was possible for labor unions, in the heyday of their power, to insist on the closed shop, which requires employers to hire only union members. The Taft-Hartley Act made the closed shop an unfair union practice and even imposed some limits on the union shop (in which workers must join the union after being hired). Even more significantly, the act provided that state laws would take precedence over the union-security provisions it contained. As a consequence, the way was open for the passage of right-to-work laws in the states. Twenty states—in general, the less industrialized— have such statutes, which specifically ban the union shop. Twelve of the state right-to-work laws also prohibit the agency shop (which permits employees to decline union membership, provided they pay the union a service fee equal to union dues), but embattled union leaders hoped that the agency shop could be used in the other eight. The Supreme Court dashed their hopes by unanimously deciding in 1963 that state courts, not the NLRB, had the right to interpret right-to-work laws.[15] Specifically at issue was a Florida court's interpretation of that state's law as forbidding the agency shop even though the statute did not flatly prohibit it. As the attorneys general of seven of the eight states (the Indiana law specifically permits the agency shop) took the same view as the Florida court, labor's use of an agency-shop clause in collective bargaining agreements in these states seems doomed to failure. Such is the fluid nature of labor's struggle with management for influence over public policy, however, that labor leaders can point to favorable results, too. In another 1963 decision the Supreme Court rejected General Motors' contention that the agency shop was illegal even in states without right-to-work laws.[16] In addition, the unions can take comfort from the reluctance exhibited by politicians in industrial states to associate their parties with right-to-work proposals. In his 1965 State of the Union message, President Johnson urged the deletion of the Taft-Hartley provision (Section 14b) that in effect permits states to pass right-to-work laws.

Public policy on labor-management relations has never been free from crisis or controversy, but it faces today an accumulation of problems that tax the skill of representatives of business, labor, and government. Many of the problems center around the vital concept of collective bargaining. Although industrial relations are presumably a private process, government action has required collective bargaining. This requirement recognizes that breakdowns in just one segment of our highly interdependent economy have far-reaching effects on third parties and the public.

Up to about 1960, when the inflationary cycle slowed, business and labor were frequently criticized for an insufficient regard for the public in their collective bargaining. The demand for civilian goods after World War II persuaded industry to pay the higher wages demanded by organized labor and to charge prices that would meet increased wage costs and still bring greater profits. The resulting inflation, blamed by industry and labor on each other, placed severe disadvantages upon salaried individuals outside of industry, pensioners, small-business men, and unorganized workers. More recently, Presidents Kennedy and Johnson have tried to minimize the importance of wage increases in collective bargaining by urging that such increases be geared to increases in productivity.

Probably the greatest public concern in collective bargaining is that it avoid crippling shutdowns in the intricately interdependent American economy. Federal mediation agencies have existed for some time, but they have their limitations. Their use has been most highly developed in the railroad and airline industries. In the settlement of more routine disputes, the National Mediation Board, which deals with both industries, and the National Railroad Adjustment Board have compiled good records. The Railway Labor Act of 1926, as strengthened in 1934 and 1936, provides for several means of settling disputes, including mediation, voluntary arbitration, and presidential appointment of an Emergency Board when essential interstate transportation services are imperiled. The Federal Mediation and Conciliation Service, created by the Taft-Hartley Act but with predecessors going back to 1917, also has mediated many disputes when a work stoppage in an essential industry has been imminent. During both world wars and during the Korean conflict, this machinery was supplemented with special boards (called the National War Labor Board in the world wars and the Wage Stabilization Board in the Korean War). While their stormy history reflects the difficulty of the problems set before them, they did manage to prevent intolerable strife during the emergencies. Even so, it was necessary for the government to seize a number of plants during both world wars in order to prevent work stoppages.

The Taft-Hartley Act recognized the problem of strikes in essential industries in peacetime by establishing elaborate machinery designed to produce a cooling-down of a dispute that imperils "the national health and safety." The President may appoint a board of inquiry to investigate and report on the issues without making any recommendations. After he receives the board's report he may direct the Attorney General to ask for a federal district court injunction prohibiting a strike or lockout. During the sixty days following the issue of the injunction, the parties to the dispute are required to try to settle their differences with the assistance of the Federal Mediation and Conciliation Service. Thereafter, the President receives from the board of inquiry a further report that contains the employer's last offer of settlement. Finally, within fifteen days after the end of the sixty-day period, the National Labor Relations Board must hold an election to determine whether the employees wish to accept the employer's offer; the court is asked to discharge its injunction; and the President reports to Congress on the dispute, together with such recommendations as he cares to make. If anything, this procedure has encouraged a more intransigent attitude between disputants. The more essential the industry involved, the more likely the disputants are to fight their case in the mass media and to rely upon governmental intervention for eventual settlement of the disagreements. In this atmosphere, disputes tend to drag on for a considerable amount of time and to gravitate toward ever higher circles in the national government. Thus, the dispute over work rules on the railroads was waged before various mediation boards, both regular and emergency, in the courts and in Congress, until, after five years of controversy, President Johnson, by dint of strong appeals and long bargaining sessions in the White House, managed a settlement in 1964. Similarly, on the question of holding the price-wage line, both Presidents Kennedy and Johnson engaged in vigorous persuasive efforts.

Governmental intervention—even at the highest levels—in major collective bargaining disputes seems likely to continue, even though its possible prolongation of disputes is recognized. For example, though President Eisenhower personally followed a hands-off policy toward such disagreements in order to encourage disputants to settle disagreements on their own, Vice-President Nixon played a crucial, behind-the-scenes role in settling a potential steel strike in 1960. Because the economy has become so interdependent, the threat of nation-wide stoppage of a vital service becomes ever more important. It has been suggested, therefore, that Congress provide the President with an arsenal of weapons for use in such disputes. Thereby the calculations of the parties-in-interest as to the President's likely course of action would be confounded and the incentive for agreement between the disputants increased. Instead of having no choice except an injunction when an impasse has been reached, the President might be authorized to choose any of these courses:

> . . . demand a postponement without a court order; establish
> a fact-finding board that would have power to make recom-
> mendations or not make them as the President desired; seize
> a struck plant or industry, with an option to keep the profits
> or turn them back at the end of the takeover; get an injunc-
> tion; or do nothing at all.[17]

While such an arsenal of remedies would better equip the President to contend with collective bargaining emergencies, it may be doubted whether Congress would be willing to grant such broad powers to any President or whether the Supreme Court would find all of them constitutional. When President Truman sought to deal with an impending national strike in the steel industry in 1952 by seizing the industry, the majority of the Supreme Court decided that he had exceeded his constitutional powers.[18] Nevertheless, though doubts exist as to the amount and kinds of governmental intervention in critical labor disputes, presidential mediation is more likely to be used as the last resort than compulsory arbitration—another suggestion for the avoidance of strikes. Though the latter has gained a measure of support, its record of use in Canada and elsewhere indicates that it does not guarantee continuity of production nor does it fit some of the ideals associated with collective bargaining and democracy itself.

The spectacular nature of occasional major disputes tends to overshadow the progress that has been made in incorporating successful collective bargaining into industrial life. In the nation's forty thousand unionized plants, collective bargaining agreements have institutionalized the roles of both management and labor. Hammered out in the clash of opinion, these agreements generally require the participation of judicious outside umpires. In 1962 more than fifteen thousand labor controversies were settled by arbitrators, whose use is provided for in 98 per cent of all collective bargaining agreements.[19] An arbitrator may be called in on an *ad hoc* basis to settle a grievance brought by an employee, or, increasingly, a company or an industry will join with a union to select a man to serve on a continuing basis. The part-time appointment of labor arbitrators, most of whom come from the ranks of college professors, is facilitated by suggestions from the American Arbitration Association, to which members of this relatively new profession belong.

In considering the future of industrial relations, one is struck by the diversity and complexity of conditions that public policy must meet. A partial listing includes the issue of "featherbedding," which is prohibited by the Taft-Hartley Act but has retained its prominence in certain industries such as the railroads, where changing technology encounters strong unions and long-established work patterns; the allegation of monopoly power against unions powerful enough to cause crippling nation-wide strikes, and the related question of whether the use of such economic power should be made a violation of the antitrust statutes; the question of labor relations practices in areas of the economy employing unskilled, unorganized, and often underprivileged workers; bitter and disruptive jurisdictional battles among some unions; allegations of dictatorship against some union leaders and lack of leadership against others; charges of corruption against some union leaders but evidence of immense dedication from others; claims of racial or religious discrimination in the practices of certain businesses and unions, but strong voluntary efforts toward equality by others; and, finally, examples of all shadings of cooperation and conflict between employers and employees in the many industries and companies that comprise the industrial economy.

CONSUMERS

Protection of consumers is a subject permeated with paradoxes. Every person and every institution is a consumer of some goods and services, but the term is usually restricted to the ultimate consumer —the individual or family who buys and consumes or uses goods and services. Though these non-institutional consumers collectively purchase nearly two thirds of the gross national product of over $600 billion, they have far less organized economic strength than the large institutional consumers and the producers who buy material for further fabrication. Although numbers often mean strength in a democracy with many interest groups, the innumerable individual consumers have aims too diverse and diffuse to permit them to organize and achieve a significant voice in policy-making circles. Even though the sovereignty of the consumer—his free choice of goods and services—is basic to the theory of our private enterprise system, the practical limitations upon this concept have produced sporadic governmental action to protect the consumer from some of the more extreme consequences of his exercise of sovereignty. The final paradox, then, is that despite the lack of effective consumer organization, government in the twentieth century has, to a degree, responded to the needs of consumers.

The extent to which the government should protect the consumer is somewhat controversial. Protection from direct hazards to health or safety draws a large measure of agreement; when entire shipments of canned fish are ordered destroyed because one or two individuals have died from eating a spoiled can, or when a fabric is outlawed because it proves to be highly inflammable, the actions of government are widely accepted. But matters become more confused and views more divergent on questions involving deception, false or misleading advertising, or incomplete statements in labels and advertising. Often there is no fine line between advertising which merely deceives and that which endangers health. For example, is it a hazard to health if a consumer is misled into believing that a patent medicine relieves the pain of arthritis? It may be dangerous if it causes a buyer with a degenerative arthritic disease to defer his trip to the doctor, yet for the vast majority of buyers it means only the purchase of aspirin or another pain-killer at a higher price than usual. This shading from the clearly hazardous misrepresentation to the fairly harmless "puffing" of products is what causes much of the debate. An actual case before the Federal Trade Commission, which has jurisdiction over the deceptive advertising of foods and drugs, illustrates the contrasting approaches found even in official bodies. A patent medicine manufacturer had advertised that his product, which was designed to make up iron deficiencies in the human system, would relieve certain symptoms. The majority of the FTC ruled that the advertising was deceptive because it omitted a warning that the symptoms it claimed to relieve were not always produced by an iron deficiency. Commissioner Lowell Mason, a colorful champion of business freedom, objected:

> To put it simply, if a man claims apples are in his basket, must he deny the presence of peaches? . . .
> When the merchants of America must all talk like Government lawyers, life will be most complicated. Advertisements will look like the Federal Register and will be read about as frequently.

We will all turn into a species of robots clicking out IBM data to one another, choosing our canned foods by code, marrying by IQ, propagating by test tube and dying by formula.

When this millennium has arrived, it will be the proper time for such an order as is here attempted.

Then will be the time for So-and-So's Cosmetic Company to tell the scullery maid that she will always look like a dope even if she uses their lotion.[20]

As in other regulatory fields, the answers to the questions of whether, when, and how the government shall act have been affected by the attitudes of the economic units upon whom the weight of the government action would fall, as well as by the attitudes of the beneficiaries of such action. Because consumers are unorganized, they may count themselves fortunate when producers' interests happen to coincide with theirs. Thus, purchasers of woolen products and furs owe a vote of thanks to producers of these materials, who decided that governmental regulatory action was preferable to loss of business due to consumer suspicion of production practices. Sheep growers and weaving firms, concerned about the increasing competition that virgin wool was receiving from what they judged to be inferior clothing materials, encouraged Congress to pass the Wool Products Labeling Act of 1940. Similarly, the concern of the more responsible furriers about competitive practices in the labeling of misleadingly named animal skins led to the passage of the Fur Products Labeling Act of 1951 which requires accurate naming and the furnishing of pertinent information on labels and in advertising. Partly because farmers were concerned at an early date about marketing their products, consumers have benefited from a variety of statutes assuring quality through the setting of standards and the use of inspections. Examples of statutes include meat inspection (1890 and 1906), animal quarantine (1901), grain standards (1901), butter standards (1923), canned goods standards (1930), and, to an extent, even the Pure Food and Drug Act of 1906.

The struggle waged over food and drug legislation mainly illustrates, however, that when powerful interests are affected, the protection of the consumer has not been accomplished easily. Some protective action by one or another level of government has existed in America since colonial days, but, as with so many regulatory topics, the action has had difficulty keeping up with economic changes. As food and drug production and distribution began to encompass larger geographical areas and to employ more elaborate processing techniques, local governments and, later, state governments sought federal regulation to supplement their own efforts.

More significant was the great public indignation aroused by revelations of food adulteration and patent medicine frauds around the turn of the century. Crusading magazines carried numerous "muckraking" articles detailing the questionable, repulsive, or dangerous practices employed. The publication in early 1906 of Upton Sinclair's *The Jungle,* set in the cattle slaughterhouses of Chicago, was extremely influential in the passage of legislation extending meat inspection to the domestic market and of the Pure Food and Drug Act of 1906. Though the latter statute was substantially weakened by the resistance of food and drug producers, who had fought a bill for a generation, and though its administration by the Department of Agriculture's Bureau of Chemistry was consistently hampered by inadequate appropriations, it constituted a notable step in consumer protection. It firmly established the precedent that government should protect not merely the consumer's health but also his pocketbook. Both misbranded and adulterated food and drugs were prohibited in interstate commerce. The definition of misbranding included imitating another article, giving false or misleading information, and failing to state the quantity of habit-forming or dangerous drugs named in the act. Adulteration was defined as including decomposed or diseased animal or vegetable substances or poisonous or other deleterious ingredients possibly injurious to health, removing valuable components, substituting less valuable components, and hiding damage or inferiority through artificial coloring or coating. Violation of the act could bring a fine for first offenders and imprisonment and a fine for second offenders. In practice, juries shied away from convicting local manufacturers and rarely imposed imprisonment, and some manufacturers looked upon the small fines as a license for doing business. Under the circumstances, the more crucial sanction provided by the act was the authority to seize adulterated or misbranded articles upon their entry into interstate commerce. The effectiveness of this remedy was increased after 1906 when many states made their food and drug laws parallel to the Pure Food and Drug Act. Adulteration was more effectively avoided than misbranding because judicial interpretation of the latter was sufficiently restrictive to permit preposterous claims of cures and beneficial effects to be made and because the failure to include advertising in the act made the efforts of unethical manufacturers and merchants easier.

Not until the Great Depression sparked a renewed interest in consumer protection in the 1930's was the Pure Food and Drug Act of 1906 replaced, after a vigorous fight, by a stronger law. Again, books and articles calling attention to abuses—this time often in advertising—generated much of the impetus. The Department of Agriculture's Food and Drug Administration (as it was called after 1931), which had taken over enforcement of the food and drug statute in 1927, publicized a grisly exhibit of spoiled food it had seized, death certificates collected from users of patent medicines, and photographs of women disfigured, blinded, or paralyzed by the use of cosmetics. In Congress an FDA-sponsored bill, first introduced in 1933, made little headway against the opposition of manufacturers and advertisers until a tragedy in 1936 dramatized the issue. After more than one hundred persons had died from taking a new, untested drug (sulfanilimide in a solvent chemically related to automobile antifreeze), the more responsible drug manufacturers ceased their opposition to stronger legislation.

The Food, Drug, and Cosmetic Act of 1938 replaced the 1906 law. It added cosmetics (an eyelash cosmetic had caused blindness) and therapeutic devices to the list of regulated items, made sanctions more severe, and strengthened the definitions of adulteration and misbranding of food and drugs. Adulteration of food, for example, now included adding substances to increase bulk, to reduce quality or strength, or to "make it appear better than it is"; for drugs, the FDA compendia had to be followed or else the precise differences therefrom had to be clearly labeled; and cosmetics were made subject to safety and purity standards. All foods with special names given by manufacturers also had to be labeled with their usual name and the ingredients declared; foods sold under the name of another had to be clearly marked "imitation"; food labels were to disclose the addition of artificial coloring, flavoring, and chemical preservatives; drug labels were to contain adequate directions for use, warnings, where appropriate, of habit-forming qualities, and warnings against unsafe dosages and dangerous ingredients. With the sulfanilimide tragedy in mind, the act also required that full information about new drugs be filed with the FDA and that samples be submitted for FDA testing.

Though the Food, Drug, and Cosmetic Act failed to deal with deceptive advertising, another 1938 statute did. The Wheeler-Lea Act prohibited the false advertising of foods, drugs, cosmetics, and therapeutic devices. The Federal Trade Commission, not the FDA, was made the enforcing authority, as the statute gave the former general control over "unfair or deceptive acts or practices in commerce." The FTC had only limited success with its new authority. False advertising was weakly defined in the statute, the courts were relatively lenient in interpreting these provisions, and the FTC's other duties limited its attention to advertising for foods, drugs, cosmetics, and therapeutic devices. It should be noted that a third agency, the Post Office, has responsibilities touching on the subject of false advertising because of its authority to forbid use of the mails for fraudulent purposes. The FDA's strategic position was somewhat improved in 1940 by its transfer from the Department of Agriculture, where it had been subject to pressure from producer groups, to the Federal Security Agency, which in 1953 achieved cabinet status as the Department of Health, Education, and Welfare.

In 1962 tragedy again gave a bill to strengthen consumer protection the fillip needed to make it the law of the land. The widespread publicity given to the birth of deformed babies whose mothers had taken the drug thalidomide focused attention on the inadequacy of existing legislation. Although the FDA's refusal—thanks to the alertness of a staff doctor—to permit sale of the drug saved many American families from the heartbreak suffered in thousands of European homes, the news that a drug company had distributed thalidomide extensively to American physicians and that it had been used experimentally without federal supervision caused great consternation. Prior to the incident, legislation to strengthen the hand of the FDA in dealing with drugs had been given little chance of passage because of considerable public indifference and industry opposition. Almost overnight the situation changed, however, and the Kefauver-Harris Drug Amendments Act became law. It placed increased responsibilities on drug manufacturers, who were to use all their facilities and controls to assure the safety, identity, strength, quality, and purity of all drugs; to keep records and make reports to the FDA as to clinical and other experience on new drugs and antibiotics; to prove the effectiveness, as well as the safety, of all drugs before marketing them; to label drugs so as to include the drug's established name in addition to any proprietary name; to register annually with the FDA; and to list in prescription drug advertisements the drug's established name, quantitative formula, and a brief summary of side effects, contraindications, and effectiveness. Further, the FDA's authority was significantly increased. It was given jurisdiction over affirmatively approving new drugs before they are marketed and withdrawing approval immediately if a drug represents an imminent hazard to public health; over the certification on a batch-by-batch basis, before marketing, of all antibiotics prepared for human use; over inspection of all domestic drug firms at least once every two years; and over complete inspection of all prescription drug firms for all matters (except certain financial, personnel, and research data) that have a bearing on violation of the act.

On the basis of the new statute, the FDA stepped up its enforcement program. It set October 1964 as the deadline for makers of nearly five thousand drugs manufactured between 1958 and 1963 to submit proof that the drugs are safe and effective. It exempted from this review about one thousand long-used drugs, pending disposal of a suit brought in federal district court by the Pharmaceutical Manufacturers Association challenging the FDA's authority. In November 1964 the agency announced a program for the enforcement of advertising provisions of the Kefauver-Harris Act. The regulations sought to assure physicians reading advertisements in medical publications of a fair balance between the information on effectiveness and that on side effects. The resources available to the FDA for meeting its responsibilities have been markedly increased during the past decade. Between 1951 and 1955 its annual budget hovered around $5 million. In 1955 a citizens' advisory committee appointed by the Secretary of Health, Education, and Welfare recommended that the long-starved FDA be expanded threefold or fourfold over a five to ten year period. This recommendation, together with the FDA's broadened responsibilities under the Kefauver-Harris law and several minor statutes enacted after 1955, stimulated an increase in appropriations to a total of more than $28 million in fiscal 1963. Still, the FDA could boast that though 30 per cent of the American consumer's daily spending is for products under FDA jurisdiction, the annual cost to each individual for all FDA activities is only thirteen cents.[21]

Regulation of food and drugs exemplifies the difficulty of working out a consistently reasonable approach to consumer protection. Faced with popular indifference and industry pressure, the Food and Drug Administration has been subject to criticism for failing to use aggressively the authority it had under the Food, Drug, and Cosmetic Act of 1938. Observers have noted, for example, that the FDA required reports on the testing of drugs only when marketing applications for those drugs were filed and thereby ignored four fifths of the testing on humans done by manufacturers.[22] This situation the FDA belatedly corrected in new regulations issued in early 1963. Corrective legislation for drugs has the difficult task of achieving a balance between protecting the public from inadequately tested drugs and denying patients the benefit of new drugs by delaying their development and availability. It has been suggested, for example, that the Kefauver-Harris Act may not prevent another tragedy because testing procedures may not discover all side-effects (thalidomide was found safe for all but pregnant women) and that it may slow down new drug development through the imposition of added costs and other burdens on pharmaceutical companies.[23] Though other observers would not only dispute these generalizations but question whether the law has gone far enough for public safety, there is widespread agreement that the drug industry's clinical testing procedures have been utterly inadequate. Responsibility for this inadequacy is more difficult to assign. In 1963 a committee of the New York Academy of Medicine noted with regret that no official or professional body has set any professional standards for clinical testers.[24] It is difficult to escape the conclusion that for this fault, as well as for other shortcomings in food and drug regulation, no single group bears responsibility. For drugs, scientific advances have at least partially transformed the regulatory problem from one of policing to one of adequate scientific evaluating. Medical advances continue to gather speed even while the complexities of drug safety seem almost insurmountable. It is said that about 90 per cent of all prescriptions written today could not have been filled before 1948. As to food, both its quantity and its quality have been greatly improved by extremely effective, but often highly toxic, pesticides that are the product of advances in chemical technology. Regulatory agencies obviously must themselves become part of the scientific community and thereby supplement their older enforcement philosophy. Pressure to adapt to an emphasis on science appears to have had repercussions on appointments within the Food and Drug Administration. The important position of chief of its Bureau of Medicine remained unfilled for a year or more after becoming vacant in mid–1962. The refusal of some nominees to accept appointment was said to stem from a belief that the Bureau (and particularly its head) was still oriented too much toward enforcement.[25]

The increased importance of scientific knowledge to governmental activity in behalf of consumers, as well as the difficulty of agreeing upon the goals of regulation, were dramatically shown in the recent public controversy over cigaret smoking. After a series of private studies had indicated the deleterious effects of cigaret smoking upon health, a study was made by a respected committee appointed by the Surgeon General of the United States. Its report, issued in January 1964, confirmed the findings of earlier studies and stated that "Cigarette smoking is a health hazard of sufficient importance in the United States to warrant appropriate remedial action."[26] The assertion, while expected, caused consternation among tobacco-state congressmen, who attempted to head off adverse action by calling for publicly-financed research to find means of making smoking less hazardous. The ingrained habits of millions of smokers, to say nothing of the importance of the tobacco industry to the economy and the unhappy experience with enforcement of the Eighteenth Amendment, obviously eliminated government prohibition of cigarets. A widely favored remedy was to require cigaret manufacturers to inform the public, on package labels and in advertising, of the dangers of their product. The Federal Trade Commission, under its authority to prevent unfair or deceptive trade practices, issued regulations to this effect in June 1964, but before the rules went into effect in 1965, the FTC, under tobacco industry pressure, withdrew them. Before the issuance of the Surgeon General's report, several bills had also been introduced to broaden the jurisdiction of the Food and Drug Administration by bringing tobacco products under its surveillance. In April 1964, while bills were pending in Congress, the major cigaret companies agreed on a cigaret advertising code to be enforced by an independent administrator. Although the code incorporated mild reforms, such as the elimination of youth-directed advertising, it carefully avoided mention of the proposal that labels and advertising warn cigaret users of the dangers to their health. In terms of tactics, the industry move clearly represented an attempt to forestall governmental action by providing evidence of industry self-regulation. The action did not, however, forestall the introduction of a bill in 1965 by the influential chairman of the Senate Committee on Interstate and Foreign Commerce that would require a health warning on each cigaret package.

In general, the emphasis of the Kennedy and Johnson administrations upon protection of the "total interest of the consumer" is probably a harbinger of an era in which the consumer will have a more prominent place in public policy than he has had in the past. Such an emphasis is consistent with ever increasing urbanization and with concern for poverty in the midst of plenty. Since elements of regulation in the interest of the consumer date from earlier decades in the present century, the novelty of consumer protection can easily be overstressed, in any case. Standardizing weights and measures, eliminating impure foods, drugs, and cosmetics, preventing unfair methods of competition and deceptive trade practices, assuring fair rates in transportation, power, fuel, and communications—all these are examples of programs bearing directly or indirectly on consumer protection. Yet vigilance in enforcing established programs, alertness to the need for new ones, and coordination of the efforts of various agencies can together produce an attention to consumers that is something of a departure in the policy of the national government. As was noted with respect to the cigaret controversy, the threat of public action often produces a chastened attitude among the relevant private groups, though not necessarily action to match the attitude. Thus, because of presidential action and congressional bills on the subject of "truth-in-packaging," a flurry of activity occurred among packagers in 1964. For example, companies redesigned packages to give prominence to statements about precise weight or capacity of contents, and leading grocery producers and suppliers met in Washington with weights and measures officials from the states to tighten up labeling laws. Whether such actions are too little and too late is a question that the democratic process will answer in this case, as it has in others dealing with the entire spectrum of public policy. What is clear is that though protection of consumers remains perhaps the most difficult portion of public policy to dramatize, a new consciousness of its importance is abroad in the land. Increasing urbanization and its recognition in legislative reapportionment will see to that better than presidential programs can.

Government
as
Buyer

To speak of government as "buyer" may seem strange. Yet a moment's reflection will show that the role is not new. Governments have always purchased supplies for armies and for many kinds of construction. Buying has not been restricted to objects; it has included services as well. In many places and times the services of tax collectors were purchased for a percentage of their collections. There were many hired soldiers in the Roman legions, and the British contracted with Hessian mercenaries to fight American colonists.

What *is* new—in American history, at least—is the size and variety of government's role as buyer. We live in an age when the national government has become the sole or largest customer of many major industries. Because this phenomenon is so recent, neither its scope nor its consequences may be adequately appreciated. This century's turbulent history has made it plain that government's role as the major buyer of goods and services is no passing phenomenon. Strain as we might to restore a popular image of government as being set apart from the economy, we would find it difficult to foresee a future in which government is not by far the economy's largest single customer. Fluctuations in spending moods, and the rise and fall of international tensions will affect the level of purchases but will not significantly change the role of government as buyer.

This role has been affected by several constitutional clauses and the interpretations given to them. One involves the first of Congress' enumerated powers in Article I, Section 8: "To lay and collect Taxes, Duties, Imposts, and Excises, to pay the Debts and provide for the common Defence and general Welfare of the United States; but all Duties, Imposts, and Excises shall be uniform throughout the United States." The portion of this statement known as "the general welfare clause" has been interpreted in widely varying ways: James Madison, who adhered to Thomas Jefferson's emphasis upon a central government of decidedly limited powers, believed that the clause conveyed no power to do anything not authorized as one of the specifically enumerated powers in Section 8; at the opposite extreme, the contention has sometimes been advanced that the clause is really a grant of broad power to legislate for the general welfare; the moderate position, and the one that has prevailed, is the view of Alexander Hamilton and Joseph Story that the clause gives the national government authority to raise and spend money for any public purpose connected with the general welfare. Justice Benjamin N. Cardozo's opinion for the Supreme Court in a 1937 case upholding federal old-age benefits is illuminating as an indication of the discretion available to Congress (so long as it avoids "a display of arbitrary powers") in spending for the general welfare. After endorsing the Hamilton-Story interpretation, Cardozo stated: "Nor is the concept of the general welfare static. Needs that were narrow or parochial a century ago may be interwoven in our day with the well-being of the Nation. What is critical or urgent changes with the times."[1]

A second relevant constitutional clause (in Article I, Section 9) requires in part that "No Money shall be drawn from the Treasury but in Consequence of Appropriations made by Law. . . ." Over the years this clause, too, has been the subject of controversy. In brief, Congress has been anxious to prevent inroads on its power of the purse, but it has been forced to recognize that when the executive branch purchases goods and services some flexibility of arrangement is necessary. As early as 1820 there were protests in Congress about the executive department's practice of making contracts in anticipation of appropriations to fulfill them.[2] So long as Congress appropriated funds haphazardly and without the guidance furnished by an executive budget, its frustration over its ability to shape and control expenditures was acute. The Budget and Accounting Act of 1921 finally authorized the President to present an annual budget to Congress and thereby enabled Congress to view executive branch requests *in toto*. Nevertheless, the demands of the twentieth century forced Congress to authorize the President to incur obligations in

anticipation of appropriations. In both world wars Congress authorized the President to establish agencies and spend funds for the
prosecution of the war; in so doing, Congress recognized the imprac-
ticability of any other arrangement. The Great Depression and the
more recent cold war have only solidified this practice.

THE SCOPE AND IMPACT OF GOVERNMENT BUYING

Government buying ranges from paper clips to manned moon
missiles. So massive and complex have even the more traditional
forms of government buying become that in 1949 Congress created
the General Services Administration to bring a semblance of order
to the picture. To this agency were assigned a variety of functions
relating to property acquisition and management, functions formerly
performed by a number of agencies. Within the General Services
Administration, specialized units handle the tasks. The Federal Supply Service purchases, stores, and distributes common-use items of
supply for all federal agencies. The Utilization and Disposal Service
manages the transfer of excess property from one agency to another
and directs the disposal of surplus property. The Transportation and
Communications Service develops and administers programs for the
procurement and utilization of transportation, public utilities, and
communications services. The Public Buildings Service designs, con-
structs, manages, maintains, and operates federal buildings and develops policies for government-wide real property management. The
Defense Materials Service acquires, stores, and manages a stockpile
of strategic and critical materials.

The stockpiling programs, some of which are administered by
agencies other than the GSA, are a good example of the broadening
of the buying function. One of the lessons taught by World War II
concerned the importance of avoiding shortages of materials essential
to the prosecution of a war. Included in this idea was the need
to maintain the productive capacity of certain industries. Beginning
with the Strategic and Critical Materials Stock Piling Act of 1946,
Congress has passed a number of statutes dealing with the acquisition
of strategic materials for stockpiling. As of September 1963, about
$8.6 billion worth of materials (chiefly metals) were contained in the
inventories administered by the GSA.[3] Other inventories included a
civil defense stockpile held by the Department of Defense, a civil
defense medical stockpile maintained by the Department of Health,
Education, and Welfare, machine tool inventories administered by
the Department of Defense and the GSA, and helium inventories
administered by the Department of the Interior. If one includes the
$5.5 billion in agricultural commodities purchased under the price-
support program—a debatable step because the program's primary

purpose is to promote agriculture—the total national stockpile inventories amount to about $14.5 billion.

Buying of this magnitude inevitably produces public debate. Undoubtedly, the purchase of various minerals has been made with a view to maintaining an active mining industry in the United States against the day when it might be needed for national defense purposes. Yet various contracts to buy have been criticized in Congress for going too far in accommodating the firms involved. Examples of criticized practices include permitting companies to make excessive profits and deferring deliveries until profit levels can be vastly increased. In recent years, criticism by the General Accounting Office and congressional committees has stimulated the tightening of contract procedures. The coordination provided by the Office of Emergency Planning in the Executive Office of the President has also helped. Among its other important functions, the Office of Emergency Planning determines the kinds and quantities of strategic and critical materials to be acquired—perhaps from other government stockpiles—and stockpiled under the 1946 statute.

Capital expenditures—what business calls spending for plant and equipment—offer another good illustration of the extent of government buying today. In 1963 all of the nation's businesses together spent about $39 billion on new plant and equipment. By comparison, the capital expenditures of the national, state, and local governments amounted to nearly $19 billion. This was a rise of almost $7 billion in a decade. The bulk of public capital outlays go into highway building, conservation projects, and educational facilities, but an increasing amount has gone into equipment—especially power-generating equipment, computing and other office devices, research equipment, and motor vehicles.[4] Public capital expenditures can obviously be an increasingly potent factor in bolstering the economy.

Considering the annual budget of the national government, one is immediately struck by its $100–billion size and by the dominant place of defense expenditures, which claim roughly half of this total. In the early 1960's defense spending approached 10 per cent of the gross national product. The economy administered by the Pentagon, Walter Lippmann has noted, is over two thirds as large as the entire economy of Great Britain.[5]

Even more remarkable than the increases in the scope of government buying is the shift in the kinds of purchases made. At the root of this change is the steadily increasing importance of scientific and technical work to the achievement of major public purposes. Procurement for national defense has been largely transformed since the early 1950's. As weapons have become more complex, the emphasis in defense buying has shifted from relatively simple contracts calling for the production of conventional weapons to highly involved contracts calling for "research and development" as a prelude to production. Weapons have become so complicated that they are often referred to as "weapon systems." Reliance on nuclear warheads—to say nothing of the search for peacetime uses for the atom—has channeled research and development funds to the Atomic Energy Commission. After Sputnik awakened the nation in 1957 to the extent of Soviet progress in conquering space, research and development became the watchword for the newly created National Aeronautics and Space Administration. President Kennedy's announcement on May 25, 1961, that "this nation should commit itself to achieving the goal, before this decade is out, of landing a man on the moon and returning him safely to earth," immensely accelerated the effort. Aside from defense and space, the National Institutes of Health and the National Science Foundation have been the chief government agencies employing research and development ("R. & D.") contracts. From 1957 onward, budgetary funds for research and development increased at an annual rate of about 20 per cent, reaching the substantial sum of $15.3 billion in the budget announced in January 1964. When it is considered that governmental "R. & D." expenditures amounted to perhaps $100 million annually before World War II and did not reach the $1 billion figure until 1950, the revolution in government buying becomes even more dramatic. Of total federal expenditures for research and development, about 80 per cent are spent through contracts with businesses, universities, and other non-government entities.[6]

The repercussions of this "new look" in government buying are so many and so widespread that they can only be sketched here in broad outline, with primary emphasis on the consequences of contracting for research and development. In our highly sensitive, interdependent economy, decisions in Washington about what may be prosaically called "government buying" produce tremendous reverberations. Within only the last few years "aerospace"—which includes firms that build airplanes and military missiles, as well as manufacturers of hardware for moon flights—has passed the automobile industry in size and has become the nation's largest industrial employer. The fifty-one companies identified by the Securities and Exchange Commission as aerospace manufacturers had combined sales of $15 billion in 1962.[7] Many substantial companies, such as General Dynamics Corporation and North American Aviation, Inc., are almost wholly dependent on their sales to the government and its prime contractors. Even such giants as Westinghouse Electric Corporation, General Electric Company, and Radio Corporation of America make from one quarter to one third of the dollar amount of their sales to the federal government. But not only big companies are involved in the aerospace industry. Development and production

of the Polaris missile that is carried aboard nuclear submarines involved thirty thousand contractors and subcontractors. The huge
Apollo program for putting astronauts on the moon involves twenty
thousand different firms and three hundred thousand workers scattered through forty-eight of the fifty states. The local impact of
activities on this scale is bound to be immense. According to estimates
of the Department of Commerce, whenever one hundred new jobs are
created in a community, they bring in a total of 296 people, generate
$590,000 in additional personal income annually, create the need for
classroom space for fifty-one more children, and increase retail sales
by $360,000.[8]

The impact of government buying associated with defense has
been accentuated by the tendency for regional concentrations of industry to develop. During World War II the Midwest was a leading
production center, for weapons were strongly tied to the automotive
technology of that area. In the 1950's there began a shift to areas
and industries considered more receptive to the needs of a new technology. A leading example was the West Coast airplane industry,
which was eager to supplement or replace declining production with
missiles, as contrasted with the reluctance of auto manufacturers to
divert resources from their booming industry. Also favoring the former
was the greater suitability of coastal areas for experimentation with
missiles and space vehicles; missile shots could be directed seaward,
and water transportation of huge missiles was available. This regional
shift was also facilitated by an important technological change. Following the lead of the Air Force, the other military services also
adopted a "weapon system" approach in recognition of the increasing complexity of modern weapons. Under this approach, a contract
is made with a single corporation to manage the development and
production of a weapon system, often a complex missile or an advanced bomber or fighter. For the sake of convenience, other prime
contractors as well as subcontractors for that weapon system tend
to cluster around the headquarters location of the system-manager
corporation. The extent of the regional shift is apparent from statistics. The five Midwestern states of Indiana, Illinois, Ohio, Michigan, and Wisconsin had over 27 per cent of total prime contract
awards in early 1950; by fiscal 1960 the percentage had fallen to
less than 12 per cent. General Motors, which had been the largest
single defense contractor between 1950 and 1955, had dropped back
to fifteenth place by 1958. By 1960 California's share of production
contracts for the federal government accounted for almost 24 per cent
of the total awards to all states.[9] In 1964 the House Space Subcommittee on Science, Research, and Development, in the first definitive government-wide survey on the extent of geographical disparity
in the award of prime contracts and grants for research and develop-

ment, found that nine Western, Eastern, and Gulf states accounted for almost 71 per cent of the monetary value of these awards in fiscal 1963, California alone for over 38 per cent of the total.[10]

Localities as well as regions find decisions about defense and space industries crucial to their economic welfare and therefore of vital political interest. About 90 per cent of California's defense business is concentrated in three counties.[11] The fierce competition between two plane manufacturers for the award of a $7-billion contract for the TFX fighter-plane in 1962 deeply involved the economic fate of Wichita, Kansas, and Fort Worth, Texas. When the Defense Department awarded the contract to the company in the Texas city, a congressional committee launched an acrimonious investigation into the decision. Though the points at issue involved the merits of the rival planes, the controversy was intensified by the territorial rivalry.

When employment under government contracts reaches substantial proportions in a state or community, that area is obviously highly vulnerable to relatively slight changes in government buying. In Washington and Kansas, for example, employment in defense industries is over 25 per cent of total manufacturing employment. In five other states west of the Mississippi it is between 15 and 25 per cent.[12] Under such circumstances, relatively obscure details in the huge federal budget become a matter of vital local political interest, and a slowdown in spending for a program may be viewed with great concern by congressmen from the affected areas.

Given the uneven geographical impact of government contracts, the question of aiding economically depressed areas naturally arises. For the Department of Defense the problem has been especially difficult. Congress has laid down guidelines that fall somewhere between the extremes of action and inaction. The Defense Department may give certain limited preferences to chronically depressed areas, surplus labor market areas, and small businesses. At the same time, the Department may not pay price differentials on contracts for the purpose of relieving economic dislocations.[13] To supplement the assistance, the Department of Defense has taken administrative steps to smooth over the impact of contract decisions upon localities. An Office of Economic Adjustment has helped communities work out plans and programs to offset the termination of contracts. An "early warning system" designed to give communities several years' warning as to expected shifts in procurement has been devised.

To turn to another kind of local impact of government contracting, when the federal government directly regulates the minimum wage and maximum hour levels of private employers, it is not surprising that government contracts deal with the subject of wages and working conditions. Actually, the first statutes to use contracts to accomplish these purposes, at least to some degree, antedate the

Fair Labor Standards Act of 1938, which is broadly applicable to private businesses operating in interstate commerce. The Davis-Bacon Act of 1931 was passed after certain construction contracts had been won by contractors who had paid wages lower than those prevailing in the immediate area of the construction site by recruiting and transporting workers from low-wage areas. To halt the practice, the Davis-Bacon Act required the payment of wage rates not less than those prevailing in the locality where the construction took place—a much stricter requirement than that for minimum wages in the Fair Labor Standards Act. Subsequently, it became the practice of Congress to insert a "Davis-Bacon provision" in statutes authorizing construction programs for airports, housing, slum clearance, and hospitals. The enactment of the Federal-Aid Highway Act of 1956, which authorized the huge interstate highway building program that will be completed about 1970, saw labor groups win a spirited fight to have the provision apply for the first time to highway contracts largely financed by the federal government but awarded by the states. In 1964 the Davis-Bacon Act was broadened in another way. After sharp debate, Congress decided to include fringe benefits usually found in labor contracts—such as health, welfare, unemployment, and retirement benefits—in the determination of the prevailing local wages.

The second pre-1938 statute that used government contracts as a lever for improving the lot of workers in private industry was the Public Contracts Act of 1936, also known as the Walsh-Healey Act. It required government supply contracts of a certain size to contain stipulations with respect to the payment of minimum wages and overtime, non-employment of child and convict labor, and the observance of certain safety and health standards. The close connection between regulation through contract provisions and the administration of minimum-wage and maximum-hour standards under the Fair Labor Standards Act is symbolized by the fact that, since 1942, both duties are handled by one division within the Department of Labor. The immense growth in government contracting since the Davis-Bacon and Walsh-Healey Acts were passed has, of course, greatly broadened their impact.

The great civil-rights controversy that has increasingly occupied the nation in recent years provides an even more ambitious example of government's use of contracting to affect an important public policy area. The President's Committee on Government Employment Policy, established by President Eisenhower's executive order, sought to persuade contractors to adopt non-discriminatory hiring practices. The Kennedy administration replaced this group in 1961 with the President's Committee on Equal Employment Opportunity. Although the new executive order empowered the Committee to use such drastic means as terminating contracts or recommending criminal proceedings for the filing of false information, it also directed the Committee first to attempt "conference, conciliation, mediation, and persuasion." In practice, great emphasis was placed on these informal methods. As in so many areas of civil rights, slow progress was made. For example, in April 1963 it was reported that of twenty-four contracting companies with branches in Atlanta, Georgia, only four Atlanta offices were complying with voluntary pledges to recruit Negroes for employment.[14] Running a parallel course with the executive order was the "Plan for Progress" inaugurated by the Committee on Equal Employment Opportunity to enroll leading government suppliers in the non-discrimination campaign. By early 1964, agreements under this plan had been executed by 135 companies which had approximately 6.5 million employees. These figures compared with the total of 50,000 industrial companies employing about 15.5 million workers and 243,000 non-industrial contractors employing about 4.5 million people estimated to be subject to the executive order.[15]

The large-scale government support of science and technology has had a substantial impact on business, universities, and government itself, as well as on science and technology themselves. Some effects are salutary, some alarming. Business has benefited considerably from the national government's huge expenditures for research and development because products for the civilian economy often are the end product of military research and development. An estimated 2500 processes that can be used commercially have already emerged from the young aerospace industry.[16] Thanks to the massive increase in the national government's expenditures for research and development, the total amount spent annually for this activity by both public and private sources has risen to almost 3 per cent of the gross national product. Because this is a much larger amount than was traditionally allocated when business was the main source of "R. & D." expenditures, the pace of technological advance has been immensely speeded throughout the economy. But with so large a proportion of these expenditures principally benefiting certain industries and firms, some observers have expressed concern about the effect of government spending upon the structure of American industry. Furthermore, whenever defense orders slacken, prime contractors tend to subcontract less in order to keep their own shops busy.

Huge government expenditures related to science have helped greatly to push its frontiers even farther, but the increasing costliness of scientific research and its involvement with national goals mean that the time may be approaching when a system of national priorities will be established. This era has already arrived for the building of expensive accelerators, or "atom smashers"; budgetary decisions are having to be made which balance expense against probable returns in valuable new information on the basic nature of matter. The prospect has alarmed many scientists, including some of those connected with governmental undertakings. The Special Assistant to the President for Science and Technology warned in 1963 against making science a monolithic "planned economy" endeavor, because there must always be "at least one other agency to which the scientist seeking support for an unusual idea can turn after being rejected elsewhere."[17] Other scientists have stressed the inherently unpredictable nature of creativity, as well as the difficulty of predicting which endeavors will bear fruit. The director of the Carnegie Institution of Washington, for example, has cautioned that proposed governmental programs for doubling the number of doctoral degrees in the physical, engineering, and mathematical sciences might not only dilute the quality of scientific scholarship but might produce "massive imbalances among delicately related elements of our research structure."[18]

Universities, too, have felt a substantial impact from the large amounts of government spending. Reliance on the campuses has greatly altered them. Huge complexes of science buildings, special institutes to handle government-sponsored research, swollen research staffs, enlarged science curricula—all these and more are, principally, manifestations of government support and interest in university resources. In the course of this development, educational purposes have also been served through such programs as graduate student fellowships and institutes for high school teachers. One university president has placed the effects of recent federal support of scientific research on a par with those of the land-grant movement of the nineteenth century in molding the modern American university and making it distinctive.[19] Beginning on a modest scale during World War II, government support of university research reached an annual total of $1.2 billion by fiscal 1961,[20] and in 1960 federal funds accounted for 75 per cent of all university expenditures on research.[21] For a number of years, federal research spending in universities was concentrated almost exclusively in the physical and biomedical sciences, thereby creating anxiety about a proper balance of research endeavors. Recently there has been some broadening, with National Defense Education Act fellowships for graduate students in the social sciences, the support of behavioral sciences by the National Science Foundation, and even a proposal for a National Humanities Foundation. Nevertheless, some educational observers have detected unfortunate overall tendencies, such as lessened university autonomy, decreased faculty contact with undergraduates, and a transfer of some professors' loyalties from the campus to the federal agency paying for their research. University presidents have also been hopeful of more university control over government research money. If national priorities on scientific research sponsored by the government actually are established, however, their hope will be dimmed.

In passing, it should be noted that many universities have also been affected by another kind of government contract. Since the early 1950's an increasing number of American universities have contracted with the United States government to furnish technical assistance to underdeveloped nations. A survey taken in 1957 and 1958 identified 136 technical assistance programs in which American universities were engaged,[22] and there is reason to believe that the number has increased since then.

Technical assistance has principally meant sending teams of faculty members abroad or having citizens of aided countries undertake training on campuses in the United States. A new international dimension has thereby been brought to American universities; they cannot remain unaffected by their contract-stimulated experience. But along with a more cosmopolitan outlook have come new problems. The universities have had to face such questions as the extent of their contracting, the availability of suitable academic resources for this assistance function as against other pressing needs, and the degree to which they can resist taking on technical assistance duties that other types of organizations could provide equally well.

Inevitably, government itself has been greatly affected by the revolution in government buying that is the product of today's era. The attempts of the Department of Defense to cushion the impact on the economy of government contracting have already been noted. A larger bureaucracy has been an inevitable concomitant of the new-style contracting. Its complexity has required the assistance of many government specialists in devising and sifting the requirements of weapon systems, space satellites, or foreign aid plans as a preliminary to drawing up contracts; and it has spawned experts in drafting and administering contracts as well as in inspecting work done under contract. Governmental defense and space efforts have also hugely increased the number of scientists connected with the national government. Taking account of government contracts with universities, industry, and research institutes, 60 to 70 per cent of the nation's scientists and engineers are said to be directly or indirectly employed by Washington.[23] The number of scientific advisory committees has inevitably proliferated, posing questions about when scientists are acting for the government and when they are members of the public. In any case, the importance of science in the councils of government has achieved unprecedented importance.

PROBLEM AREAS IN GOVERNMENT CONTRACTING

The size and complexity of government contracting in the age of the atom and the missile has raised many perplexing questions. Three problem areas are singled out here for discussion: formulas for awarding contracts, conflicts-of-interest, and patent rights to inventions deriving from government contracts.

In the nineteenth century, open advertising for bids and firm prices became the hallmark of government contracting. Even today, competitive bidding prevails in almost all procurement by state and local governments, though it governs far less than a fifth of federal government procurement.[24] This is still a substantial sum, however; in 1962 it amounted to $5.1 billion.[25] The sharp percentage decline in federal procurement through competitive bidding stems, of course, from the immense increase in defense and space procurement and from the unsuitability of buying unstandardized items through the older method. Departures from competitive bidding came during both world wars, when war goods had to be procured hastily; though defense procurement reverted to competitive bidding after the first World War, the cold war situation prevented a similar course of action after World War II.

Negotiated contracts with various forms of reimbursement are heavily used in defense buying. Of the $25 billion in purchases made by the Department of Defense annually, as much as 80 to 90 per cent is accomplished through negotiated contracts.[26] These contracts are most frequently associated with research and development, an area in which specification of end products and advance estimation of costs is difficult. Procurement by negotiation is limited to use in seventeen situations, specified in the Armed Services Procurement Act of 1947, in which procurement on the basis of advertised bids and award procedures is either impracticable or inappropriate. Still, even with these limitations, negotiated contracting was adopted with some trepidation. President Truman, in signing the act, warned that "This bill grants unprecedented freedom from specific procurement restrictions during peacetime."[27]

Anxiety about negotiated contracts stems partly from their departure from ordinary norms of competition. In competitive bidding there is open advertising for bids, a basis for exact comparison of bids, and a fixed price. Under the newer procurement method these elements are largely lacking. The government selects the contractor by negotiation and agrees to reimburse him for the *actual* costs he incurs (subject to certain exclusions), and he is paid a fee based upon a percentage (often about 6 per cent) of his *estimated* costs. This form of contract thus avoids some of the inefficiency inherent in the cost-plus-percentage-of-costs contracts widely used during the two world wars. Competition is not lacking in negotiated contracting, though cost competition is often secondary to such factors as design and the engineering, production, and managerial capabilities of the respective companies. Competition also appears in the subcontracting process, though, again, considerations other than price may be crucial. Subcontracting may extend through several tiers. In weapon-system contracting, the first-tier subcontractors are likely to be on a cost-plus-fixed-fee basis, just as the prime contractor is, with the fee again paid by the government. Subcontracting contracts at the second tier and below may be on a cost-plus-fixed-fee basis or a fixed-price basis, depending on the end item to be obtained.[28]

The Comptroller General of the United States, whose responsibilities as head of the General Accounting Office include the review of agency contracting, has often been critical of military procurement under negotiated contracts. During fiscal years 1957 through 1964, he reported to Congress findings of excessive prices and other excessive costs totaling over $109 million; more than half of this amount was recovered from the contractors.[29] The Comptroller General was also largely responsible for a 1962 amendment to the Armed Services Procurement Act of 1947 that tightened up the use of negotiated contracts. The amendment was intended to require more purchasing by formal advertised bidding, require clearer written justification when certain negotiating authority is used, require and produce more competition in negotiated purchasing, and safeguard the government against inflated cost estimates on negotiated contracts. The effects of the amendment will become clear in time. Though the Comptroller General submitted forty-eight reports on defense contracts in fiscal 1964, the principal findings in the reports were related mostly to contracts awarded before the 1962 amendment became effective.[30]

Much of the criticism of negotiated contracts has centered on their failure to provide incentives for economy. The pyramiding of fixed fees through contracting and subcontracting is costly. Other factors that tend to inflate costs include the concentration on design and technical and managerial competence, the assurance given to a successful contractor that all of his costs will be covered by the government, the liberal allowances for overhead, and the contractors' advantage over the Defense Department in judging cost estimates. The last-named factor was at the heart of some of the Comptroller General's findings. An example drawn from another source, a Tax Court case, is that of a well-known plane and missile manufacturer that initially submitted cost estimates $80 million higher than its secret cost estimates made at the same time, a fact uncovered by the Federal Bureau of Investigation.[31] Higher estimates mean a larger fixed fee, of course. At the opposite extreme, some concerns purposely make low estimates to obtain a contract and then include unwarranted profits in their charges for design and procurement changes.[32]

Although complaints of hidden profits have been rife, formal profits have been modest. The combined profits of 4680 contractors for defense items in fiscal 1963 amounted to about 3 per cent of the total business done, and this was before taxes and before the deduction of any costs that might be disallowed by the government.[33] Since fixed-fee contracts, which would constitute a major part of this business, usually provide for about twice this amount, the likely explanation is that actual costs of furnishing the items exceeded estimated costs, upon which fixed fees are calculated. The Defense Department was disturbed about low profit levels and even more so about the fact that the 3 per cent level seemed to apply "regardless of whether contractors had a record of good work at low cost, whether they used their own facilities and capital and whether they were willing to undertake work at substantial price risks."[34]

In January 1964 the Defense Department modified its system for awarding negotiated contracts in the direction of providing incentives for holding down costs and improving quality of performance. Under the new procedure, contractors are chosen on the basis of secret semiannual reports evaluating their past performance in fulfilling contracts in terms of costs, time, and quality. Extra profits can be earned by a contractor's staying within his estimates, producing on time, employing his own funds instead of getting advances from the government, contributing his own technology rather than relying on the government's, and accepting a fixed-price contract rather than cost-plus-fixed-fee.[35] The Department argued that fixed-price contracts alone could save up to ten cents on the defense dollar and that the system as a whole, judging from a limited test run, could produce profits of 10 per cent for an efficient firm. Administration of the plan was facilitated in late 1964 by the creation of a department-wide contract audit agency to consolidate the contracting functions of the three military services. Further, more careful inspection procedures were instituted for judging the quality of a contractor's work, partly for purposes of determining whether that contractor should be awarded future contracts. An increasing problem in both defense and space contracting has been a quality of performance inadequate for today's stringent demands. Newspaper stories during one week in October 1963, for example, reported failings in two important programs; a Navy spokesman charged that the atomic submarine construction program had been delayed because of poor workmanship, and the National Aeronautics and Space Administration complained that space capsules for the astronaut globe-circling project had been delivered with more than five hundred defects and that spare parts were 50 per cent defective.[36]

Though there have been difficulties with new methods of government contracting, it would be a mistake to infer that the older system of open competitive bidding is free of defects. The advantages usually cited for competitive bidding—that bidders are in open price competition and that they, not the government, bear the economic risks—do not always exist in practice. Collusion among contractors may interfere. One such instance was disclosed in the government's successful antitrust suits in the early 1960's against manufacturers of electrical equipment (reviewed in Chapter Three). The Tennessee Valley Authority was one of the many buyers of such equipment to recover damages against manufacturers who had been found guilty of conspiring to fix prices. At the state and local level, particularly on minor contracts, there is often a practice of rotating business among several suppliers, who in turn encourage this practice by making identical bids. Business sources frequently explain identical prices in terms of the similarity of production costs for standardized items. In 1961, after the electrical equipment cases, President Kennedy issued an executive order that required federal agencies to transmit to the Attorney General reports of identical bids submitted in advertised procurement of property or services exceeding $10,000 in total amount. It also instructed the Attorney General to invite state and local agencies to make such reports to him. Six hundred cases of identical bids were reported, involving about 1 per cent of the estimated $10 to $11 billion of advertised public procurement.[37] Though the sample was regarded as too slim for firm conclusions to be reached, the percentage of identical bidding was lower than the Attorney General had expected. The statistics were thought to have been influenced by the deliberate publicity given to the survey and by its proximity in point of time to the electrical equipment cases. Nevertheless, identical bidding was found to be a significant problem in about ten broad product categories, including such major items as asphalt road materials, chemicals, and textiles. As the Attorney General's first report under the executive order covered only the first seven months of 1962, his second report was awaited with interest. For all of 1962, about $155 million of advertised public procurement was affected by identical bidding.[38] This again represented only about 1 per cent of all such public procurement, which totaled $15.4 billion in 1962. In federal procurement, iron and steel plate, sheet, and strip was the commodity class most often affected by identical bidding, but fuel oil was a more important item in terms of dollar value. At the state and local levels, asphalt road materials and chemicals led the list. A survey of state and local agencies indicated that the actions under the executive order had reduced identical bidding in their procurement. Another kind of difficulty that has emerged with competitive bidding is concentrated largely in the construction field. In 1962 the House Armed Services Committee expressed serious concern about the award of military construction contracts to "entrepreneurs" with little or no building experience. Aside from the delays and the poor quality that were the frequent products of such awards, the Committee noted that "entrepreneurs" were, in effect, paid "over-head and profit merely for having consolidated a number of sub-contractor quotations."[39]

Under the new technology in defense and space, conflict-of-interest problems have sharpened. In the past, when defense con-tracting usually involved production engineering and the manufacture of final products, the contractors had various customers besides the government. Now, to a considerable extent, defense and space con-tracting is for purposes of research and development, and the indus-tries involved (such as those dealing in aircraft, rockets, electronics, and atomic energy) often have the government as their sole customer. They have, moreover, the strongest incentive to seek research and development contracts in order to gain the know-how necessary for follow-up production contracts. Reviewing this situation in 1962, a presidential committee headed by David E. Bell, then Director of the Bureau of the Budget, was impelled to ask: "In what sense is a business corporation doing nearly 100 percent of its business with the Government engaged in 'free enterprise'?"[40] The committee concluded that "the developments of recent years have inevitably blurred the traditional dividing lines between the public and private sectors of our Nation."

The Bell report, while accepting close government-business inter-dependence as necessary, noted three conflict-of-interest areas in need of clarification: (1) where individuals serve simultaneously as govern-mental consultants and as officers, directors, or employees of private contractors; (2) where there are "interlocking directorates" among the boards of universities, research agencies, and corporations en-gaged in government-sponsored research; and (3) where organiza-tions are involved in varying activities on one weapon system.[41]

Conflict-of-interest statutes applying to individuals exist at every level of government, but their application has changed somewhat over the years. The federal statute stems from Civil War days and was intended to apply principally to petty officials who might be tempted to procure supplies for the Army and divert them to their own private uses. In more recent times, conflict-of-interest provisions have tended to involve major officials. Still the most blatant example of conflict of interest is that of certain cabinet members during the Harding administration whose involvement in the granting of leases on Navy oil properties to private interests on unduly generous terms has become known as the Teapot Dome scandal. Because the federal statute prohibits federal employees from having a personal financial interest in the private organizations with which they deal, cabinet members now follow the practice of ridding themselves of shares in companies with which their departments may do business. Secretaries of Defense are the most obvious candidates for this practice, Charles E. Wilson and Robert S. McNamara together having disposed of $4 million in stock of the automobile companies they headed. Two quite different questions have been raised about this procedure. Some critics have asked whether too much of a financial sacrifice is demanded of able men who are asked to serve in high positions with the government. Others have wondered whether the severing of pecuniary ties produces the desired impartiality in an official or, alternatively, makes him lean over backward to avoid his former firm— which may be a valued contractor.

In practice, when an official has clearly used his position to improve his private situation, his resignation has been swiftly obtained. Thus, in the late 1950's, the Secretary of the Air Force was forced out when it was discovered that he was using Air Force stationery to solicit business for his private firm, and the Deputy Secretary of Defense found himself without portfolio after intervening to get a manufacturing contract for his wife's company. More ambiguous, however, are such instances as one involving the Secretary of the Navy in 1963. A congressional committee investigating the award of the large TFX plane contract to a Fort Worth firm publicized the fact that the bank formerly headed by the Secretary was one of nineteen banks jointly making a loan to the contract-winning firm. Several months later, the Secretary resigned his post, though the Kennedy administration insisted that the resignation was unrelated to the incident and though the Secretary's critics had not directly accused him of a conflict of interest. Thus, it is probable that the practical criterion of conflict of interest in ambiguous cases is political embarrassment rather than transgression of the law.

The subtlety of the conflict-of-interest problem is further indicated by another incident involving the same Secretary of the Navy. In order to foreclose even the appearance of temptation, he voluntarily withdrew from any role in the award of a contract for a new type of vertical takeoff plane because he had formerly been a director of one of the companies competing for the contract. How difficult it was for him to withdraw completely was demonstrated by the fact that the Deputy Secretary of Defense, in amassing information on which to base a decision, asked the Secretary for his evaluation of the company's management. For this the Deputy Secretary earned the wrath of a congressional committee, after the company won the contract. The committee emphasized that military evaluators had preferred another company's plane and that the Navy Secretary's advice might have been decisive.[42]

A factor that has contributed to sensitivity about the conflict-of-interest issue is the larger role in the choice of contractors recently accorded to civilians in the Department of Defense. Secretary of Defense McNamara's award of the TFX plane contract apparently contradicted the judgment of most of the evaluation teams in the Department.[43] Especially when a contract is lucrative, civilian officials are likely to come under heavy congressional criticism if their decision runs counter to a recommendation made by evaluation boards heavily populated by military men. This is so even though the civilian officials are not legally required to take the advice of military evaluators in awarding contracts.

As to government consultants, as distinguished from officials, the Bell report suggested that the standard proposed in President Kennedy's memorandum of February 9, 1962, on "Preventing Conflicts of Interest on the Part of Advisers and Consultants to the Government" be followed, namely, that "no individual serving as an adviser or consultant should render advice on an issue whose outcome would have a direct and predictable effect on the interests of the private organization which he serves."[44] Full disclosure of a consultant's private interests was requested, as well as alert action by government officials to avoid conflict-of-interest situations involving consultants. At the same time, another plaguing problem has involved the hiring of persons with special knowledge and skills whose principal employment is outside the government. Because such individuals were subjected to the same restraints under the conflict-of-interest laws as full-time employees, recruiting proved to be difficult. To meet this situation, Public Law 87-849 was passed in 1962. It imposed a lesser array of prohibitions on temporary and intermittent employees than on regular employees.

At the heart of the interlocking-directorate problem, the second conflict-of-interest area identified by the Bell report, is the scarcity of men of ability, who are often asked to serve in a variety of roles. The Bell report observed that such multiple service could give rise to a conflict of interest because "Members of governing boards of private business enterprises, universities, or other organizations which advise the Government with respect to research and development activities are often simultaneously members of governing boards of organizations which receive or may receive contracts or grants from the Government for research, development, or production work."[45] Unless the board members actually are government consultants, present conflict-of-interest laws do not apply. The Bell report suggested that boards and their members be guided by the standards applied to government consultants.

The third area identified by the report dealt with possible conflicts of interest for organizations, rather than individuals. The committee noted that a conflict of interest could occur "if a private corporation received a contract to provide technical advice and guidance with respect to a weapons system for which that same private corporation later sought a development or production contract, or for which it sought to develop or supply a key sub-system or component."[46] Both the defense and space agencies have taken steps to improve this situation. In September 1962 the Defense Department, taking note of the Bell report, established a rule stating that a company serving as a technical adviser in a research program cannot later compete in the "hardware" phase. The rule was first applied to the communications satellite program, in which the International Telephone and Telegraph Company helped the Department's Defense Communications Agency to coordinate the efforts of the Air Force and Army in planning for the construction of defense satellite communications systems.[47] Even before the Bell report was issued, the National Aeronautics and Space Administration had attempted to limit the role of the General Electric Company, its technical adviser on the Apollo rocket and capsule program, to non-production activities. The practical problem that emerged was that of defining what should be covered by the "hardware exclusion clause."[48] An even knottier problem has arisen as to the proper role of quasi-government corporations spawned by the contracting process. One such company was Space Technology Laboratories, which won a contract as technical director of the Air Force's ballistic missile program. In May 1960 the General Accounting Office recommended that this wholly-owned subsidiary of Thompson Ramo Wooldridge, a private, profit-seeking corporation, be absorbed by the Air Force because of the conflict that had developed between its public responsibilities and its private interests. Because it was a profit-seeking organization, participating contractors had been reluctant to give it full cooperation, fearing it as a competitor. At the same time, the government was apprehensive that the company would desert its tasks as technical director in favor of the greater profit-making potential in manufacturing missiles, once it had gained the requisite competence.[49] Situations such as these have led to periodic suggestions that defense and space agencies should act as their own managers. Needless to say, there are various obstacles involved, including the fluid, technical nature of many defense and space projects and the salary differential in favor of industry.

PATENT RIGHTS

The growth of research and development contracts to the startling figure of $15.3 billion annually by the 1964–1965 fiscal year has immensely increased the urgency of determining rights to patents for inventions made with government funds. The ubiquity of the patent question may be illustrated by the impact it has had on universities. Largely because much of its research involves government funds or equipment, all employees of one large state university must sign a patent agreement stating that they agree to have the university patent their inventions if it so desires and to assist the university in performing its obligations to grantors of funds for research or contracting agencies. In fantasy one can perhaps imagine a Shakespearean scholar disputing with the government about poetic innovations, but a real development has been that the university's patent agreement requirements have had to be broadened to cover students and visiting scholars.

Perhaps inevitably, government policy has not been consistent toward patent rights. The Department of Defense, the Post Office, and the Treasury Department have operated under laws or regulations giving title to contractors, while the Atomic Energy Commission, the Department of Agriculture, the Tennessee Valley Authority, and the National Aeronautics and Space Administration have, under most circumstances, retained title for the government. The variations in policy have become particularly significant since the great growth of research and development contracts. Three agencies, the Department of Defense, NASA, and the Atomic Energy Commission, accounted for about three fourths of the $12 billion spent in fiscal 1962–1963 for research and development. In line with the policy developed during both world wars, the Defense Department has permitted contractors to get patent rights to inventions developed under contract, although it has acquired for the government a license to use all such inventions. The other two agencies lack this tradition and are associated with awesome new inventions. In both cases Congress has decided that patent rights shall be held by the government instead of by the contractor. These two agencies can waive government title if they believe a waiver to be in the public interest. Between 1958, when NASA was established, and mid-1964, there were 2240 contractor inventions, and waivers were granted on only 104, or less than 5 per cent.[50] The Atomic Energy Commission has tended to be even more conservative with its waivers.

Should the government obtain title to patented inventions resulting from government-financed work or should title be retained by the contractor subject to irrevocable, royalty-free license for government use? The question has provoked much heated discussion. Contractors naturally prefer to obtain patent rights themselves, though an article appearing in a magazine friendly to business has conceded that "No matter who gets the patents, it is still possible to use R. & D. funds so that young scientists can be trained, research departments upgraded, and the production techniques of nuclear energy and space science learned at government expense."[51] This suggests that contracts will not go begging even if contractors are denied patent rights.

How one answers the question of patent title depends strongly on one's value system, as a review of the arguments demonstrates. Those who favor the contractor tend to put their argument on four grounds: tradition, democracy, equity, and incentive. Each of these points will be reviewed briefly, together with the rebuttal made by those who favor government retention of patent rights.

The argument from *tradition* is that our country has grown great on the basis of a constitutional system that preserves patent rights for the inventor, not for the government. Why change a successful arrangement? On the other side, it is pointed out that one of the firmest traditions of American business is that the patent rights to inventions made by employees while working for companies are assigned to their employers. From this it is argued that the actual tradition favors government title to patent rights. The opposite system, it is said, would mean a double standard, one for companies and their employees and one for the government and its contractors.

The argument from *democracy* also seems to see quite different things. Those favoring contractor ownership of patent rights emphasize that "a major identifying difference between democracy and communism lies in the legal concept of property" and that "we tend to break faith with our inventors when we insist upon the Government taking title to their inventions."[52] The rebuttal is two-pronged: (1) when competition is discouraged through permitting a single contractor the advantage of patent rights he acquired through government-financed operations, democracy is undercut, and (2) when the government "taxes the citizens of this country to secure funds for scientific research, on the ground that such research promotes the general welfare[,] and then turns the results of such research over to some private corporation on an exclusive, monopoly basis," there ensues "public taxation for private privilege, a policy that is clearly in violation of the basic tenets of any democracy."[53]

The argument from *equity* is that:

> The Government does not claim rights in the private property of the shippers, airlines, or farmers, nor does it claim the crops or any part thereof as a result of the subsidy payments made. Why should it claim rights to the inventions resulting from the research and development work it finances?[54]

The rebuttal is somewhat oblique and distinguishes among government contractors. Contractors that have invested their own resources and that occupy established commercial positions in fields in which the government is interested should have their equities recognized when patent rights are awarded. Similarly, "if the Government uses public funds, its equities also should be recognized."[55] Under this philosophy, an actual company that started with an investment of $7500, had only modest additions of outside capital, and yet found the market value of its stock increased to $300 million after seventeen years of dealing with the government as its only customer would be permitted to retain patent rights to few inventions or none.

The final argument centers on *incentive*. Those favoring contractor ownership have expressed fears that economic progress will be adversely affected by any other arrangement. More specifically, Representative Overton Brooks has stated that under NASA's ownership of patent rights "the American space effort suffers because contractors (a) do not put forth their best efforts, or (b) they increase the cost of their research services, or (c) they refuse to take on the work which the government needs."[56] Senator Russell B. Long, on the other hand, has claimed that the government pays no more for comparable research and development under one patent policy than under another and that the benefits of government contracts are such that there is no dearth of firms willing to accept contracts when some refuse to take on work. On a broader scale he has argued that incentive is not dulled by government ownership of patents for a variety of reasons: first, a patent monopoly has not been essential for private companies in the development of most civilian commodities and services; second, businesses do take licenses on government patents and produce items for the civilian market (e.g., frozen orange juice concentrate, the aerosol bomb) even though the businesses are not assured of exclusive commercial rights; third, since a contractor's costs are covered and his market assured, he does not require the incentive of a patent monopoly usually given to inventors; and finally, agricultural productivity has increased by leaps and bounds because "the bulk of agricultural research in this country was financed by Federal funds, and its results were put at the disposal of the potential users free of charge."[57]

Taking account of this sharp conflict over patent policy and the interest aroused in Congress, President Kennedy in 1963 issued to executive agencies a Memorandum and Statement of Government Patent Policy.[58] While the policy declaration recognized that complete uniformity was not feasible in view of "the differing missions and statutory responsibilities of the several departments and agencies engaged in research and development," it insisted upon greater consistency than had existed. A middle-of-the-road position was articulated. The government should "acquire the principal rights to inventions in situations where the nature of the work to be undertaken or the Government's past investment in the field of work favors full public access to resulting inventions." Exclusive commercial rights should be accorded to the contractor in situations "where the contractor has an established nongovernmental commercial position and where there is greater likelihood that the invention would be worked and put into civilian use than would be the case if the invention were made more freely available." The policy declaration attempted to guard against failure to practice the invention by requiring that the contractor "take effective steps within 3 years after the patent issues to bring the invention to the point of practical application or to make it available for licensing on reasonable terms." In addition, the government should also have the right to insist on the granting of a license to others "to the extent that the invention is required for public use by governmental regulations or to fulfill a health need, irrespective of the purpose of the contract."

In applying the new patent policy, the two agencies chiefly concerned with research and development expenditures moved toward greater uniformity but without obscuring significant differences.[59] In the Defense Department, patent title became a matter for negotiation with the contractor, rather than one of automatic transfer to him. The impact of the change was limited, however, by the fact that most defense contracts fall outside the fields for which the Kennedy statement prescribed government ownership. NASA, which had usually kept government title, brought its conditions for granting a waiver of government title into line with the Kennedy guidelines, but the change was not expected to result in a noticeable increase in the percentage of waivers granted. More significant and more controversial was NASA's decision to permit a waiver to be granted when a contract was signed rather than, as in the past, to grant it only after the inventions were reported, sometimes several years after the contract date. This procedure soon came under criticism from some congressmen, who asserted that NASA was giving away patent rights before learning what inventions might result.[60]

THE FUTURE OF GOVERNMENT BUYING

By 1964 indications had developed that the pace of expansion in government buying was slowing down rapidly in the very areas most responsible for the enlargement of government's role as buyer: defense, space, and atomic energy. In President Johnson's 1964–1965 budget the combined spending for defense and space actually was scheduled for a slight decline. Though research and development spending was pegged at the huge total of $15.3 billion, this figure represented an increase of only 3 per cent over the 1963–1964 fiscal year, compared with previous annual increases of about 20 per cent since the Soviets orbited Sputnik in 1957. That a plateau had been reached was confirmed by the 1965–1966 budget, issued in January 1965. Total defense spending was reduced $300 million; the increase in spending for NASA programs was only $200 million, compared to average increases of $1 billion a year since 1960; and research and development expenditures rose only $200 million.

A number of reasons can be adduced for the leveling off of government's role as buyer in 1964. In general, the reasons reflected the international situation and American reaction to changes in it. The nuclear test ban treaty of 1963, a degree of progress in disarmament talks between the nuclear giants, and a generally more conciliatory attitude toward the United States by the Soviet Union after its open quarrel with Red China led to a decreased sense of urgency about defense expenditures. These developments undoubtedly also spurred a change of attitude toward the problem of defense preparedness in the nuclear age. In 1963 policy-makers began giving serious attention to the argument that the United States, at unnecessarily high cost, was overbuilding its arsenal of nuclear weapons, with the result that such weapons could be used only by hitting conceivable targets many more times than needed. In January 1964 the budget submitted to Congress, as well as the explicit statements of the President and the Secretary of Defense, gave official recognition to this argument. Undoubtedly, the timing was helped by the Johnson administration's economy drive. Basically, however, after some years of frantic construction of missiles and missile sites, strategic weapons investment had virtually reached the aims set for it; because missiles remain ready for use, replacement needs tend to be slight. Another factor was the discovery that instead of a "missile gap" favoring the Soviet Union, the United States had a clear lead in missile production. Another was the greater emphasis placed on conventional military forces after 1960 because of an increasing number of small, guerrilla-type actions around the globe. Some of the urgency of the space program, too, began to lessen in 1963. Economic difficulties in the Soviet Union and pressure from its people for more consumer goods suggested that that nation's "race to the moon" might be adversely affected. Both defense and space programs would continue to demand high expenditures, of course. With both the Soviet Union and the United States striving to develop an effective anti-missile missile, with Red China's explosion of an atomic device in 1964, and with the possibility of heavier American involvement in Vietnam and elsewhere, a sharp reduction in American programs was not even contemplated. The portents of the future, uncertain though they are in international relations, point to a stabilization and perhaps even a gradual decline in the size of the bill for defense and space buying. The forecasts of the Department of Defense, for example, envisaged a 4 or 5 per cent decline in military spending over the five years after 1964, assuming no startling developments.[61]

Even before the expansion of government buying had begun to

slacken, some of the events noted in the preceding paragraph had engendered talk of the necessity to plan for such an eventuality. Although reconversion to a peacetime economy had occurred with a minimum of dislocations after World War II, it was widely noted that a much slighter shift in economic emphasis might bring weighty problems in its wake in the 1960's. The reasons cited included the absence of a large backlog of consumer demand in contrast to that accumulated by 1945; the limited adaptability to civilian use of the technical skills required in today's defense production; and the greater concentration of defense production, both geographically and by industry, than in the past.[62] In addition, the slowness of defense industries to develop reconversion plans in the early 1960's caused considerable uneasiness. Companies in the aerospace industry, whose main customer, and often virtually its only one, had been the government, lacked the knowledge of the consumer market and the skilled sales force necessary to step easily into another role.

This general situation produced an increased clamor for government itself to cushion the impact of a change in its buying needs. As noted earlier, the Department of Defense had established a unit with the responsibility for helping communities plan their readjustment to shifts in production of materials for national defense. When the likelihood of more major shifts became apparent in late 1963, President Johnson appointed a Committee on the Economic Impact of Defense and Disarmament. Believing that congressional action was warranted, fourteen senators and twenty representatives co-sponsored bills in each house to create a National Economic Conversion Commission in the Executive Office of the President. The Commission, to be composed of the heads of nine federal agencies, was to plan action by government to facilitate conversion. Defense contractors were also to be required to develop alternative production possibilities.

In these times, government's role as buyer of goods and services is notable not only for its size and scope but also for its effect upon innumerable aspects of American society. As we have seen, the transformation of this role under the pressure of international events and evolving technology has so intertwined government with the economy that it cannot escape the responsibility of planning for anticipated change. Government, being the kind of consumer it is, cannot deal with its suppliers of goods and services in the manner of a householder who casually purchases items at this store and that. It cannot even buy in the manner of a giant corporation, for it cannot pretend to the same disinterest in the fate of its suppliers. In our day, government, acting as buyer, cannot forget such other concerns as a prosperous economy, the elimination of pockets of poverty, and the building of a better society.

Government
as
Manager

What does the national government manage? A comprehensive answer is hardly feasible here, so multifarious are its managerial functions. In the interest of orderly presentation, certain arbitrary groupings must be made. Without doing too much violence to the topic, government may be said to manage natural resources, business-type services, social services, and economic growth and stability. Several words of caution are in order. First, the categories are not mutually exclusive. For example, managing the production and sale of electricity from multipurpose dams involves both the first and second headings. Second, the word "manage" may have somewhat different connotations from one category to another and even within categories. Thus the government, though broadly concerned with natural resources, finds itself in a position to act directly upon certain segments (such as national parks) and more indirectly upon others (such as water pollution). Some business-type services are wholly owned by the national government; others are only partially owned by the government or are entirely privately owned but managed by the government. Granting the enormous difficulties of categorizing so vast and amorphous a subject, the four categories offer a reasonably consistent way of viewing "government as manager."

In the museum at Big Basin State Park in California, established in 1902 as the first of a number of parks designed to save the coastal redwood trees from destruction, placards tell of the astonishment, anger, and contempt that greeted the efforts of those who sought to halt the cutting of the majestic trees. Lumber representatives vigorously asserted their right to cut them as equivalent to the right of the fishermen to take fish from Monterey Bay. This reaction illustrates the ambiguity and shifting nature of concepts about conservation. Today, as population pressure focuses more attention on the food resources of the sea, there is a growing concern about the conservation of that remarkable resource. When oyster beds are destroyed by oil discharge from ships, when shrimp and fish die in great numbers near the mouth of the Mississippi apparently because of insecticides washed down the river from hundreds of miles away, and when Soviet trawlers use such efficient ways of netting fish that other nations worry about the overall supply, conservation takes on added meanings.

In order to understand better the evolving nature of resources conservation, it will be helpful to consider why conservation came to the forefront of American public policy. Two events—the closing of the frontier about 1890 and the immense spurt in industrialization in the latter part of the nineteenth century—probably deserve much credit.[1] The former produced the realization that resources were finite and could even be exhausted. The latter vastly stimulated the search for raw materials and their efficient accumulation. A nation that had been primarily concerned with land settlement exhibited impatience with natural resources. Settlers tended to regard forests as mere obstacles to farming, for example. As land became scarcer and industrialization increased, natural resources became valuable. Minerals and timber, once regarded as useless or in abundant supply, became valuable commodities. Industrialization spurred the search for familiar resources and the discovery of new ones. Machine processes were developed for harvesting and extracting resources, often with great economic and social consequences. A simple but graphic example is furnished by timber cutting. Trees in the East were cut selectively because of limited demand and the use of manual methods, but by the time timber cutters reached the Midwestern timber stands in post-Civil War days, mass assaults upon timber stands were both possible and demanded. Railroad tracks were laid into forests, and when the trees had been decimated the tracks were extended and the process repeated. As a result, where Eastern forests had usually survived lumbering, forests around the Great Lakes disappeared and entire lumbering communities with them.

Historians of the conservation movement have detected at least three major approaches to conservation. Because each approach is still prominent today, conservation is anything but a settled issue. In point of fact, whenever a natural resources issue is discussed in the public forum, each of the approaches tends to find its vigorous spokesmen. They have been labeled the neo-Malthusian, the technician, and the naturalist.[2] The first approach pays tribute to Malthus' fear that population will outstrip resources. The "population explosion" has given a new urgency to the warnings of the early nineteenth-century English economist that unless population is checked, disappearing resources will bring poverty and degradation to man. Critics of this position believe that it is fallacious to regard resources as fixed. Many of them espouse the "technician" approach—a faith in the application of scientific techniques to the problem of resources. This position may be dominant today, thanks to American optimism and rapidly evolving technology, which constantly seeks and finds new resources. It places stress on efficient use of resources rather than on preserving them against a rainy day and on treating resources in the same manner as manpower and materials in the economic calculus. The "naturalist" school of thought on conservation abhors the "technician" position. Its adherents stress the obligation to preserve wilderness areas, protect fish and wildlife, and provide more parks and recreation areas. They fear that the rapid encroachment of civilization, if unreversed, will soon completely despoil nature.

The differences in emphasis among conservation groups have blunted their political impact, even though they have been able to unite against those who are not conservation-minded. The question of whether to build dams in lovely mountain canyons provides a case in point. Should the scenery be left in its natural state, or is it a criminal waste of resources to forego water power, navigation, and flood control or irrigation? Over such issues bitter battles have been fought for generations. Yet it is possible for those who want forests left unspoiled, for example, to combine with those who desire scientific timber management in battles against those who would denude the land altogether.

A characteristic aspect of resources politics is the extent to which governmental action has been accepted as necessary and desirable.[3] Government presumably can take a longer-range view of natural resources, balancing the needs of the present generation against the needs of those yet unborn and balancing many private interests against those of the public at large. In some instances, even producers of raw resources for industry have found it expedient to turn to government. After the Texas oil boom of the 1920's producers found themselves in such ruinous competition that the Texas Railroad Commission was authorized to administer quotas for them. Government action of quite another kind—the oil-depletion allowance allowed producers by federal law—has been justified by its sponsors as an incentive to the industry to enlarge oil reserves. While those concerned about natural resources were able to agree on government as the appropriate vehicle for action, it is consonant with democracy—especially the American version—to produce vociferous disagreement about what, specifically, government shall do. In addition, some specific limitations upon the attainment of coherent policies for natural resources should be mentioned. We may note the effects of private ownership of land, federalism, government agencies, and interest groups.

Conservation of resources cannot help but be affected by the extensive private ownership of land. Agricultural land, for example, is divided among several million farmers. Should they be expected to conserve the soil for future generations when they are faced with immediate economic necessities? Natural resources management by government must here be largely indirect. It has consisted in furnishing incentives to farmers for soil conservation. The program was instituted only in the 1930's, however, and partly as a consequence of the actions of "suitcase farmers," who plowed up marginal land during periods of high prices and abandoned them to erosion when grain prices declined.

A second limitation on government management of resources derives from *federalism*. Though some states have been conservation leaders, the states as a whole have varied widely in their efforts, thereby exacerbating the problem of coordination with their neighbors and the national government. In general, the states needed the stimulus of the first conservationist President, Theodore Roosevelt, who called a governors' conference on conservation in 1908. Many of the more recent difficulties over federalism have centered on the development of large river basins. The example of the Tennessee Valley Authority has both stimulated thought about developing other river basins and intensified the efforts of states to find other means of administering such development than a federal government corporation. Attention has been given to the possibilities of the interstate compact, a device authorized by the federal Constitution. To date, experience with it has been rather spotty. As of July 1964 there were forty-eight agencies based upon interstate compacts,[4] most of which were created to deal with interstate problems involving water, usually a river. The range of their complexity may be illustrated by considering two of the agencies that affect the Delaware River. The Delaware River Joint Toll Bridge Commission has the relatively simple task of operating and maintaining five toll bridges and fourteen free bridges that span the Delaware between New Jersey and Pennsylvania. The Delaware River Basin Commission, on the other hand, not only involves the three additional states of New York, New Jersey, and Delaware but has the stupendous task of guiding the multipurpose planning, development, and management of the water resources of the Delaware Basin. This agency was formed in 1961 after many years of agitation and controversy over unwise use of the river basin. It has authority to construct and operate river works and to own projects and finance them through loans, grants, or the issuance of bonds. In spite of its impressive mandate, however, its modest performance since 1961 indicates the more or less typical scope of operations under an interstate compact.[5] It has concentrated upon planning activities and has operated under a moderate budget of less than a half-million dollars, over one fifth of which is contributed by the federal government. The federal representative on the Commission coordinates the work of some nineteen federal agencies that have functions in the basin. Although no projects may be constructed in the basin without the Commission's approval, the Commission itself had by 1963 neither undertaken nor planned any capital projects. Various federal projects were authorized after 1961, some of which were to involve state contributions to the cost. In general, the interstate compact device has been more suited to the settlement of the legal rights and duties of two or more states in the use of a common resource than to situations involving continuing policy and administrative problems.

Much the same may be said of another device, the interagency coordinating committee, that employs coordination by an unwieldy group. In natural resources at least, such committees tend to consist of both federal and state officials. An example is the Missouri Basin Inter-Agency Committee, formed after World War II and composed of five governors from the ten basin states plus representatives of five federal agencies, that began meeting to coordinate the development of the basin within the framework of the pertinent federal and state laws. States at opposite ends of the Missouri River soon found themselves in sharp conflicts of purpose over the use of the available water (e.g., irrigation vs. flood control, consumption, and sanitation). Discontinuity developed when incumbent governors were defeated in elections, which changed the party composition of the governors on the committee.

A third limitation upon policy coherence is the remarkable *proliferation of governmental agencies* dealing with natural resources. For example, in 1955 the second Hoover Commission noted disapprovingly that twenty-five federal agencies were concerned with one or more aspects of water resources.[6] More specifically, twelve agencies were concerned with flood-damage abatement, nine with irrigation, eight with drainage, ten with watershed treatment, seven with improvements to navigation, nine with pollution control, ten with recreation and fish and wildlife conservation, nine with power transmission and distribution, fifteen with power generation, and thirteen with water supply. Though the array of agencies is less formidable in other natural resources policy areas, a neat, orderly picture obviously is lacking. Nevertheless, the proliferation of agencies is not as senseless and irrational as it may appear to be at first glance. A 1957 description of the growth of federal responsibility for just one of the above-mentioned fields indicates the parts played by some of the major agencies.

> Initially, federal flood-control activities were associated with the development of navigation, and prior to 1936, they were largely localized in the Mississippi Valley. However, the Flood Control Act of 1936 marked a radical departure, declaring that ". . . flood control . . . is a proper activity of the Federal Government in cooperation with States, their political subdivisions, and localities thereof." To this end, it authorized the Corps of Engineers to undertake ". . . Federal investigations and improvements of rivers and other waterways for flood control and allied purposes . . ." and the Department of Agriculture to undertake ". . . Federal investigations of watershed and measures for run-off and waterflow retardation and soil erosion prevention. . . ."
>
> Today, the federal government has a large-scale flood-management program, with many ramifications. The Corps of Engineers is actively engaged in the construction of flood-control works to protect the main river and tributary valleys. Flood-control storage is included in multiple-purpose reservoirs constructed by the Bureau of Reclamation. The Department of Agriculture . . . has a nation-wide program for the reduction of flood damages in the upstream tributary valleys. The Weather Bureau maintains a flood-warning service. The Housing and Home Finance Agency has been directed to establish a flood-insurance program under the Federal Flood Insurance Act. . . . And finally, the Office of Civilian Defense, the Corps of Engineers, and other federal agencies cooperate with state and local authorities in relieving distress when major floods occur.[7]

Agencies dealing with natural resources have been noted for their close relationships with *clientele groups* and, more openly than in other policy areas, have engaged in public battles with their rivals. The profusion of agencies and interest groups, as well as the vigorous conflicts over policy, testifies to a lack of consensus. Both Hoover

Commissions were alarmed at the overlapping and duplication of effort among resources agencies. Other observers have viewed this phenomenon with little concern, however; they have reasoned that the multiplicity of agencies stems from unresolved controversies over goals and that the process of reaching greater agreement cannot and should not be hurried. Merging resources agencies would often encounter strong opposition from their clientele groups and even from the bureaucracies themselves. The three major agencies involved in managing the nation's forest land, for example, have sharply differing approaches and supporting groups, and interagency cooperation has been largely lacking. The Forest Service, which administers all public lands reserved as national forests, has a highly professionalized bureaucracy resistant to outside control, but its production orientation has made it sympathetic to the lumber industry. The public lands controlled by the Bureau of Land Management include choice timber on the West Coast and in Alaska, but the Bureau's major attention is upon its relations to Western ranchers who have consistently sought liberal grazing privileges on public lands for their cattle and sheep. The National Park Service, which has jurisdiction over areas of special scenic or historic significance and draws the support of many conservationists, looks at its forests primarily from the recreational standpoint. The Forest Service has successfully avoided transfer from the Department of Agriculture to the Department of the Interior, where the other two agencies are located. Because Congress has granted all three agencies considerable discretion, their lack of a close relationship with the general public has often been a matter of concern.[8]

Though it is impossible to deal with the many and varied details of natural resources policy in so brief a space, a notion of the urgency and complexity of the policy-making process in this vital area may be gained by reviewing one aspect, the problem of water use. Its increasing complexity can be attributed both to the accelerating competition for available supplies of water and to technological advances in the use and control of these supplies. The second Hoover Commission predicted in 1955 that in the next quarter century industrial needs for water would rise by 138 billion gallons per day and domestic consumption by 7 billion gallons per day, even while sewage and industrial wastes would increasingly pollute the sources from which the water is drawn.[9] The consequences of technological advances can be illustrated from the history of multipurpose dams. As their name implies, the construction and operation of these dams are geared to such disparate purposes as irrigation, flood control, navigation, and power generation. In the nineteenth century the Corps of Army Engineers undertook various projects in the Eastern half of the country. Primarily, these projects involved the deepening of harbors and river channels, in addition to some flood control works. The twentieth century raised the question of how to integrate this older water policy with the entirely different needs of the West. Under Theodore Roosevelt's leadership, Congress passed the Reclamation Act of 1902, which made irrigation a major water use. Into a reclamation fund for the planning and construction of irrigation works went the proceeds of the sale of public lands and, later, a share of the oil and mineral royalties from public lands and of license fees for water power sites. This fund also receives repayments from water users, who are expected to repay the construction cost, without interest, within a period of forty years, though in practice Congress has permitted longer repayment periods for a number of projects. As water users hoped to keep their fees at a minimum, they encouraged the development of electric power in connection with the building of irrigation projects so that power revenues could help in repayment. Other factors also stimulated the growth of hydroelectric power. The Federal Power Act of 1920 envisaged the coordinated development of water resources for power and related purposes, and the development of the multipurpose dam provided the means. As a result, by 1927 the Corps of Army Engineers had drawn up several hundred surveys of multipurpose projects, and by 1928 the Bureau of Reclamation of the Department of the Interior had begun construction of Hoover (Boulder) Dam, the first of the giant Western dams.

When it became technically feasible and economically desirable to build multipurpose dams, all the potential users of water became rivals in a way that had not been true in the days of small, isolated, single-purpose projects. The needs of entire river basins had to be considered. Also, though the process is highly value-laden, especially when social factors are considered, costs and benefits had to be allocated between flood control, navigation, irrigation, and power generation. All these purposes had different backgrounds. Historically, flood control and navigation costs had been borne by the taxpayer at large, while the beneficiaries of irrigation were expected to repay costs. Hydroelectric power introduced several important issues. Should power rates be set sufficiently high to aid landowners in carrying irrigation costs, or should they be set low enough to encourage wider use of electricity? Those who saw hydroelectric power as a resource fully as important as the other water uses naturally argued for the latter policy. The issue led inevitably to the question of whether the government or privately-owned electric utilities should generate, distribute, and sell the electricity. Deep feelings were aroused about the propriety of government mixing into business or, alternatively, about the propriety of private utilities profiting from dams built at taxpayer expense.

Further complexities were posed by the rivalry of government agencies with contrasting points of view and, consequently, with backing by different groups. The Bureau of Reclamation was restricted to the seventeen states west of the 100th meridian, which roughly marks the eastern boundary of the nation's arid lands. This was a mild restriction, however, for the principal multipurpose projects have been in that region. The Bureau's natural supporters have been the small landowners who fit into the acreage limitations placed by the Reclamation Act upon recipients of irrigated water. As a means of broadening its appeal, the Bureau has sponsored hydroelectric power generation under government auspices and at low prices. Because the Reclamation Act permits a landowner to irrigate, from a federal project, only 160 acres (320 in community property states), large landowners have tended to gravitate toward the Corps of Army Engineers. The Corps' dams, though constructed under flood-control statutes, may provide water for other purposes. The Flood Control Act of 1944 was the first to dictate that irrigation features of Corps projects be planned, constructed, and operated in accordance with reclamation law. Enforcement, however, has been lax.[10] Local water users find that the Corps' tendency to weigh flood control heavily (a 100 per cent federal contribution for reservoirs) is a favorable factor. They also often prefer the local autonomy in hydroelectric power favored by the Corps, for they can apply for a federal license to develop the power and set power rates sufficiently high to help retire the local contribution for irrigation benefits. Unconfined by geographical limitations on its operational area, the Corps has been able to generate strong nation-wide support in Congress. In its long history of concern with internal improvements, the Corps has developed a working relationship with Congress that largely ignores the separation of powers. Once a congressman has gained the Corps' approval of a project in his constituency, he can submit it for inclusion in an omnibus rivers-and-harbors and flood-control bill. A measure of the close alliance between congressmen, contractors, and Corps engineers is provided by the existence of the powerful National Rivers and Harbors Congress. Drawing its membership from all three groups, it has often acted as a preliminary sifter of projects that the Corps ultimately backs. With this kind of support, the Corps was able to defy even so strong a President as Franklin D. Roosevelt and virtually to ignore a provision in the Flood Control Act of 1944 that required the Corps to apply the acreage limitation of the Reclamation Act to irrigation projects that it built.[11]

Because water resources for a fast-growing national population appear increasingly limited, effective planning has become an urgent necessity. Since so many interests must be satisfied, public policy often becomes a patchwork affair. For example, the question of whether there will be enough water in the Missouri River to take care of all the purposes envisaged in the so-called "Pick-Sloan" plan was largely ignored. The "plan" was basically an amalgam of the Bureau of Reclamation's proposal for irrigation and hydroelectric projects for the upper Missouri and the Corps of Army Engineers' proposal for navigation and flood-control works for the lower Missouri. With the entire nation a battleground for rival proposals, their backers, and government agencies, it is not surprising to find water-resources planning taking the form implied in a 1962 news dispatch that began as follows:

> The Federal Government's dam builders have signed a peace treaty. It marks a major step in the development of more hydroelectric power in the Pacific Northwest and toward settlement of the Columbia River dispute with Canada.
>
> President Kennedy is expected to announce soon that the Bureau of Reclamation in the Department of the Interior and the Army Corps of Engineers have resolved their long-standing jurisdictional dispute over water-resources development in Alaska and in the Columbia and Missouri River valley.[12]

Chaotic as water-resources planning has been in the dry-lands area of the United States, the confusion over public policy for water pollution demonstrates that the situation is not unique. Sewage and industrial wastes have produced endless problems, particularly in the populous East. Though the problem was initially viewed as local—a view often encouraged by industries that feared the high costs resulting from federally-enforced standards—meaningful federal action was finally taken in 1948. The Water Pollution Control Act of that year made the Public Health Service responsible for preparing pollution-abatement plans for interstate streams, encouraging the states to enact uniform laws, helping municipalities in pollution investigations, and promoting the formation of interstate authorities. A number of interstate compacts were formed under the statute. The Ohio River Valley Water Sanitation Commission, for example, enabled eight states to coordinate their efforts in trying to rid the Ohio River of pollution. By 1960 most of the communities and many of the industries had adequate installations, but 225 industries still had not met the basic control requirements.[13] The original statute was replaced by the Federal Water Pollution Control Act Amendments of 1956, which included provisions for comprehensive programs for water-pollution control; interstate cooperation; research, investigation, and training; grants for water-pollution control programs; grants for construction of sewage-treatment works; and enforcement measures against pollution of interstate waters. Amendments passed in 1961 vested all functions under the statute in the Secretary of

Health, Education, and Welfare and, among other things, expanded the enforcement authority, increased maximum grants for construction of treatment works, and authorized the establishment of field laboratory and research facilities. In January 1965 the Senate passed a bill further expanding the federal role in curbing water pollution; the bill appeared to have a good chance of becoming the first item enacted in President Johnson's 1965 legislative program. It provided for the creation of a Federal Water Pollution Control Administration within the Department of Health, Education, and Welfare; higher maximums for grants to municipalities for sewage-treatment projects; and procedures for the establishment of standards of quality applicable to interstate waters.

The enforcement procedures under the amended statute emphasize the gingerly approach often characteristic of laws that envision federal-state-local cooperation. Whenever a state or a municipality (with the state's consent) calls the attention of the Secretary of Health, Education, and Welfare to a pollution problem that extends beyond the jurisdiction of the state, the Secretary is directed to call a conference of the local, state, or interstate agencies involved. If he finds that "effective progress" in pollution abatement is not being made after such a conference, he is to recommend to the appropriate agency what action should be taken. If, after six months, no action is forthcoming, he is empowered to call a public hearing in the geographical area concerned. The hearing is held before a hearing board composed of five or more persons, including one representative of each state allegedly causing the pollution or claiming to be adversely affected by it, one representative of the Department of Commerce, and one or more representatives from the Secretary's own department. If the hearing board finds that pollution is occurring and that effective progress in abating it is not being made, it makes recommendations to the Secretary, who in turn notifies the relevant state or interstate agencies to take corrective action. If action is still not forthcoming, the Secretary may request the Attorney General to bring suit in a federal district court. Federal authorities have been slow to follow these involved procedures to their ultimate end, despite notorious delays by municipalities in pollution control. The first federal suit was filed in 1960 after the government had spent three fruitless years attempting to get a city to refrain from dumping its raw sewage into the Missouri River.[14] In short, federal action has so far resulted in only limited progress in fighting the battle against pollution. The states, which theoretically have great control over municipalities, have been reluctant to act boldly, often because of a fear that they will frighten industry away from their borders. Further steps at the federal level may be seen as necessary in view of the ever increasing urbanization and the statement of the head of the

Public Health Service that there is now nearly six times as much pollution in our rivers, streams, and lakes as sixty years ago and that the amount is still increasing.[15]

"Public enterprise" is an ambiguous term. Though, in a sense, it might be applied to all governmental activities, it is usually restricted to those somewhat analogous to "private enterprise." Within this admittedly broad category, one may distinguish (1) industrial and commercial services provided for the government itself and (2) those provided for the public.

"Government service" enterprises have been scrutinized carefully from time to time during the last decade in order to determine their essentiality in the light of the availability of privately-owned businesses. Stimulated by criticism on this score from the second Hoover Commission in 1955, the Bureau of the Budget required reports from federal agencies on their enterprises, broadly defined, and their plans for curtailing services wherever they competed with private enterprise.[16] Over 19,000 commercial and industrial installations were identified in civilian agencies and about 5000 in the Department of Defense. It was found that about 17,500 of the civilian installations did not represent substantial or significant competition with private enterprise and that compelling reasons existed for not procuring the goods or services involved through ordinary business channels. About 2000 installations were discontinued and about 500 others were curtailed. The minor nature of most of the "enterprises" that were continued is indicated by the fact that about 8000 of them were custodial or janitorial activities carried on in post offices and about 3900 were grain storage bins owned by the Commodity Credit Corporation. Of the Department of Defense enterprises, about 10 per cent were eliminated or curtailed. The remainder, consisting mostly of support activities for military bases, were deemed worthy of continuing for a mélange of reasons, including national security, geographic location, excessive costs of private procurement, and training of personnel.

Commercial activities conducted by the government for its own benefit can easily become controversial in the United States, which is often labeled a business civilization. Should government-owned shipyards be operated when private shipyards are not busy? Congressional policy has reflected the political attractiveness of employment in shipyards, regardless of ownership. In 1962, when work in private shipyards was at a low ebb, Congress required that 35 per cent of the contracts for naval repair, alteration, and conversion be awarded to private yards. Two years later, when the Secretary of Defense proposed the closing of several government shipyards as an economy measure, a number of congressmen sought unsuccessfully to eliminate the 65–35 provision in the hope of giving more work to government shipyards.[17] The decision in late 1964 to close the Brooklyn Naval Yard set off a widely publicized controversy, even though Secretary McNamara had promised alternative employment to the workers. Another example of the ambiguity inherent in some government service enterprises is provided by post exchanges or commissaries. The low prices charged armed service personnel and their families in these government-owned stores have been criticized by the General Accounting Office as causing losses of $150 million a year to taxpayers.[18] For their part, the armed services have pleaded that the stores and their favorable prices serve as badly needed incentives to offset the relatively low level of military pay.

In general, these examples and others that might be cited suggest that government service enterprises will continue to exist but not without challenge. Policy toward them is likely to vary somewhat, depending upon the temper of the country. For example, under the Eisenhower administration the Bureau of the Budget issued instructions to federal agencies establishing a presumption in favor of government procurement from commercial sources.[19] Though the instructions were not repealed by the Kennedy administration, increasing emphasis was placed on using government installations and staffs rather than commercial or contractual arrangements when the latter would be more costly on a truly comparable basis.[20] For example, an Assistant Secretary of Defense reported in 1964 that federal employees replaced 135 technical representatives, provided by an electronics contractor, at the Army's Air Defense School. Savings were calculated at $283,000 annually, or more than $2000 per employee.[21]

The term "public enterprise" is most often associated with governmental activities having at least a quasi-commercial flavor and involving service to the public. The Post Office is undoubtedly the most familiar example, with the Tennessee Valley Authority perhaps running second. A host of other activities are often known only to specialized publics. There is perhaps no better way of showing the number and variety of these activities than by naming the agencies (minus the familiar Post Office) handling them and briefly describing their major functions.[22] Those marked with an asterisk are government corporations.

A. AGRICULTURAL DEVELOPMENT

1. *Commodity Credit Corporation.** Capitalized at $100 million and with authority to borrow up to $14.5 billion, it uses personnel and

facilities of the Agricultural Stabilization Service to conduct price-support operations and make payments for directing excess acreage to conservation. It acquires (through nonrecourse loans) and sells certain agricultural commodities, owns and maintains storage facilities, and makes loans for farm storage facilities.

2. *Federal Land Banks* (12).* Established in 1916 and now fully owned by about 750 federal land bank associations, they make long-term mortgage loans to farmers through these associations. The banks obtain the money to make loans principally from the sale of consolidated federal farm loan bonds to the investing public. The farmers' notes and mortgages serve as security for the bonds. The borrower purchases stock in an association in an amount equal to 5 per cent of his loan. The association in turn purchases a like amount of stock in the bank. When the loan is repaid, the stock in the bank and in the association is retired.

3. *Federal Intermediate Credit Banks* (12).* Established in 1923, they make loans to, and discount agricultural paper for, production credit associations, state and national banks, agricultural credit corporations, livestock loan companies, and similar lending groups. They may make loans to, and discount paper for, Banks for Cooperatives and Federal Land Banks. Loan funds are obtained principally from sales to the investing public of bonds that are the joint and several obligations of the Federal Intermediate Credit Banks. In 1957, when the twelve Production Credit Corporations merged with the twelve Intermediate Credit Banks, each bank assumed the additional responsibility of supervising production credit associations, which make loans for general agricultural purposes. In 1963 these associations totaled 487, of which 480 had retired all government capital and the remaining four were largely owned by farmer-members. The associations were originally capitalized by the government-owned Production Credit Corporations.

4. *Banks for Cooperatives* (1 central and 12 district).* The district banks make commodity, operating capital, and facility loans to farmers' cooperatives. The central bank makes loans to the district banks and participates in loans that exceed the latters' respective lending limits. As the 2770 cooperatives using the credit facilities increase their capital stock in the district banks, the government capital is retired.

5. *Federal Crop Insurance Corporation.* Its purpose is to protect farmers against loss from causes beyond their control, such as weather, insects, and disease. Premiums paid by the farmers who elect to take this protection are set at levels to cover anticipated losses and to build the premium reserves necessary for a sound insurance operation. Most of the administrative costs of the insurance program, however, are financed by annual congressional appropriations. The

Corporation's original financing came from an authorized capital stock of $100 million.

6. *Farmers Home Administration.* Through almost 1500 local offices, it provides a variety of loans to rural residents. Purposes of the loans include the operation, development, and purchase of family farms; home building and improvement on land owned by farmers or certain residents of towns with populations of 2500 or less; aid to farmers in cases of natural disasters; and projects for water development, soil conservation, and shifts in land use undertaken by groups of farmers. Loans are supervised by county or area committees of three farmers, and they are granted only to those applicants who cannot obtain credit elsewhere at reasonable rates and terms.

7. *Rural Electrification Administration.* It makes loans to cooperatives for the purpose of bringing electricity service (authorized in 1935) and telephone service (authorized in 1949) to rural areas without them. By 1963 Congress had authorized over $5 billion in loan funds for electrification, of which somewhat less than one third had been repaid in principal and interest (at 2 per cent). As rural electrification now exceeds 97 per cent, loans have increasingly been used to strengthen the generating and transmitting capacity of existing systems.

B. HOUSING AND HOME FINANCE

1. *Community Facilities Administration.* It makes a variety of loans— to colleges for dormitories; to political subdivisions of states for planning and constructing public works that meet an essential public need and contribute to the reduction of unemployment; to private nonprofit corporate sponsors, consumer cooperatives, or public bodies for rental or cooperative housing for the elderly; and to states, political subdivisions, Indian tribes, and private nonprofit corporations to assist industrial expansion under the Area Redevelopment Act of 1961.

2. *Federal Housing Administration.* Through seventy-six field offices it insures mortgages on FHA-appraised homes. Its income from fees, insurance premiums, and interest on investments has been sufficient to pay all its operating expenses and losses to date and to build substantial insurance reserves.

3. *Public Housing Administration.** Created in 1947 but with antecedent agencies extending back to 1937, it administers the program of federal financial assistance to local communities for the construction of low-rent public housing. Such assistance is given in the building of about 35,000 housing units annually.

4. *Federal National Mortgage Association.** Known as "Fanny May," this agency increases the supply of investment capital available for home mortgage financing by buying and selling home mortgages, finances home mortgages when special assistance is needed

for certain segments of the population or when a decline in home building is threatened, and manages a mortgage portfolio.

5. *Federal Home Loan Banks* (11).* Under the supervision of the Federal Home Loan Bank Board, the banks act in support of the member institutions that own them: savings and loan, building and loan, and homestead associations; savings and cooperative banks; and insurance companies. The Secretary of the Treasury is authorized to purchase consolidated Federal Home Loan Bank obligations up to $1 billion outstanding at any one time, but the record of loan repayment by the approximately 5000 member associations has been good enough to avoid the use of this emergency power to date.

6. *Federal Savings and Loan Insurance Corporation.** It insures the safety of individual investors' savings up to $10,000 in accounts with member institutions of the Federal Home Loan Bank system. Premiums for the insurance are paid by member institutions. Under the statutory requirement that 50 per cent of net income each year be used to retire government capital, all of the original $100 million furnished by the government has been returned to the Treasury.

C. BANKING AND FINANCE

1. *Federal Reserve Banks* (12). Supervised by the Federal Reserve Board and owned by member banks (all national banks and such state banks and trust companies as have applied to join and have been admitted), the Federal Reserve Banks perform various operations to reinforce and make more flexible the nation's banking system.

2. *Federal Deposit Insurance Corporation.** Financed by assessments on member banks in the Federal Reserve System and income from investments, it insures individual deposits to a maximum of $10,000. In connection with this principal function, it examines insured banks that are not members of the Federal Reserve System, terminates the insured status of banks with unsafe and unsound practices, acts as receiver for all national banks placed in receivership, and takes various other steps to protect depositors.

3. *Export-Import Bank of Washington.** It aids in financing exports and imports and the exchange of commodities between the United States and any foreign country or its agencies and nationals. In doing so, it is directed by Congress to supplement but not compete with private capital. The bank is authorized to have a capital stock of $1 billion and, using its own bonds and notes, may borrow from the United States Treasury amounts not exceeding $6 billion outstanding at any one time.

D. TRANSPORTATION AND COMMUNICATIONS

1. *Alaska Railroad.* Built in 1914, it was given the tasks of providing transportation, developing areas along the 483-mile railroad line,

and stimulating settlement and industrial and agricultural development. It has incurred heavy losses, but it has provided services
attempted unsuccessfully by private railroads at an earlier date.

2. *Panama Canal Company.** It maintains and operates the Panama
Canal and conducts a variety of business operations (including even
restaurants, theaters, and bowling alleys) in the Canal Zone, where
private parties may not own land. The Company's operations have
usually earned a profit; in fiscal 1963 the profit amounted to over
$2 million, down $5 million from 1962.

3. *Saint Lawrence Seaway Development Corporation.** With the Saint
Lawrence Seaway Authority of Canada, it has constructed and now
operates the Saint Lawrence Seaway. It has the task of financing the
United States share of the seaway cost on a self-liquidating basis
through the imposition of tolls whose level is set jointly with its
Canadian counterpart. Because seaway traffic has not reached the
expected proportions, there has been debate as to whether to raise
toll charges in the hope of reaching a self-sustaining level or to
retain present rates as a deliberately promotional course of action.
The question is complicated by a division of opinion in the United
States (e.g., Great Lakes ports vs. Atlantic ports) and by Canadian
eagerness to increase seaway traffic even if the seaway is not self-
sustaining.

E. HYDROELECTRIC POWER

1. *Tennessee Valley Authority.** As part of its varied activities in
the development of the Tennessee River Basin, it sells electric power
to municipalities, nonprofit cooperative associations, and industrial
customers. This power is sold at rates that encourage the wider use
of electricity but also assist in liquidating the portion of TVA's cost
assignable to electricity generation and transmission. With the added
requirements imposed by the Atomic Energy Commission's heavy use
of electricity, TVA has depended more and more upon steam plants
as a generating medium.

2. *Bonneville Power Administration, Southeastern Power Administration,
Southwestern Power Administration,* and *Bureau of Reclamation.* These agencies carry out functions assigned to the Secretary of the Interior under
various laws relating to the sale and transmission of electric power
generated at federal dams. Preference in power sales is required to be
given to public bodies and cooperatives and is offered at the lowest
possible rates consistent with assignable costs.

F. MISCELLANEOUS

1. *Virgin Islands Corporation.** Created to promote the economic
development of the Virgin Islands, it grows sugar cane, manufactures

raw sugar, and makes development loans to industrial, commercial, and agricultural enterprises. Until it decided in 1963 to sell the facilities to the government of the Virgin Islands, it also distributed electric power and distilled salt water.

    2. *Federal Prison Industries, Incorporated.** Using the labor of federal prisoners, it manufactures a variety of products, such as mail sacks, primarily for the federal government.

    Because the agencies listed above have functions that in varying degrees resemble those of a private business, the question of whether their operating methods should also resemble those of business arises quite naturally. The Post Office represents the outstanding example of an agency with quasi-commercial functions for which essentially no concessions in the way of operating methods have been made. With over a half-million employees, it is probably the largest public enterprise in the non-Communist world, but it operates under rules that fit ordinary government agencies. Basically, this means that it does not retain its revenue but turns it over to the Treasury and that it is dependent upon annual appropriations by Congress. Whereas a private business can set its own policies, the Post Office must look to Congress to set the prices of the services it sells and the salaries of its employees; to the Interstate Commerce Commission for parcel post rates and the charges made by railroads for carrying the mail; to the Civil Aeronautics Board for airmail-carrying charges; to the Civil Service Commission for rules on most postal employees; and to politicians for the filling of the top twenty thousand jobs. No wonder that the Post Office has often been charged with inefficiency! Nevertheless, its situation points up the fact that motives other than business efficiency frequently are associated with public enterprise. Some of the major public service factors associated with the Post Office operation have been discussed in Chapter Two. Here it is enough to point out that, empirically speaking, policy-makers have felt that other considerations have been more important than the question of whether the Post Office, or certain of its services, should consistently make a profit.

    Whatever may be said by way of defending the Post Office's operations, the demands of twentieth-century government have led to the widespread use of a form of public enterprise more suited to quasi-commercial operations, namely, the government corporation. Of the public enterprises listed above, sixteen (marked *) fall into this category,[23] and at times during the twentieth century the number has been much higher. The two world wars and the depression of the 1930's were the principal occasions for use of this device. Though the powers of individual government corporations vary widely, the reasons for the adoption of the corporate device can be inferred from its general characteristics, which include (1) legal status, which permits a government corporation to sue and be sued, to enter into contracts, and to acquire property in its own name; (2) authority to make expenditures on its own; (3) authority to retain revenues in its own treasury; (4) use of commercial budgeting, accounting, and auditing methods; and (5) authority to use its own personnel system. The last characteristic is not as common as the rest, but Congress has exempted the Panama Canal Company, Tennessee Valley Authority, Virgin Islands Corporation, Banks for Cooperatives, and Federal Intermediate Credit Banks, in whole or in part, from the laws that apply to the federal government's merit system.[24]

Though the government corporation provides needed flexibility for the operation of public enterprise, there is another criterion applicable to democratic administration, namely, accountability. During the Franklin D. Roosevelt era, Congress became concerned that the creation of government corporations by the executive branch might constitute a serious inroad upon responsible government. Even within the Roosevelt administration there was a feeling that under the impetus of the depression emergency, inadequate attention had been paid to the structure and practices of the new corporations. In 1935, for example, President Roosevelt directed certain corporations to submit their budgets for administrative expenses to the Bureau of the Budget for review, a rule extended to all corporations in 1942. For its part, Congress imposed restrictions on corporate administrative expenses, brought most corporations under the merit system, and approved the placing of most corporations under departments—at least for "housekeeping" purposes. In 1945 Congress passed the Government Corporation Control Act, which still determines the boundaries of corporate activity. As a number of corporations had been chartered under the laws of various states and the District of Columbia, the act required reincorporation under federal law. By imposing other restrictions upon the creation of corporations, Congress, in effect, reasserted its power to authorize new executive agencies of any kind. Corporations wholly owned by the government were required to submit annually a business-type budget for review by the Bureau and Congress. The General Accounting Office was given authority to audit the accounts of all corporations.

The effect of the restrictions placed upon government corporations was to narrow, but certainly not to remove, the differences between them and other agencies. Their essential characteristics, reviewed above, were largely retained, though supervision was tightened. Supervising executive departments and the Bureau of the Budget may, in fact, exert considerable influence, particularly in those cases where departmental officials serve on the board of the corporation. The coordination of corporate action with that of other agencies in the executive branch is generally thought to be in line with democratic theory. Considerable autonomy remains in the relations of corporations with Congress and the General Accounting Office. A wholly-owned corporation seeks approval from Congress of its budget program as a whole, and while Congress has authority to limit corporate expenditures, it rarely does so except for administrative expenses. To the extent that a corporation is dependent upon congressional appropriations to finance its program, it is, of course, more nearly in the position of a regular agency. The business-type audits of the General Accounting Office, too, recognized the special character of corporations. For ordinary agencies, the General Accounting Office performs a type of audit that scrutinizes the legality of an expenditure as well as the propriety of bookkeeping procedures. If its interpretation of legality differs from the agency's, the expenditure is disallowed. Although the Comptroller General strongly urged subjecting corporations to this rule, Congress stipulated a business-type audit in the Government Corporation Control Act.

The 1945 statute also recognized that corporations wholly owned by the government should be treated differently from those privately owned. The latter, except for the Federal National Mortgage Association, are not subject to any form of budget control. It may be observed at this point that there is much flexibility in the process by which some corporations wholly owned by the government at their inception can pass through the stage of mixed ownership and finally reach private-ownership status. This has happened to the Federal Land Banks and the Federal Home Loan Banks. It is in the process of happening to three groups of corporations that now have mixed ownership: the Central Bank for Cooperatives and the twelve District Banks for Cooperatives, the twelve Federal Intermediate Credit Banks, and the Federal National Mortgage Association. The usual device for accomplishing private ownership is to require those obtaining loans from a corporation to purchase capital stock in an amount proportionate to the size of the loan. One advantage for the government is that government capital is retired and can be used again in the same fashion.

That government capital is retired from government corporations where it is feasible to do so is itself some indication of the place that public enterprise occupies in the federal government. A scrutiny of the various examples of public enterprise listed above demonstrates that, in general, they play a supplementary role in the economy. Principally, they have been used to promote the welfare of groups that policy-makers have considered lacking in the wherewithal to obtain credit or insurance without assistance. The transfer of corporate ownership to private hands is consistent with the idea that the government will step out of its support role when a private group has gained the means to finance its own operations. The corporation is not dissolved at that point because it still has a role to play. But it is not always feasible to obtain a transfer of ownership. The extreme vagaries of the weather, for example, make it difficult for even a government corporation to provide crop insurance to farmers at premium levels within their means. Private insurance companies would find the task far more difficult because of their higher borrowing rate for money and the necessity to earn a profit. Another indication that the government is not ideologically committed to public enterprise as a goal is found in the method by which it aids housing. Low-rent housing has been provided by direct means, it is true, but for the reason that private builders have preferred to construct housing for middle- and upper-income groups. Even in this case, the Public Housing Administration operates chiefly through financial assistance to local communities that wish to replace slum housing. The principal role of public enterprise in housing has been to insure mortgages (through the Veterans Administration and the Federal Housing Administration) and to stabilize the mortgage market (through the Federal National Mortgage Association). Thereby private financing of housing has been encouraged.

Despite what has been said, the question of competition with private enterprise can hardly be said to be irrelevant. It raised its head, for example, when the Communications Satellite Act of 1962 was passed. As a result of a lively argument between those members of Congress who wanted a wholly-owned government corporation to operate a communications satellite program and those who wanted a privately-owned communications giant to operate it, a compromise was reached. By the terms of the Act, the Communications Satellite Corporation was incorporated in 1963 under District of Columbia law as a private corporation subject to regulation by the Federal Communications Commission. That the Corporation is something other than an ordinary private business, however, is indicated by other provisions of the statute. No more than half of the common stock can be owned by communications carriers. The board of directors is to consist of six directors chosen by the carriers, six chosen by the investors who buy the other half of the common stock, and three chosen by the President of the United States with the advice and consent of the Senate.

A perennial controversy over public vs. private enterprise has long characterized electric utilities. The privately-owned utilities have waged a vigorous campaign against public power on the ground that it competes unfairly and unnecessarily. These companies emphasize that their charges must be higher because, unlike public enterprise, they pay taxes and borrow money at commercial rates. Public power defenders assert in turn that public power meets needs that private companies find unprofitable and that electric power generation is often only one aspect of a multipurpose natural resource development. TVA, for example, has prevented flood damage in the hundreds of millions, provided a 900-mile waterway over which thirteen billion tons of traffic move annually, experimented in the development of fertilizers and in conservation practices, and promoted a remarkable recreation area. When pressed more directly to answer the charge of unfair competition, public power advocates argue that (1) privately-owned utilities are legal monopolies with assured returns on investment and so should not cloak themselves in the mantle of competitive enterprise; (2) the taxes that these utilities pay are business expenses and therefore are charged to the consumer in the rates he pays; and (3) some government-owned projects make payments to local and state governments in lieu of taxes and pay interest at the rate it costs the government that authorized them to borrow the money. Such assertions of course do more to explain the private-power/public-power differential in rates charged customers than to allay fears of those who regard public enterprise, by its very existence, as a threat to private enterprise.

The conflict over public power has turned in considerable measure upon the question of whether it serves as a "yardstick" for privately owned utilities. Since the Tennessee Valley Authority not only fixed the wholesale rates at which it sold electricity to distributors but also fixed the retail rates which distributors charged, the early view that the retail rates charged by privately-owned utilities should be measured against those set by the TVA caused consternation. Such a comparison was obviously unfair because it overlooked the low costs of generating electricity in a multipurpose dam. Ultimately, a more reasonable definition of the yardstick was put forth by defenders of public power. The new yardstick sees public power merely as an adjunct to regulation in bringing about lower electrical rates by example. More importantly, low public power rates demonstrated to privately-owned companies that demand for electricity is so elastic that profitable operations are possible with relatively low rates. In support of this meaning of the yardstick, it is often pointed out that privately-owned companies operating in areas adjacent to public power have rates that are lower than those operating farther away, that electricity use and the purchase of electrical appliances have climbed dramatically when rates have been lowered, and that companies have prospered under the TVA-pioneered formula.

An example of an agency whose practices may indicate the limit of tolerance for public enterprise in America is the Rural Electrification Administration. Because of the regulated utilities' slowness in bringing electricity to rural areas, the REA was created by

Executive Order in 1935 and given statutory status in 1936. As amended, the statute permits the REA to make loans to finance electric distribution, transmission, and, if need be, generation facilities in order to bring initial and continued adequate electrical service on an area-coverage basis to persons in rural areas who do not have it. Similar loans can be made to furnish and improve rural telephone service. The REA statute directs that preference in making loans shall be given to public bodies and cooperatives. It also establishes the low interest rate of 2 per cent on all REA loans and fixes the permissible loan repayment period at a maximum of thirty-five years. The REA's aggressiveness in backing cooperatives stimulated a great expansion in rural electrical service by regulated utilities as well as by the REA cooperatives. By 1964 about 98 per cent of the farms in the nation had electricity. Though REA cooperatives and regulated utilities have always regarded each other warily, a sharp intensification of their rivalry developed in the postwar period. The swift urban and suburban expansion raised the question of who should sell electricity in rural areas annexed to urban and suburban communities. The REA cooperatives have argued that they supplied the areas initially, when there were only scattered homes, and that they should be allowed to continue doing so rather than be forced to let the power companies "skim the cream" off milk they did not produce. The private companies—or, in some cases, municipally-owned utilities—have contended that the REA cooperatives should be held strictly to the law, which limits them to communities of 1500 inhabitants. The private companies have also claimed unfair competition by the REA cooperatives because of the low interest rate on loans made to them. The REA and its cooperatives appear to be under increasing pressure to yield at least some of their privileges. In 1963 the appropriations committees of both houses of Congress initiated a requirement that the REA submit to their scrutiny all applications for large loans for generation or transmission projects.[25] In 1964 the REA administrator conceded that the 2 per cent interest rate could be supplanted by some other type of financing arrangement for those REA cooperatives more advanced than others in meeting their power needs.[26]

Often overlooked in the heat of the public-power/private-power battle are both the extent of their cooperation and the immense and expanding need for electric power from any source. The cooperation of the City of Los Angeles Department of Water and Power and the Southern California Edison Company in operating the generating equipment at Hoover Dam and in purchasing the power produced has been a vital element in Southern California's development since the 1930's and in the operation of war plants and defense industries. In the Pacific Northwest, a power pool drawn from both public and private sources was voluntarily created during World War II in order to handle wartime demands, and this arrangement has continued since then. The rate of growth of power needs is indicated by the fact that residential consumption almost tripled in the decade of the 1950's, not to mention the rapid increase in industrial demand. Though the United States produces almost 40 per cent of the world's electricity, supply has had difficulty keeping pace with demand, which is now doubling every ten years. Privately-owned utilities have prospered and seem destined to prosper more. Two factors restrict the competition from public power: (1) because hydroelectric power sites are limited in number, even TVA produces about three fourths of its power by burning coal to make steam to run generators; and (2) private companies are taking advantage of such technological advances as extra-high-voltage lines to transmit electricity great distances and are quicker to seek out new power sources. Under these circumstances, the share of electricity produced by private companies, which now stands at about four fifths, is likely to increase.

ECONOMIC SECURITY

By no strange coincidence, a systematic federal program for providing economic security to individuals dates from the Great Depression. It was not merely that thirteen million workers—about one fourth of the labor force—were unemployed nor that private philanthropic groups and local and state governments had inadequate resources to provide sustenance for them. Even more significant was what this situation symbolized. For the first time in American history, tangible proof was provided to the most faithful disciple of nineteenth-century individualism that loss of earning power was involuntary for millions of Americans. A second lesson provided by the depression of the 1930's was that neither private philanthropy nor local and state governments could deal with the consequences of a major breakdown of the industrial system.

In earlier years the needs of the poor had been dealt with in a variety of ways. The American colonists inherited the English system of poor relief, whereby a township or county levied a poor-tax to support the indigent. Bare subsistence was given, provided that relatives were unable to help. Able-bodied aid recipients were considered morally defective, and to the aid were attached conditions such as the pauper's oath, which gave clear indications of the place of public assistance in the scheme of things. As industrialization spread, a system of poor relief designed to take care of a handful of ne'er-do-wells and unfortunates appeared increasingly incongruous. The waves of immigrants who settled in our cities often relied upon the largesse of political machines to counteract the effects of unemployment.

Nevertheless, increased urbanization and the growth of slums forced a gradual increase in local and state expenditures for "relief."

The philosophy of these programs remained basically unchanged, however. By the early twentieth century, the states had begun to assume a heavier burden in providing economic security. Their concern was chiefly the disabled. They built and operated institutions for the blind, deaf, insane, and delinquent. Largely through assistance to local communities, they provided aid to needy persons outside of institutions, such as the blind, the aged, and widows with dependent children. In practice, many of these programs suffered from a shortage of funds at the local level. Aside from aid to special groups, the states acted to correct an inequity that faced industrial workers who were injured on the job, and by 1930 all but four states had passed workmen's compensation laws designed to make industry responsible for compensating workers or their survivors. During all this time, federal welfare activity was even more limited. Chiefly, it consisted of pension grants to veterans, emergency aid in disasters, and, in the 1920's, grants-in-aid for maternal and child care.

The urgency of the depression crisis after 1929 led to a number of emergency relief measures. Because of President Hoover's hope that prosperity would speedily return of its own accord, these measures were limited at first. By 1932 the depression had deepened, unemployment had soared, and the states had largely exhausted their resources. The time was ripe for the New Deal's experiments in work relief. In the 1933–1935 period, grants for "relief" were provided to the states on both a matching and a nonmatching basis, work camps were established for youths from families receiving aid, and work programs were established for employable workers. Many of these work programs were of the leaf-raking variety, for the confusion characteristic of the period prevented a broad achievement of the goal of priming the economy with solid public works projects. What the frenetic activity had accomplished was to establish firmly the principle that the federal government would take steps to alleviate widespread economic insecurity.

Perhaps even more significant for the long run was the federal government's assumption of responsibility for economic security programs of a more permanent nature. The Social Security Act of 1935 launched the government on a course of action that involved a variety of approaches to meet the uncertainties of our industrial age. That these approaches have met widespread approval is indicated by the broadening of original programs and the addition of new ones in subsequent years. As this process has occurred under Republican as well as Democratic administrations, "social security" may be said to have become thoroughly bipartisan. This country's economic security programs have lagged well behind those of many European countries, however. Chancellor Bismarck, for example, instituted social insurance for German workers in the 1880's as a tactical device to undercut the appeal of the Social Democratic Party, and Great Britain's "cradle to the grave" plan, drafted by Lord Beveridge in the 1940's, far exceeds the dimensions of the American arrangement. The latter contains unique concepts stemming from this country's regard for individualism and federalism. One may divide a discussion of the programs involved under the general headings of assistance and insurance. Different assumptions guide each.

ASSISTANCE

Assistance programs are basically an extension and systematization of the venerable idea of poor relief. Those aided are the needy in several categories (hence the familiar term "categorical assistance"). Assistance programs are administered by the states with financial help from the federal government. These "grants-in-aid" depend upon the states meeting certain standards, both financial and administrative. Table II summarizes the amounts of federal grants-in-aid to the states for selected years. The decade-by-decade costs have risen substantially, partly because aid levels have been increased as the cost of living has risen, partly because of expansion in programs, and partly because of population increases. The per capita cost figures for each program, based on total United States population, in effect correct for the last cause of increase and so yield a better measure of inflationary and programmatic increases than do the absolute totals.

As Table II indicates, the costs of the various forms of assistance contrast sharply. Aid to the blind, aid to permanently and totally disabled adults, and medical assistance to the aged are relatively low-cost programs. Old-age assistance and aid to dependent children, on the other hand, involve substantial federal payments. Even so, the adequacy of old-age assistance has scarcely kept pace with rising prices since it was instituted in 1935. While the level of monthly payments to the needy aged are set by the states, the matching provisions of the federal government's grants-in-aid attempt to assure a certain minimum level to the aged, to encourage states to go beyond the minimum, but also to take into account a state's capacity to provide assistance. Thus the federal government pays monthly twenty-nine thirty-fifths of the first $35 awarded to each recipient. Of the next $35 (the maximum payment is $70), it pays a proportion that varies according to the average per capita income in the state for the most recent three years, except that the federal percentage in any state shall not be less than 50 per cent nor more than 65 per cent. Without such

TABLE II

Federal Grants to States Under the Social Security Act for Selected Years: Amounts (in thousands of dollars) and Per Capita Costs (in parentheses)

Program	Fiscal Years		
	1940–41	1950–51	1960–61
Public Assistance			
Old-age assistance	$259,781 ($1.96)	$825,636 ($5.44)	$1,215,165 ($6.66)
Aid to dependent children	62,991 ($0.48)	316,477 ($2.08)	701,302 ($3.85)
Aid to the blind	7,073 ($0.05)	26,195 ($0.17)	48,123 ($0.26)
Aid to the disabled		17,456 ($0.11)	182,817 ($1.00)
Medical assistance for the aged			19,579 ($0.11)
Children's Bureau Programs			
Maternal and child health services	5,471 ($0.04)	12,854 ($0.08)	18,114 ($0.10)
Services for crippled children	3,928 ($0.03)	9,666 ($0.06)	19,795 ($0.11)
Child welfare services	1,532 ($0.01)	5,538 ($0.04)	13,613 ($0.07)

SOURCE: Adapted from U.S. Department of Health, Education, and Welfare, Social Security Administration, *Social Security Bulletin, Annual Statistical Supplement, 1961*, Table 18, pp. 16–17.

provisions, the monthly payments made by states would undoubtedly differ even more widely than they do. As it is, these payments have sometimes not reached the amounts authorized under the above formulas because the states have failed to appropriate adequate funds. Severe restrictions have sometimes been imposed on aided individuals. In addition to the usual test of means, some states do not aid persons who have legally responsible relatives who could help them, even though the relatives actually do not give any help.[27] Some states require recipients to give a lien on an owned house so that the state may ultimately recover some of the money it has given them.

In recent years the most controversial program, as well as the largest in terms of numbers of recipients, has been aid to dependent children (called "aid to families with dependent children" since 1962). As with old-age assistance, recipients must be in need. States have the discretion to define this condition and, at least theoretically, are to develop a budget of need for each category of assistance. In practice, the standards are frequently developed in relation to the maximum payments permitted by the state law. Any income received by the recipient is deducted from the amount determined, by whatever means, as the need. The federal law provides guidelines for the meaning of dependency. Until 1961, children aged eighteen or younger who were living with relatives and who had suffered deprivation of parental support or care by reason of a parent's death, disability, or continued absence were eligible. Amendments in 1961 permitted payments to assist children who are in need because of the unemployment of a parent (expanded in 1962 to cover both parents); they also made eligible for assistance children no longer living with relatives but placed in a foster home by court action after a finding that the welfare of the child demanded the change. In general, the statutory provisions have had the humane objective of maintaining children in their homes. The program has run into the moral objection that illegitimacy is being encouraged because no distinction is made between needy children born in and out of wedlock. Adding parental unemployment as a basis for eligibility has also intensified objections from some quarters.

Medical assistance for the aged was begun in 1960 in order to encourage the states to help persons over sixty-five meet the cost of medical services. The Kerr-Mills Act of that year amended the Social Security Act to provide for two programs. One increased the amount of federal matching funds available for medical care of persons eligible for old-age assistance. The other established a new public assistance category, medical assistance for the aged, which provides care for medically needy aged persons who are not poor enough to qualify for old-age assistance funds. The latter program reflected the increasing public concern over the problems faced by low-income aged persons who generally have sufficient income to meet their needs except for medical care, the costs of which have been rising steeply. The states were given considerable latitude in determining the scope of medical assistance for the aged, with regard to both the individuals who are eligible and the kind and extent of services to be provided under the program. As with old-age assistance, federal contributions vary in terms of per capita income in the states; federal funds range from 50 to 80 per cent of the total payment.

The adequacy of medical care under the Kerr-Mills formula has been a matter of dispute. Most states were slow to take advantage of the provisions of the Act. By August 1963, however, every state was participating in the old-age assistance medical care program, and by

October 1963 thirty-two jurisdictions out of fifty-four (the District of Columbia, Guam, Puerto Rico, and the Virgin Islands were included along with the states) had medical assistance for the aged, the second Kerr-Mills program.[28] Average individual payments under the latter program varied widely, ranging from $5.56 in Guam and $27.93 in Kentucky to $437.92 in Illinois. Critics of this program charged that its lack of adoption by twenty-two jurisdictions indicated that it was not a truly national program, and they pointed out that, where the program had been adopted, aged persons needing medical care fared best in the wealthier jurisdictions.

Aside from the adequacy of the Kerr-Mills program, its critics doubted that medical care for the aged should be handled as public assistance at all. The approach adopted by Presidents Kennedy and Johnson involved a program of compulsory old-age health insurance tied to contributions under the social security system. The so-called King-Anderson bill ("Medicare"), debated in Congress in the years after 1960, required no means test, covered all persons over age sixty-five, and was to be financed by an increase in the social security tax. The bill would provide for inpatient hospital care for periods of from 45 to 180 days, subject to various rates of deductibility depending on the period of hospitalization elected. It would also provide up to 180 days of skilled home nursing services after transfer from a hospital, and up to 240 home health service visits per year. This program also drew criticism, on the one hand for resembling "socialized medicine" and on the other for not covering payment of drugs, nurses', or doctors' bills. President Johnson's sweeping victory in the 1964 presidential election enhanced the chances for a social insurance approach to the gnawing problem of medical care for the aged.

The development of an omnibus bill by the powerful House Ways and Means Committee and its passage by a vote of 313 to 115 in the House of Representatives in April 1965 gave strong indications that Congress would vastly enlarge various features of health care. The bill provided for two health insurance programs for persons aged sixty-five or more: a compulsory plan providing hospital and related care, financed mainly by a payroll tax under social security; and a voluntary supplementary program to pay physicians' costs and other expenses not covered by the basic plan, financed by $3 monthly premiums from those aged persons joining the program and matching Treasury funds. The latter plan was sponsored by the Republicans and met the objections of the American Medical Association that Medicare did not cover doctors' fees. Though the foregoing portion of the bill represented a triumph of the social insurance approach, another portion extended the Kerr-Mills concept of medical assistance for the aged to include needy persons under the dependent children, blind, and disabled programs and increased the federal share of funds for the expanded program under the Kerr-Mills Act. Finally, the 296-page bill proposed a 7 per cent increase in cash benefits under the old-age, survivors, and disability insurance program (see below) as well as higher social security tax rates and a higher annual taxable-earnings base.

The health and welfare service programs for mothers and children do not involve payments to individuals but rather to states to support state services. The federal grants are used to help states pay doctors, nurses, and other medical workers who aid needy children and to pay for hospital care, convalescent care, and foster home care for such children. The grants also help support prenatal clinics, child-health conferences, and public postgraduate education in the care of mothers and children. The increasing problem of juvenile delinquency prompted the passage of a 1961 statute that authorized federal grants to states for demonstration projects and training programs.

There are a number of other grants-in-aid, falling into the broad category of assistance, that are administered by units of the Department of Health, Education, and Welfare other than the Social Security Administration. About a dozen "formula" grants (i.e., grants that match in various ratios state appropriations with federal funds) dealing with aspects of community and environmental health are administered by the Public Health Service. Another half-dozen similar grants are handled by the Vocational Rehabilitation Administration.[29] Approximately another dozen grants by the former are not formula grants (i.e., do not involve matching contributions by states).

INSURANCE

The contrasts between the assistance programs just reviewed and the economic security programs based on insurance principles are illustrated by the largest program under the Social Security Act—old-age, survivors, and disability insurance. The discussion that follows is organized around the ten principles listed by a former commissioner of social security, Charles I. Schottland.[30]

1. *All workers should be covered by the system.* Almost all persons who are gainfully employed are now covered, are eligible for coverage, or are under another governmental retirement system, such as that for railroad workers. Over the years coverage has been extended from wage earners in industry and commerce to embrace most farm workers, domestic servants, self-employed persons, and military and government personnel.

2. *Benefits are paid as a matter of right.* The statute assures claimants of rights to administrative appeal and judicial appeal.

3. *Benefits provide protection against the risk of income loss resulting from*

old age, disability, and death. Benefits are based upon the worker's earnings, though those with low income receive proportionately more—a compromise between the principles of social need and private insurance. In general, a person becomes insured if he has forty quarter years of coverage ("fully insured") and has at least six quarters of coverage during the thirteen-quarter period immediately preceding his death, disability, or retirement ("currently insured"). All types of retirement and survivor benefits are generally payable if a person is fully insured; certain survivor benefits are also payable if the deceased is only currently insured. A fully-insured worker becomes eligible for retirement benefits at age sixty-two, although he can receive only a percentage of his "primary insurance amount," which is calculated upon a retirement age of sixty-five. The minimum primary insurance amount in 1964 was $40 per month, and the maximum was $127 (double these amounts if both husband and wife were covered workers). Since 1939 a covered worker's dependents have also received benefits calculated upon the primary insurance amount. Since 1957, benefits, computed on the same basis as for retirement, have been paid to workers who have been disabled for six months and are not able to engage in any substantial gainful activity. A disabled, dependent child of a retired, disabled, or deceased insured worker may also receive such benefits if he is over eighteen and became disabled before that age. Survivor insurance benefits are paid to a surviving widow, dependent widower, dependent parent, or child of an insured worker who has died. At the end of 1962, almost three million individuals were drawing survivor benefits.

4. *The system is contributory.* Unlike some foreign social insurance programs, which depend upon general governmental revenues, the American system relies upon equal contributions from employers and employees (in 1964, 3⅝ per cent). Self-employed persons pay approximately one and one-half times the rate for employees. Relating benefits to payments in this manner has made the program more politically acceptable, reduced the likelihood of political manipulation, and minimized the resemblance to a "government handout."

5. *Sound financing has been a goal of the system.* Whether this goal has actually been attained depends upon the degree to which one expects the government to imitate a private insurance company in setting up reserves for the payment of benefits. Actuarial soundness for a private company means an ability to pay off its contractual obligations in the event it goes out of business or if all of its policyholders cash in their policies. A government insurance program, it is argued, can assume that its life will be as permanent as the country and that new "premium payers" will continually enter the program. In any event, the taxes collected under the program are kept in two trust funds (the Federal Old-Age and Survivors Insurance Trust Fund and the

Federal Disability Insurance Trust Fund), the money not needed to pay benefits or administrative expenses is invested in government securities, and the interest earned is added to the funds. By the end of 1961 the two trust funds totaled more than $22 billion. The funds are managed by a board of trustees composed of government officials, and since 1956 the statute has provided for periodic appointment of an advisory council to scrutinize the soundness of the funds. The first advisory council gave a favorable report in 1959. The second, after one and one half years of study, reported in early 1965 that "The social security program as a whole is soundly financed, its funds are properly invested, and on the basis of actuarial estimates that the Council has reviewed and found sound and appropriate, provision has been made to meet all of the costs of the program both in the short run and over the long-range future."[31] It did find a need for some reallocation of the contribution income between the two trust funds.

The second council noted that the contribution and benefit base is now substantially out of date because of large advances in the general wage level. When the program was enacted in 1935 the $3000 base upon which taxes were based would have covered 95 per cent of total earnings in covered work. In 1965, with a base of $4800, only about 72 per cent of earnings in covered employment will be taxed to support the program, and only 66 per cent of all workers and 36 per cent of regularly employed men will have all their earnings covered. The Council recommended that the base should be increased to at least $6000 effective in 1966 and $7200 effective in 1968 "in order to maintain the wage-related character of the benefits, to restore a broader financial base for the program, thus keeping the contribution rates lower than they would otherwise have to be, and to apportion the cost of the system appropriately."[32]

6. *Participation is compulsory.* This feature, which has been achieved in the main, was designed to prevent adverse selection of risks and to accomplish wholesale protection against the risks, to themselves or their dependents, of wage earners' age, disability, or death. Amendments in 1950 and subsequent years made some inroads into compulsory participation. For example, voluntary participation was provided for clergymen because of the principle of church-state separation. Also, because of the principle of federalism, groups of state and local government employees join the system only after a vote of their members; a favorable vote means compulsory participation of all members, however.

7. *Benefits are wage-related.* In contrast to some European systems, the American system reflects the individualistic bent of this country by relating benefits to earnings.

8. *The system is family-oriented.* The emphasis upon survivor and disability benefits accords with the American emphasis upon main-

tenance of the family in times of adversity.

9. *Benefits replace lost earnings.* In general, benefits are paid only to those who have suffered a loss of income. A sanction imposed is that retired workers between the ages of sixty-two and seventy-two may not earn more than $1200 per year without penalty in the form of reduced benefits. This provision has been rather controversial, but a clue to its rationale comes from the circumstances surrounding the passage of the Social Security Act. Its enactment in the depression year of 1935 was greatly aided by the prospect that the payment of benefits would enable a worker to retire and thereby help meet the immense unemployment problem.

10. *The system is administered by the federal government.* The largest social insurance program in the world is a highly mechanized program covering 140 million earnings records and paying benefits to more than 18 million persons.

While the program of old age, survivors, and disability insurance contrasts sharply with the federal assistance programs, another insurance program—unemployment insurance—contrasts less sharply. It incorporates such insurance principles as the payment of benefits as a matter of right, the collection of taxes to pay benefits, and the use of a trust fund. On the other hand, unemployment insurance is administered by the states, just as the assistance programs are. While grants-in-aid have served as the incentive for state assistance programs, a tax offset has been used by the federal government to encourage the adoption of state unemployment insurance programs.

An unemployment insurance scheme was made part of the Social Security Act of 1935 after state action had failed to fill the gap. As with other economic security programs, a number of European countries had provided unemployment insurance in the early decades of the twentieth century. America's need became acute when the Great Depression struck, but the fear of driving out industry and the general impoverishment of states kept all but a handful of them from instituting unemployment insurance. A further factor, one that also influenced federal policy-makers, was the reluctance to provide benefits as a matter of right to the able-bodied unemployed. Nevertheless, unemployment insurance was one of the proposals made by President Roosevelt's Committee on Economic Security in 1934, and it received Congress' approval the following year. In view of the fact that unemployment insurance was less widely adopted in European countries than other economic security programs, its relatively easy adoption in a more conservative country may appear surprising.

Aside from the favorable timing traceable to the depression and the New Deal's vigorous attack on the problems it produced, the major explanation for the easy adoption appears to lie in the tailoring of the bill to fit American conditions. One commentator has labeled the program "competitive collectivism" because (1) it encourages each state to establish its own system of unemployment insurance and (2) through experience ratings it encourages each employer to strive to lower the taxes he pays to support the program.[33] These features need explanation.

As previously indicated, state unemployment insurance statutes spread quickly under the federal government's strategy of permitting a tax offset. The Social Security Act provided that employers of eight or more (now four) workers pay a 1 per cent tax on the first $3000 paid to each worker. The tax rate was increased to 2 per cent in 1937 and to 3 per cent thereafter. But up to 90 per cent of the federal tax was credited to any state that set up an unemployment insurance scheme of its own that met federal standards of administration. Thus, after 1937, 2.7 per cent of the 3 per cent federal tax could be offset by a state. The remaining .3 per cent was used by the federal government to make grants to the states for the administrative expense of their programs. In 1960 this amount was raised to .4 per cent, making the total tax allowed by the statute 3.1 per cent. Under the tax-offset stimulus, all states adopted programs within a few years after the Social Security Act had been passed. The taxes collected by the states from employers are placed in state reserve funds in the United States Treasury, and from these funds the states make weekly payments to unemployed workers. The leeway in state programs shows up most graphically in these payments. As of January 1963, weekly payments that could be made ranged from a low of $30 in four states to a high of $70 in Alaska, where living costs are much higher than in the rest of the Union. Eligibility for payments also varied; six states permitted less than 26 weeks, thirty-six states permitted 26 weeks, and nine states allowed 27 weeks or over. Six of the states with a 26-week rule extended eligibility to 39 weeks in times of high unemployment, and one state extended the period to 34 weeks.[34] Usually benefits are wage-related, and the Bureau of Employment Security of the Department of Labor, which administers the federal end of the system, has urged that benefits approximate 50 per cent of a worker's wages. Though benefit levels have risen notably in the last twenty years, they have not kept pace with the increase in wages. In 1963 the average weekly wage of covered workers was about $90, but the average benefit was only about 37 per cent of this figure.[35]

This relatively autonomous system of unemployment insurance has both accomplishments and defects. The states have succeeded in raising the benefit level over the years since 1935. Furthermore, the large industrial states usually have higher benefits. Nevertheless, many observers argue that the federal government should establish nation-wide benefit levels in view of the great disparity in benefits.

There has also been a case made for federal equalization grants to aid those states whose unemployment benefits have averaged more than the national average. The present system has already required the help of federal loans in the recession year of 1958, when state funds were inadequate to deal with an extended period of unemployment. Congress established a temporary fund from which those states that wished to extend the duration of their unemployment insurance benefits could obtain interest-free loans. Still another problem is that thirteen million workers are not covered, notably agricultural workers. Unemployment insurance appears to be a broadly accepted principle in the United States, but this is far from saying that it is free from criticism. For example, there have been well-documented cases of recipients who have made little or no effort to find work. Though government officials insist that they constitute only a small minority of all recipients of unemployment compensation, such cases keep criticism of the program alive—particularly since it is for able-bodied workers.

Another controversial feature has been the experience-rating plan for employers, the second feature of "competitive collectivism" in the unemployment insurance system. The decision to tax only employers was unusual in the first place. In other countries with an unemployment insurance program, employees or the government or both contribute to the cost of the program.[36] Under the American system, not only are employers the only contributors, but in addition tax rates are varied to reflect the amount of unemployment experienced by their employees. This "experience rating" was not a requirement of the Social Security Act, but it was permitted by it. The states may have fallen into experience rating because they found that the 2.7 per cent tax rate permitted under the tax-offset arrangement was excessive in relation to the benefits that the states had chosen to provide. Experience rating provided a means of reducing the tax. The method has both its defenders and its detractors. Those who favor experience rating argue that it gives employers an incentive to stabilize employment, that it makes employers more active in policing improper claims, and that it is compatible with a competitive price system. The main criticism of experience rating is that it makes the tax rise when unemployment rises, thereby threatening the ability of the employer to pay and, in times of large unemployment, the solvency of the program itself. Whatever the merits of the claims and counterclaims, experience rating appears to be a firmly established feature of unemployment insurance.

One of the major activities of twentieth-century governments has been to provide a measure of economic security to their citizens. While the outlines have varied, such programs have in common the aim of guarding individuals against some of the major risks inherent in industrial society. In general, American measures have not come as soon nor gone as far as those of other industrialized countries. The principle of government action has gained acceptance, nevertheless, and the arguments are mainly over such questions as levels of benefits, assignment of costs, and administrative techniques to avoid abuses. This is not to say that United States economic security programs ignore the spirit of individualism; as we have seen, these programs often incorporate this quality. Nor do new economic security programs have easy sailing, as witness the generation-old battle over government health insurance schemes.

ECONOMIC STABILITY AND GROWTH

Government management of economic stability and growth is a decidedly new phenomenon in the United States. Though promotional measures adopted as long ago as Alexander Hamilton's days have had effects upon the economy, neither their nature nor their scope was such as to constitute management. Even today, governmental action of course rests upon the assumption of a private enterprise economy. What is new and merits the term "management" is that (1) the size and variety of government's roles in relation to the economy are significant, and (2) governmental actions are consciously intended to work in concert to achieve national aims for the economy.

How did this situation come about? Previous chapters have noted the occasions for the exercise of governmental promotion, regulation, and purchasing, all of which have given the national government a voice in the economy. These actions have proceeded rather autonomously, however, with little thought given to the effect they had upon placing government in a strategic position to encourage national economic aims. In a sense, one might say that they developed while the nation was still holding to the idea that government has little to do with business cycles.

Conscious and concerted action to influence the state of the economy emerged in the twentieth century. Of all the epochal events of this turbulent century, the Great Depression was the strongest factor in producing government management of the economy. The onset of this economic emergency after a decade of strong business activity that had led to hopes of permanent prosperity was a sharp blow to the traditional business philosophy. In addition, the depression's unprecedented severity and the persistence of mass unemployment even after there had been a business upturn combined to shake the confidence of Americans in the inherent stability of the economy. Less traumatic twentieth-century economic worries also played a part in encouraging governmental action to achieve economic aims. It was feared that after the booming wartime employment of 1942–1945 mass unemployment would once again stalk the land. In more recent years such phenomena as creeping inflation, recessions, unemployment rates of about 5 per cent, and growing automation have all contributed to uneasiness about the self-correcting ability of the economy.

To all these stimuli for governmental action was added an economic philosophy that awarded to government an essential role in the economy. Classical economics had assumed that the downswings of the business cycle would correct themselves. Unemployment would disappear as falling labor costs lowered prices and stimulated a greater demand for goods, thereby putting people to work again. This theory was first exposed to systematic criticism in Great Britain. High unemployment persisted there throughout the years after 1921 and became markedly more severe when the world-wide depression of 1929 struck. John Maynard Keynes, an economist who in 1919 had written perceptively of "the economic consequences of the peace," contended in 1930 and later that depression and unemployment were not necessarily self-correcting and that positive government measures were often necessary to establish the levels of aggregate demand sufficient for full employment.[37] When earlier depressions had occurred in Great Britain and the United States, the national governments, acting on classical economic principles, had cut expenditures in an effort to balance the budget, thereby further lowering aggregate demand and intensifying unemployment and economic distress.

The severity of the Great Depression prevented such a stance. Franklin D. Roosevelt, who had begun his administration in 1933 with orthodox ideas of balancing the budget, was quickly forced to abandon this goal in the face of mass unemployment and the utter inadequacy of relief measures originated by local and state governments or private philanthropy. Well before the New Deal had received or assimilated the more sophisticated Keynesian doctrines, it was forced by circumstances to adopt a pragmatic program of pump-priming. To adherents of the classical economic school, Keynesian economic thought appeared to be nothing but a handy rationalization of Roosevelt's deficit financing. Keynes and his American followers, however, believed that economic resources, particularly the resources of labor, must not be left idle. Governmental spending had to take up the slack in the economy if private enterprise could not generate sufficient demand to keep economic resources engaged. Keynes' prescription rested upon an analysis of the incomes received by economic units—consumers, businesses, and government—and upon the relation of these incomes to the expenditures of the units. The governmental remedy consisted of restoring the level of total spending in the economy either by lowering taxes or by increasing government expenditures, or both. Under this theory, government spending should be useful to the economy, if at all possible, but even relatively useless expenditures were better than letting the economy dawdle along at levels that left many resources idle.

In practice, though the spending programs of the New Deal only lessened unemployment somewhat without ending it, the enormous deficit financing of World War II did put all economic resources to work. But what would happen when the war ended? Memories of prewar days led to passage of the Employment Act of 1946. In its original version it placed great stress upon full employment, but in the course of passage this aim was somewhat diluted. The Act, nevertheless, represented a considerable endorsement of the new economics. "All practicable means" were to be used by the government to "promote" employment. Maximum production, purchasing power, and employment were stated as goals. A Council of Economic Advisers was authorized to study the economy and make recommendations to the President for attaining economic well-being. The President was directed to furnish Congress at the beginning of each regular session with an "Economic Report" containing legislative recommendations relating to the economy. A Joint Committee on the Economic Report, composed of seven members from each house, was established by the Act to advise Congress on the presidential recommendations.

In the United States, as in other industrialized countries, the propriety of governmental action to assure economic stabilization and growth is today well established. The outlines of such action are still in the process of evolution, and in the United States, at least, there is still much controversy over the new economics, though very recently it appears to be diminishing somewhat.

So far the discussion has been quite general as to what government might do in managing the state of the economy. Because the notion of concerted action by government has evolved in the twentieth century and undoubtedly is still evolving, a definitive statement is not possible. What is clear is that as the government's economic instruments have become more numerous and diversified, its deliberate exercise of its economy-influencing role has become more pronounced. Most of the instruments at the disposal of the government relate to management of the volume of money and credit (monetary policy) and of the balance of government expenditures and tax receipts (fiscal policy).

The management of money and credit is primarily in the hands of the Federal Reserve System, which was established in 1913 as a means of overcoming the inelasticity of the national currency and disjointedness in the use of bank reserves. Under the direction of the seven-member board of governors of the System, the twelve Federal Reserve Banks attempt to regulate the volume of money and credit and the terms upon which they become available to consumers and investors. All national banks and those state-chartered banks that agree to be subject to the requirements of the Federal Reserve Act are members of the System. Every member bank subscribes to the capital of the Federal Reserve Bank in its district an amount equal to 6 per cent of its capital and surplus.

The Federal Reserve System has three means of influencing credit and monetary conditions by affecting the reserve position of member banks. The first of these is the authority to raise or lower the rediscount rate of the Federal Reserve Banks. These banks accept the commercial paper (i.e., loans) made by member banks, in order to enlarge the latter's funds for use as reserves or as a basis for additional loans. By raising the rediscount rate employed by the Federal Reserve Banks, credit given by member banks may be contracted; by lowering the rate, credit may be expanded. The second means by which the Federal Reserve System can influence money and credit consists of raising or lowering reserve requirements of member banks, thereby affecting the amount they have available for lending. Wide fluctuations in reserve requirements are possible under amendments to the Act adopted in 1935, though the Board has found that this instrument of credit policy is not adapted for day-to-day changes in banking and monetary conditions. Open market operations constitute the third weapon in the Federal Reserve arsenal. If the flow of money and credit is judged to be too sluggish, the Federal Reserve Banks buy government securities in the open market. When a securities dealer deposits his check from such a sale in a member bank, the bank's reserves are increased, thereby expanding its power to lend. This expansion is at a greater level than the amount of the check because the reserve requirement is only a fraction of the sum that can be loaned. A deflationary effect, on the other hand, can be created through the sale of government securities. In this case, the securities dealer draws a check on a member bank, thereby decreasing its reserves and its lending power.

The Federal Reserve System also can affect money and credit by the use of selective credit controls. Since 1934 it has been empowered to vary the margin on which stocks may be purchased. On a temporary basis it has had authority in crisis situations to regulate the terms on which banks can make installment loans on consumer goods, as well as the terms of certain types of real estate credit.

The monetary controls available to the Federal Reserve System have been indispensable to the growth and stability of the economy. At the same time, they appear to work better when the situation calls for restraining the flow of money and credit than when it calls for expanding the flow. Credit expansion can be checked quickly by using one or more of the controls. To expand the use of money and credit, however, may require more than building bank reserves. If the business outlook is very uncertain, bankers may be unwilling to lend, businesses to borrow, and consumers to buy.

Even when the economy is operating relatively smoothly, the Federal Reserve may be criticized for the way in which it is employing its weapons. Its critics have often charged it with being too secretive, too independent, and too insensitive to the needs of small borrowers. These three charges are interrelated and reflect the public-private status of the System. The Federal Reserve Board has generally resisted the efforts of the Treasury to bring monetary policy into conformity with the requirements of Treasury borrowing and public debt management. Under the Truman administration the Board did agree to employ open-market operations for the purpose of keeping the interest on government securities at a low level. Under the inflationary pressures released by the Korean War, an agreement between the Board and the Treasury was negotiated in 1951, leaving the Board free to pursue a deflationary monetary policy. During the Eisenhower administration the Board continued to battle inflation vigorously, and its critics contended that the recessions of 1958 and 1960 were triggered when the Board raised interest rates and reduced the credit supply. In 1964 the Board again faced a dilemma in trying to anticipate whether to apply deflationary action after a tax cut had taken effect or whether to assume that any tightening of credit policy might throttle the expansion of the economy. One may anticipate continued criticism of the Federal Reserve Board, but its independent status appears likely to continue despite the introduction of bills in Congress in 1964 to end it.

While monetary policy is thus coordinated by a single agency, fiscal policy may be said to be an amalgam of the actions of numerous government agencies. As the latter involves a variety of expenditures as well as the tax system, Congress has a vital part to play. Though the exercise of fiscal policy is therefore cumbersome, governmental efforts to employ it as a countercyclical weapon are increasing.

Government's ability to fill this role has been enhanced by the general expansion in its other economic roles, particularly its role as buyer. In the early 1930's, for example, government spent less than 3 per cent of the gross national product, whereas in recent years the Defense Department alone has spent three times that percentage. Furthermore, most government expenditures are less affected than those of private economic units by the oscillations of the economic system. Regardless of the expected pattern of prices and markets, the government continues to need defense weapons, supplies for permanent services, and civil servants. The existence of this huge autonomous element in the total use of resources in the country is a stabilizing factor in the business cycle.

Another factor that greatly aids government in steering the economy is the existence of "built-in stabilizers," which automatically move against the trend in the business cycle. These can be found on both the revenue and expenditure sides of the federal budget. On the revenue side is the progressive income tax. Income tax payments by individuals and businesses automatically decline when there is a slump in business activity, thereby cushioning the impact of the decline. When the economy is booming, the increased tax payments that result help prevent inflation. All this takes place without a change in tax rates. Many of the government expenditure programs also move automatically against the current of business activity. Unemployment compensation, old-age insurance and assistance payments, and farm price-support payments tend to rise when a business and agricultural recession occurs. Prosperity tends to reduce these payments. Again, the countercyclical action is automatic.

Modern economic analysis, while admitting the importance of government's expenditures and of the built-in stabilizers, leaves a large role for positive action as well. No American government today could or would stand idly by while a serious economic emergency developed and the economy ground to a halt. In all probability it would undertake such steps as vastly enlarging public works, liberalizing unemployment compensation, and furnishing freer credit aids to businesses and consumers. It might also advance the timing of veterans' payments, accelerate military stockpiling, and, more questionably, increase defense expenditures. On the revenue side, a tax cut might be ordered.

When it comes to more moderate variations in the business cycle, governmental discretionary action is most evidently in the process of evolution. Attitudes appear to be shifting toward the employment of devices to stimulate economic growth even while prosperity is at a high level.

Concern over the national growth rate has recently intensified for several reasons. In 1960 the American economy had suffered its second recession in two years and its third in seven years. Even in times of relative prosperity, unemployment was persisting and there was unutilized industrial capacity. Meanwhile, the Soviet Union, operating on a smaller economic base, seemed to be achieving a higher growth rate. The Federal Reserve's monetary policy had not only failed to prevent the setbacks but was accused of having contributed to them. Thus the climate was receptive to the proposals of Presidents Kennedy and Johnson for a tax cut. In 1964 Congress, with the general approval of the business community, enacted the proposals into law. The reasoning behind the tax cut was that it would place an additional $8 billion or so into consumers' pockets and thereby add fuel to the economic machine at a time when the rate of economic growth might otherwise decline. Through the "multiplier" effect—the rippling action of money as it spreads through the economy—additional consumer expenditures of about four times that amount were anticipated. Though the effect of the cut was not felt as quickly as had been thought, a stimulation of the economy did occur. Furthermore, the economy was sufficiently stimulated so that tax revenues—even at the reduced rates placed into effect in March 1964—increased sufficiently to reduce the anticipated deficit in the national budget for the fiscal year ending in June 1964. Though the danger that this stimulation of the economy would bring about a resurgence of inflation could not be discounted, the friendly reception given President Johnson's proposals for excise tax cuts in early 1965 suggested that the predominant worry involved the possibility of a deflationary trend after four years of prosperity.

Under more traditional budgetary reasoning, 1964 tax levels would have been left unchanged and used to attain a balanced budget. Even the Keynesian-minded New Dealers justified budgetary deficits only to offset recessions, and they favored budgetary surpluses in times of economic upswings in order to avoid inflation. The tax cut was thus a notable departure in American fiscal policy. It was, nevertheless, consistent with the trend toward regarding the national budget as part of a much larger picture. To those who so view the budget, it was reassuring to find, for example, that the gross national product—the total income earned in the American economy—had increased to twice the size of the national debt from a position of relative equality immediately after World War II. This took place even while most postwar budgets, under both Republican and Democratic administrations, were producing deficits and therefore increasing the size of the debt. In effect, the debt became "smaller" because of the more rapid growth in national income.

Obviously, the other Keynesian remedy for stimulating the economy—increased government spending—is not likely to earn such widespread support as does the tax cut during "normal" times. In fact, congressional support for the tax cut in 1964 was forthcoming partly because of President Johnson's well-publicized attempts to reduce government spending. Nevertheless, the principal point to note probably is that there is a developing consensus about the need for governmental action of some kind even when the economy is relatively stable. According to the philosophy of the Johnson administration, a balanced budget should be sought only when the economy is at or near the level of full employment, i.e., 4 per cent or less of the labor force unemployed. A cost of such a low level of unemployment may be moderate inflation. Thus future policy may have to strike a balance between tolerable rates of unemployment and inflation. If it can, the new economic philosophy should gain wide acceptance.

Frontiers

This concluding chapter attempts to relate governmental efforts to promote the general welfare to a larger context. To deal with the entire range of American governance of course is impracticable. Instead, attention will be focused upon two matters. The first is the growing interdependence of public policy in all fields and its consequences for the task of promoting the general welfare. The second consists of the prospects for the government-economy relationship.

INTERDEPENDENCE AND ITS CONSEQUENCES

The interdependence of modern industrialized society has often been noted, but the consequences may be more vividly appreciated when disaster strikes a modern community and normal services are disrupted. Specialization is so much a part of our lives that we tend to forget how fragile its underpinnings are. Nonetheless, specialization is increasing all over the world, for even the underdeveloped nations, with their new-found desires to industrialize, are taking long strides in this direction. In the United States one need only think of such phenomena as urbanism, assembly-line production, the mobility of the labor force, and mass communications to be reminded of the extent of economic and social interdependence.

Specialization and interdependence in American society at large have been paralleled by similar tendencies in government. This is not to say that our vast, sprawling government always demonstrates its understanding of the increasingly close relationships among individual policies in various fields. Policies have generally been made in response to the particular exigencies of time and place; their interdependence tends not to be uppermost in the minds of policymakers. Yet the very range and complexity of modern governmental problems is gradually forcing recognition of the importance of policy coordination.

Ready illustrations of the interdependence of policies are to be found in the connection between American economic policy toward other countries and actions on the home front to promote the general welfare. The examples are legion, but the few presented here will suffice to make the point.

Measures taken in 1963 to reduce the steady outflow of gold, itself primarily a consequence of the huge American foreign aid effort, constitute one illustration. Earlier, the federal government had taken such mild steps as reducing the dollar amount of duty-free goods that returning American tourists could bring home. When the balance-of-payments deficit continued, stronger measures were used. Ever since the First World War the Federal Reserve Board had employed its authority to alter rediscount rates as a weapon in promoting economic stability. In 1963, for the first time, this instrument was used with foreign, rather than domestic, considerations in mind. The Board raised its discount rate to member banks from 3 per cent to 3½ per cent in an effort to discourage foreign borrowers, who had raised over $1 billion in the United States capital market during 1962.[1]

Another measure to help the balance-of-payments problem similarly involved a departure from past practice. Though American investors had always been free to invest anywhere in the world, President Kennedy asked Congress to tax foreign stock purchases by Americans. His request had an immediate effect upon the level of such purchases, even though congressional action was not taken until 1964. Together, the two moves were made with the general aim of indicating to other countries that the United States was determined to prevent devaluation of the dollar. They were viewed as essentially temporary measures whose continuation would have to be balanced against the risk of hindering economic growth at home.

A second example of broadened interdependence can be found in recent measures to facilitate international trade. Consider first the Trade Expansion Act of 1962. Its emphasis on policy interdependence is evident in its stated intent of promoting the "general welfare, foreign policy, and security of the United States through international trade agreements and through adjustment assistance to domestic industry, agriculture, and labor, and for other purposes." The Act was another in a long series of steps since World War II away from political and economic isolationism and toward international economic cooperation intended to avoid a world-wide depression.

On a more mundane level, backers of the statute were concerned about excess productive capacity in various domestic industries, such as steel, and the need to develop a basis for dealing with the European Common Market. In practice, negotiations with the Common Market over some of the five thousand items in international trade proved disappointingly slow in the first two years of the Act's history. The problem hinged largely upon the difficulty encountered by both the United States and the Common Market in answering cries for protection from their own producers. One of the best-publicized struggles was "the chicken war." It began when the Europeans raised their common outer tariff on poultry in an effort to give their own poultry producers a larger share of the European market, in which the more efficient American producers had made sharp inroads. American retaliatory action, strongly demanded by domestic poultry producers, was inhibited by the fact that the Common Market countries were purchasing about one fourth of all United States agricultural exports. An armistice of sorts was reached when the United States agreed to permit an international arbitration board to fix the amount of financial loss suffered by the American poultry industry. The United States then raised its tariffs on certain imports from Europe to an amount equal to the $26 million announced by the board as the loss to poultry producers.

The incident demonstrates the difficulty of relating foreign economic policy to the fortunes of particular domestic industries. In order to get the support of the cotton textile industry for the Trade Expansion Act, President Kennedy offered it a package that included the negotiation of a five-year international agreement for voluntary restrictions on textile exports to the United States, a $30 million tax reduction in the form of liberalized allowances for depreciation of textile machinery, and a promise to support the industry's case for a special tariff on cotton goods.[2]

And in yet another area the general pursuit of foreign trade expansion has produced a broadening of the concept of promoting the general welfare. In order to compete with other nations, the United States has had to follow their example in providing export credit guarantees. For a number of years, various European countries have insured their exporters against the failure of a foreign buyer to pay for goods and against the risks of losses due to war or expropriation. Private insurance companies found it difficult to provide such broad protection. In 1960 and thereafter, with the active intervention of Presidents Eisenhower and Kennedy, the Export-Import Bank began offering an increased measure of protection to American exporters.[3]

Agriculture provides a third example of the close connection between foreign and domestic economic policies. In 1954 Congress, concerned about the amassing of almost $4 billion worth of surplus farm commodities in connection with the agricultural price-support program, enacted the Agricultural Trade Development Act, familiarly known as P.L. 480. Under this statute, over $9 billion worth of farm commodities were disposed of abroad within eight years. Some commodities were bartered or donated (P.L. 480 now is the major vehicle for the Food for Peace program). Most of the commodities were shipped to underdeveloped countries to be paid for in their own currency, a valuable concession to dollar-short nations. The United States has used a portion of these funds to make loans to these countries and to finance its expenses in them, including expenditures for technical assistance, educational exchanges, and research. The funds have also been used to develop and expand markets for American farm products. The program has had obvious domestic and foreign benefits, and the intertwining of purposes is apparent.

The production of specific agricultural commodities often is affected by this same intertwining. The Sugar Act of 1937 authorized the Department of Agriculture to determine annual sugar requirements of American consumers and to fix marketing or import quotas for the various sugar-producing areas, domestic and foreign, supplying this market. The program, adopted when the sugar industry was in great distress, was designed to promote the interests of American producers, both at home and in the then territories, and of friendly sugar-producing nations, and to provide American consumers with an assured sugar supply at reasonable prices. In the early 1960's this system of market stabilization was upset when the actions of the Castro regime in Cuba provoked the United States into embargoing Cuban products. The Department of Agriculture made up for Cuban sugar by decreeing higher production and import quotas for other production areas, both foreign and domestic. By 1964 domestic sugar production had increased to the point where additional acreage allotments for sugar beet production were being turned down. This, together with the question in Congress of renewing sugar import quotas, provoked a bitter battle between supporters of domestic and foreign sugar producers, the latter being aided by American refiners of imported raw sugar.

Another commodity that has been the subject of a tug of war between domestic and foreign interests is cotton. In order to sell raw cotton abroad, American exporters have been paid a subsidy designed to make up the difference between the world price and a much higher domestic price. The latter has been paid to cotton growers as a part of the system of agricultural price supports. These two subsidies—to cotton growers and to cotton exporters—worked a hardship on a third group, the domestic cotton mills, who had to pay the federally-supported price for the raw cotton they purchased from domestic suppliers. Farm legislation for 1964 provided a third subsidy as the answer to this problem. This plan provides textile mills with a direct subsidy to offset the similar subsidy paid to exporters for cotton shipped abroad for competing foreign mills.

If anything, the interaction of domestic policies is even greater than that between foreign and domestic economic policies. To illustrate briefly, an increased consciousness of inequities in the enjoyment of civil rights produced reverberations in governmental policies toward business and labor in the first half of the 1960's. The Civil Rights Act of 1964, which outlawed segregation in hotels, restaurants, and other places of public accommodation, brought various types of small businesses under federal surveillance to an extent never before envisioned. The hiring practices of offices, factories, and businesses, and laws less directly related to civil rights were also brought under scrutiny by the Act. A decision of the National Labor Relations Board in July 1964 made it an unfair labor practice under the Taft-Hartley Act for a labor union to discriminate against a Negro.[4]

The interdependence of governmental policies and private actions is also of increasing importance. A vital fact for government in its relations with other nations is the increase in foreign investment by American business from $11.8 billion in 1950 to more than $37 billion in 1963.[5] Foreign policy must also take into account private American ownership of $15 billion worth of foreign common stocks and bonds and foreigners' ownership of American common stock worth about four fifths of this amount.[6] Promoting the general welfare, in short, has become a subtle and complicated task.

Among the major consequences of this growing interdependence of policies is a greater need for the coordination of policy-making and policy administration. There is, for example, no single transportation policy but rather a variety of policies for the various modes of transportation. They evolved seriatim, as one mode succeeded another and was made commercially practicable. Fitting a particular public policy to each transportation medium as it developed was a process particularly well suited to American pragmatism. Promotional and, later, regulatory programs were adopted that seemed to fit the time and place, and, quite often, they were enacted in response to considerable agitation. The net result is that today competing modes of transportation operate under different rules, causing friction. To coordinate these rules is a more difficult and at the same time a less spectacular task than that which faced policy-makers of an earlier age. There is little drama and much hard work involved. Furthermore, the coordination of transportation policies and of other policies is hampered by the diffuse nature of American government and politics. Each mode of transportation has built up its relationships with regulatory agencies and is wary of what change may bring, even though it may not cherish the present situation. Because divisions among agencies and their backers tend to be reflected in Congress itself, its mediating function has limits. Against this situation must be placed the fact that lack of coordination becomes an ever greater luxury as the governmental function of promoting the general welfare becomes more complex. The coordination required for the maintenance of a competitive economy, for example, is stated by two economists in the following terms:

> All actions of the government which have implications for the goal of maintaining a workably competitive economy should be subjected to conscious coordination. Our tariff policy, taxation, the allocation of government contracts, and the leading policies of our banks should be subjected to scrutiny in the light of the requirements for the maintenance of vigorous competition.[7]

Jurisdictional lines among agencies may not always be kept clear—a problem that is often attributable to Congress and that sometimes comes back to plague it. In July 1964 a long-standing dispute between the Comptroller of the Currency and the Federal Reserve Board concerning jurisdiction over investments by national banks in foreign banks reached the name-calling stage.[8] A month later, at hearings held before the House Banking and Currency Committee, the Comptroller of the Currency clashed with a third regulatory agency in the banking field. The Comptroller and the Federal Deposit Insurance Corporation differed vigorously over a proposal that banks be required to report any change in ownership to the FDIC. One committee member was prompted by the debate to remark:

> How much this is like the Romans in the old Coliseum when they used to watch the lions and tigers tear each other apart. I think it would be a good idea if one of these years our committee turned its attention to the whole group—to the role of the Fed, the FDIC, and the Comptroller to see if we cannot produce a more rational and harmonious bank regulatory structure, but that is another story.[9]

Though examples of the need for policy and organizational coordination could be multiplied, it is more important to pass on to a subtler consequence of interdependence, an increasing recognition by economic groups that in order to achieve their particular aims they must strive for a favorable public image. In an era of mass communications, no businessman is likely to be found repeating Commodore Vanderbilt's statement, "The public be damned." Some businessmen have indicated that profit making must always take place in the context of advancing the broader purposes of society.[10] At the very least, many businessmen today might echo the statement of a public relations director for one of the nation's largest corporations: "We can preserve our freedom of enterprise only if it fulfills the aspirations of our society."[11] Even the ownership of corporations is undergoing changes that reach across traditional lines and have far-ranging implications. Over 150 industrial corporations have profit-sharing plans. Furthermore, union pension funds and trusts administered by banks are buying controlling blocks of stock in blue-chip firms.[12] Independent of these developments but related to the theme of this paragraph is the changing character of labor disputes. In recent years both business and labor have conducted contract negotiations with one eye on the public. Undoubtedly, their acceptance of high-level government mediation has been motivated partly by a fear that the public, either on its own or because of statements by government officials, will condemn an economic group that appears to be overly recalcitrant. Granted that interdependence may not produce greater love among these and other groups, their actions tend increasingly to bespeak their status as members of a larger community.

Another consequence of interdependence is the increased burden placed upon government to anticipate the complexities of emerging policy issues. In each segment of the economy, policy questions are emerging whose dimensions are not clear but whose seriousness is unquestioned. Automation, for example, promotes economic progress but causes worries about technological unemployment and the retraining of workers. The federal government is beginning to move in this area. The Vocational Education Act of 1963 authorized federal grants to the states for vocational training not only of persons preparing to enter the labor market but also of "those who have already entered the labor market but need to upgrade their skills or learn new ones. . . ." The Manpower Development and Training Act of 1962 established federal-state training programs to retrain 400,000 unemployed persons in an effort to overcome the "structural unemployment" of workers whose skills had become obsolescent through automation. Significantly, this statute also charges the federal government with a continuing responsibility for defining the nation's manpower goals and requirements and for initiating policies to meet them. President Johnson's 1964 Manpower Report to the Congress, an annual report required by the Act, initiated two administrative actions: a study of the impact of automation and technological change on workers, unions, and firms; and an appraisal by a committee of present and future labor-force requirements of the economy. In 1965 the President signed a liberalized and extended Manpower Development and Training Act. Another emerging problem with vague but far-reaching implications concerns migratory farm labor. Essential in the production of some perishable crops, it raises questions about the adequacy of housing and wages, the quality of education for children of the workers, and the desirability of employing temporarily imported workers. Growing concern with "pockets of poverty" in a prosperous nation means that migratory farm labor is increasingly viewed in a context extending far beyond the traditional one of the economics of growing fruit and vegetables. Interdependence, in short, tends to broaden the scope of governmental concern, particularly in an age that stresses equality of opportunity.

THE SHAPE OF THE FUTURE

Perhaps the broadest form of interdependence on the public policy scene is that between politics and economics. Jefferson, for example, recognized their close relationship in his preference for a democracy based upon economically equal farmers and small-town merchants and artisans. Evolving industrialization not only eliminated that possibility but made the interdependence of politics and economics more intimate. Thus, President Eisenhower's Commission on National Goals emphasized in 1960 that:

> The economic system must be compatible with the political system. The centers of economic power should be as diffused and as balanced as possible. Too great concentrations of economic power in corporations, unions, or other organizations can lead to abuses and loss of productive results of fair competition. Individuals should have maximum freedom in their choice of jobs, goods, and services.[13]

While this statement undoubtedly meets with almost universal approval in the United States, its precise interpretation is cause for controversy. Businessmen, for example, tend to believe that labor unions embody an undue concentration of economic power, and the unions often have the same sentiments about giant corporations. The precise application of national economic goals, then, is always under debate. In a study of "tides of American politics," Arthur M. Schlesinger, Sr., found an alternation between "conservative" and "liberal" eras in the years between 1841 and the 1930's.[14] He concluded that "conservative" eras averaged about fifteen years in length and "liberal" ones about sixteen and one-half years. Furthermore, at any given time, governmental and political institutions may have varying emphases. The interests of producers, for instance, have traditionally been strongly represented in Congress, whereas, in the twentieth century at least, the President has often been the principal defender of consumers. As to party differences, the Democrats, to the occasional annoyance of the Republicans, have since the thirties identified their policies with human rights. The Republican candidacy of Senator Barry Goldwater in 1964 can be traced in part to an attempt by economic conservatives to reassert the importance of property rights.

Though there will undoubtedly continue to be eras of reform and conservatism as well as contending social philosophies, violent swings of the pendulum of government economic policies seem, on the evidence of the past, to be unlikely. First, in contrast to Europe, a broad consensus about problems arising from industrialism has been maintained. Neither the radical right nor the radical left has been able to gain a firm foothold in American politics. The elder Senator La Follette could sound like Karl Marx when he diagnosed the ills of American industrialism: ". . . there has, in my opinion, been only one great issue in all the history of the world. That issue has been between labor and those who would control, through slavery in one form or another, the laborers."[15] Yet his remedy was the mild one of firm governmental regulation of powerful private interests. Reformers of the Progressive era regarded regulation as but a limited cure. Louis D. Brandeis once conceded that "Regulation may compel the correction of definite evils. . . . But regulation cannot make an inefficient business efficient."[16] Though discouragement with the remedial effects of regulation sometimes led reformers like the Progressives to urge public ownership of railroads or other regulated industries, even this recommendation was customarily so hedged about with conditions that it cannot be said to have approximated a socialist ideology. Also, as the twentieth century has progressed, foreign experiments with nationalization of industry have driven home the point that taking over industries is not itself a panacea but only the beginning of a host of new problems. In the 1960's even a Democratic administration has sponsored legislation entrusting communication satellites to a private corporation.

A second factor contributing to a conclusion that alternatives in the government-economy relationship are not likely to be extreme is the considerable similarity in the policies of the two major parties when in power. After the twenty years of Democratic hegemony that began with the inauguration of Franklin D. Roosevelt in 1933, there were some who predicted that the Eisenhower administration would undo much of what had been done. Though there was considerable rhetoric about "getting the government out of business" and though some steps were taken to reduce governmental ownership and operation of economic instruments, by and large remarkably little was changed. The Tennessee Valley Authority, cited by President Eisenhower as an example of "creeping socialism," not only was continued but grew substantially. And though many Republican congressmen had been lukewarm toward "social security" when it became law in 1935, the Eisenhower administration successfully urged its expansion by Congress. The similarity of party viewpoint can easily be overemphasized; some economic conservatives, in fact, rallied behind Goldwater in 1964 to accentuate their disagreement with economic liberalism in the Republican party. On the basis of recent history, however, it appears that a Republican administration is not likely to reduce government's role in the economy. At most, it might be inclined to slow the pace at which government responds to pressure to enlarge its role further.

A third factor that has contributed to stability in public economic policies is the growing realization that governmental instruments are essentially neutral and can be used to advance the social philosophies of the party or group that controls them. This possibility was recognized a half-century ago by Samuel Gompers, the first president of the American Federation of Labor, when he warned labor about the likely consequences of the creation of a governmental agency administering social insurance of various kinds: "Whoever has control of this new agency acquires some degree of control over the workers. There is nothing to guarantee control over that agency to the employed. It may also be controlled by employers."[17] Probably the most apt illustration of the truth of this statement is to be found in the history of the National Labor Relations Board. Created to protect the interests of employees, it has since gone through various changes in statutory and administrative philosophy. The only certainty is that the statutes under which it operates and the social outlook of its members will continue to be items of concern to those interests most involved. The pertinent point is that once proponents of differing social philosophies fight for control of governmental agencies instead of over the abolition of such agencies, the range of possible governmental roles is significantly narrowed. Plainly, in such a case laissez faire is not even in the picture.

Two final and related factors that tend to prevent wide alternation in government's economic role are the parlous international situation and the acceptance of government's stabilizing role in the domestic economy. The cold war is the cause of governmental purchases of defense goods and foreign aid materials (80 per cent of the latter are purchased in the United States[18]). Powerful private economic groups thus have a vital stake in the continuance of governmental economic activity. The lesson of the Great Depression, the frequency of "soft spots" in even a prosperous economy, and increasing acceptance of the need for governmental action to encourage the continuing growth of the economy tend to promote an active role for government in economic stabilization.

Though these factors limit fluctuations in the level of government activity in promotion of the general welfare, they have little effect upon the way in which emerging problems are viewed by policymakers and those they represent. Controversy over general welfare problems and ways of dealing with them can be expected, and rightly so. Poverty provides a good example. Postwar prosperity has thrown into sharp relief the distressed condition of about thirty-four million Americans who live at or below the threshold of poverty (defined as an annual income of less than $1250 for a single person, less than $1750 for a couple, and less than $2700 for a family of four).[19] Who are the poor? They are found by sociologists to have such "poverty-linked" characteristics as the following: "nonwhites, families with no earners, families whose heads are females, males aged fourteen to twenty-five or over sixty-five, individuals with less than eight years of schooling, inhabitants of some farm areas, and families in which there are more than six children under eighteen."[20]

Perceptions of poverty as a problem varied widely in the four years after 1960, when President John F. Kennedy had made it one of his campaign themes. Kennedy's emphasis, and that of his successor, was upon attacking this formidable problem from various directions. Kennedy's first executive action upon taking office was to double the quantity of surplus agricultural commodities being distributed to the poor. Soon after, Congress endorsed his plan to establish an Area Redevelopment Administration that would supply long-term, low-interest loans to induce private industry to locate in depressed areas. The Manpower Development and Training Act of 1962 and the Vocational Education Act of 1963, described above, also played a part in the attack on poverty. The major "antipoverty" bill, however, was the Economic Opportunity Act of 1964. It called for a job corps to get teen-agers out of slums into rural camps, a domestic Peace Corps to act as teachers and counselors or other aides, a work-training program to lower the dropout rate in high schools, a work-study program to subsidize needy college students, a fund for community antipoverty programs, and loans to low-income farmers and small businessmen. Allied to the attitude that poverty could be alleviated through the use of various government techniques was the thought that the elimination of poverty was almost within grasp. Pointing to a decline in the percentage of Americans in the poverty group from 26 per cent in 1947 to 19 per cent a decade later, a prominent business magazine argued that "Indeed, it is precisely because the U.S. has made such progress in reducing the margin of poverty that its further reduction is not just a distant hope but represents rather a tremendous practical opportunity."[21]

On the other side of the question were various attitudes that ranged from minimization of the problem to caution about proposed solutions. Paradoxically, in a time of prosperity poverty has not been universally visible. The poor are politically weak, and they are often concentrated in the slums of large cities or in depressed regions such as "Appalachia." Thus, their problems may seem remote to more fortunate Americans. A few books of social protest that appeared in the early 1960's dramatized the plight of the poor. Michael Harrington's *The Other America* and Harry Caudill's *Night Comes to the Cumberlands* set forth indictments of the failure of local, state, and national governments to deal adequately with the question.[22] Urban renewal programs displacing slums with dwellings that the poor cannot afford, social security programs in the main helping employed workers, school-lunch programs covering only those children whose parents can afford even the token payments—governmental efforts such as these have been cited by those who feel that poverty demands a drastically new dimension of government action. Still other commentators relate the poverty problem to the welfare state. In an article entitled "Is the Welfare State Obsolete?" one writer declared that "The famous pragmatic approach to government regulation and intervention, it has been discovered, has one slight drawback: the agencies and institutions that are created soon achieve a life of their own, beyond all trial and error."[23] From another writer's viewpoint, however, the welfare state does not exist in America today because welfare payments are below subsistence levels and because the United States does not meet the criterion that "In a welfare state, the benefits an individual receives are political rights, not charity. . . ."[24]

What the poverty example suggests is that governmental activity in promoting the general welfare has entered upon a critical phase. Optimism that a dynamic democratic society can find the means of dealing with emerging problems is countered with uneasiness about whether governmental action can be effective in meeting the particular problem and can avoid bureaucratic stultification.

Yet in a socially responsible democracy there can be no escape from the task of organizing to deal with problems adequately without sacrificing individualism and democratic freedom. Organization is an overwhelming fact of life for modern man, and the most important organizing force in his world is the government. If this is so, then the preservation of individualism and democracy depends upon the attainment of creativity and sensitivity within the large organizations, private as well as public, that exist on every side. All large organizations—but government in particular—affect economic and political goals that promote the general welfare.

Can American society find the means to solve its economic and social problems? A discouraging unwillingness to view problems anew is sometimes noticeable. For example, while welfare expenditures have risen greatly, neither liberals nor conservatives seem able to develop a creative solution to the problems of human waste and degradation. Also, ugliness and squalor have been too long accepted as the price of industrial progress. Finally, many have viewed the federal budget as analogous to a housewife's instead of to that of American Telephone and Telegraph, which has borrowed $7 billion for productive investments since World War II and constantly refinances its debt.

Inventiveness in governmental affairs is far from lacking, however. The former chairman of the Council of Economic Advisors during the Eisenhower administration proposed, in 1962, the creation of an Economic Policy Board to coordinate economic policies in much the same way as the National Security Council is supposed to deal with national defense. To give another example, in 1964 a cabinet-level council on aging recommended to President Johnson that elderly homeowners be permitted to supplement their incomes with benefits based on their equities in their homes. Under the proposal, the government would issue to homeowners bonds convertible to cash on a monthly basis up to the total of their equities. A homeowner would continue to live in his home, but upon his death the property would be turned over to the government for resale and recovery of the government investment in the bonds. In addition, certainly at least some of the devices in the Economic Opportunity Act of 1964 were imaginative.

Needed most is inventiveness to produce, wherever feasible, a stimulative, rather than an operating, role for government. Despite qualms that the 1964 tax cut violated traditional fiscal principles, its results produced the stimulating effect on the economy for which its proponents hoped, meanwhile avoiding the necessity for direct public works expenditures to maintain employment. On the industrial relations front, the example of Sweden may be instructive. As Gunnar Myrdal has pointed out, the central organizations for collective bargaining in the national interest that Swedish workers and employers have voluntarily formed have forestalled the necessity for governmental intervention, even to set a minimum wage.[25] Though the American situation is infinitely more complicated, such ideas are worth exploring more seriously than they have been. Paradoxically, more government intervention may be required in American than in Swedish industrial disputes because a much lower percentage of workers belong to unions in the United States. This is a reminder that governmental activity can stem from under-organization of the private economy as well as from the need to mediate between powerful groups.

The government-economy relationship in the United States would appear to be more Darwinian than Newtonian, more flexible than fixed. Evolution toward what? It is a question of great moment to both conservatives and liberals, though they perceive the present system from vastly different perspectives. Conservatives fear that "creeping socialism" may soon begin to pick up speed, if it has not already done so. Liberals are concerned that a failure to integrate the depressed one fifth of this nation's population into the mainstream of economic and political advance may well mean the downfall of democracy. How the general welfare is to be promoted remains for each generation of Americans to work out in countless public policy decisions.

FOOTNOTES

CHAPTER ONE

1. John C. Miller, *Origins of the American Revolution* (Stanford: Stanford University Press, 1959), p. 11.

2. Oscar and Mary Flug Handlin, *Commonwealth: A Study of the Role of Government in the American Economy: Massachusetts, 1774–1861* (New York: New York University Press, 1947).

3. Louis Hartz, *Economic Policy and Democratic Thought: Pennsylvania, 1776–1860* (Cambridge, Mass.: Harvard University Press, 1948), p. 88.

4. *Ibid.*, p. 97.

5. Cecil Woodham-Smith, *The Great Hunger: Ireland, 1845–1849* (New York: Harper & Row, 1963), pp. 410–411.

6. Veto Message for H.R. 10203, 49th Cong., 2nd Sess., February 16, 1887 (appears in *Congressional Record*, February 17, 1887, p. 1875).

7. Andrew Carnegie, "Wealth," *North American Review*, 148 (June 1889), 654–655; cited in Thomas G. Manning, David M. Potter, and Wallace E. Davies, *Government and the American Economy, 1870–Present* (New York: Henry Holt & Company, 1950), pp. 10–11.

8. Adam Smith, *An Inquiry into the Nature and Causes of the Wealth of Nations,* ed. James E. Thorold Rogers, 2 vols. (Oxford, Eng.: Oxford University Press, 1869), II, 273.

9. *Dartmouth College* v. *Woodward,* 4 Wheaton 636 (1819).

10. *Charles River Bridge* v. *Warren Bridge,* 11 Peters 420 (1837).

11. *Chicago, Burlington and Quincy Railroad Co.* v. *Iowa,* 94 U.S. 155; *Peik* v. *Chicago and Northwestern Railway Co.,* 94 U.S. 164; *The Chicago, Milwaukee and St. Paul Railroad Co.* v. *Ackley,* 94 U.S. 179; *The Winona and St. Peter Railroad Co.* v. *Blake,* 94 U.S. 180; *Stone* v. *Wisconsin,* 94 U.S. 181. The grain elevator case, *Munn* v. *Illinois,* 94 U.S. 113, was considered with the railroad cases, and the general doctrine was worked out for all of them at the same time. These six cases were decided in 1877.

CHAPTER TWO

1. 4 Wheaton 316 (1819).

2. William Letwin (ed.), *A Documentary History of American Economic Policy Since 1789* (New York: Doubleday & Co., Inc., 1961), p. xix.

3. *Loc. cit.*

4. Reprinted *ibid.*, pp. 54–65.

5. U.S. Congress, Joint Economic Committee, *Subsidy and Subsidylike Programs of the U.S. Government,* Joint Committee Print, 86th Cong., 2nd Sess., p. 18.

6. *Ibid.*, p. 10. The list from which the compilation is taken appears on pp. 10–16. Adaptations have been made in the interest of achieving greater clarity.

7. For most examples, more complete references will be found in Chapters Three and Four.

8. *Subsidy and Subsidylike Programs of the U.S. Government,* p. 7.

9. *Ibid.*, p. 75.

10. *Ibid.*, p. 34.

11. *Ibid.*, p. 61.

12. *The New York Times,* September 2, 1962.

13. *Subsidy and Subsidylike Programs of the U.S. Government,* p. 39.

14. *Loc. cit.*

15. *The New York Times,* August 30, 1963.

16. *Ibid.*, May 22, 1963.

17. *Ibid.*, July 10, 1963.

18. Carl Kaysen, as quoted in *Subsidy and Subsidylike Programs of the U.S. Government,* p. 4.

19. Quoted *ibid.*, p. 5.

20. U.S. Congress, House, Select Committee on Government Research, First Progress Report, *Federal Research and Development Programs,* 88th Cong., 2nd Sess. (Washington, D.C.: 1964), p. 8.

21. *Time,* 81 (June 21, 1963), 83.

22. National Science Foundation, *Research and Development in Industry, 1961* (Washington, D.C.: 1964), pp. 11–13).

23. Longstreth Wright, "For Subsidies That Make Sense," *The Reporter,* 25 (September 27, 1960), 29.

CHAPTER THREE

1. *Northern Securities Co.* v. *United States,* 193 U.S. 197 (1904).

2. *United States* v. *Standard Oil Co. of N.J.,*

221 U.S. 1 (1911); *United States* v. *American Tobacco Co.*, 221 U.S. 106 (1911).
3. *Congressional Quarterly Weekly Report*, 21 (May 24, 1963), 813.
4. *United States* v. *McDonough Co.*, 180 F. Supp. 511 (1959); *The New York Times*, February 6 and 7, 1961. See also Myron W. Watkins, "Electrical Equipment Antitrust Cases—Their Implications for Government and for Business," *University of Chicago Law Review*, 29 (Autumn 1961), 97–110.
5. *United States* v. *U.S. Steel Corp.*, 251 U.S. 417 (1920).
6. *United States* v. *Columbia Steel Co.*, 334 U.S. 495 (1948).
7. *Federal Trade Commission* v. *Western Meat Co.*, 227 U.S. 554 (1926).
8. *United States* v. *E. I. du Pont de Nemours & Co.*, 353 U.S. 586 (1957).
9. *Brown Shoe Co.* v. *United States*, 370 U.S. 294 (1962).
10. *United States* v. *Continental Can Co.*, 12 L. ed. 2d 953 (1964).
11. *United States* v. *Aluminum Co. of America*, 148 F. 2d 416 (1945).
12. *American Tobacco Co.* v. *United States*, 328 U.S. 781 (1946).
13. *United States* v. *Aluminum Co. of America*, 91 F. Supp. 333 (1950).
14. *United States* v. *E. I. du Pont de Nemours & Co.*, 351 U.S. 377 (1956).
15. *United States* v. *United Shoe Machinery Corp.*, 110 F. Supp. 295 (1953), and *United Shoe Machinery Corp.* v. *United States*, 347 U.S. 521 (1954).
16. *United States* v. *First National Bank and Trust Co. of Lexington*, No. 36, October term, 1963, decided April 6, 1964.
17. *Arrow Transportation Co.* v. *Southern Railway Co.*, 372 U.S. 658 (1963).
18. *The New York Times*, April 6, 1962.
19. Morris Forgash, "Our Transportation Problems: Time for Action," a speech reprinted in the Appendix to the *Congressional Record*, 108 (October 2, 1962), A7267.
20. E. R. Quesada, "The Pressures Against Air Safety," *Harper's Magazine*, 222 (January 1961), 58–64.
21. *The New York Times*, October 2, 1963.
22. *Nebbia* v. *New York*, 291 U.S. 502, 536 (1934).

23. *Smyth* v. *Ames*, 169 U.S. 466 (1898).
24. *Federal Power Commission* v. *Natural Gas Co.*, 315 U.S. 575 (1942).
25. *Federal Power Commission* v. *Hope Natural Gas Co.*, 320 U.S. 591 (1944).
26. *Federal Power Commission* v. *Southern California Edison Co.*, 11 L. ed. 2d 638 (1964).
27. Merle Fainsod, Lincoln Gordon, and Joseph C. Palamountain, Jr., *Government and the American Economy*, 3rd ed. (New York: W. W. Norton & Co., Inc., 1959), p. 668.
28. *Phillips Petroleum Co.* v. *Wisconsin*, 347 U.S. 672 (1954).
29. Dissenting in *Federal Power Commission* v. *Hope Natural Gas Co.*, 320 U.S. 591, 649 (1944).
30. John C. Mason, "Problems in Regulation of Interstate Operations of Producers Under the Natural Gas Act," *Administrative Law Review*, 14 (Fall 1961), 62.
31. *Wisconsin* v. *Federal Power Commission*, 369 U.S. 870 (1963).
32. *The New York Times*, April 8, 1964.
33. U.S. Congress, House, Hearings before a subcommittee of the Committee on Interstate and Foreign Commerce, 85th Cong., 2nd Sess., and 86th Cong., 1st Sess., 14 parts (Washington, D.C.: 1958–1960); *Interim Report*, H.R. 1602, 85th Cong., 2nd Sess. (Washington, D.C.: 1958).
34. Bernard B. Smith, "A New Weapon to Get Better TV," *Harper's Magazine*, 225 (July 1962), 27–34.
35. William L. Cary, quoted in *The New York Times*, November 29, 1962.
36. *Silver* v. *New York Stock Exchange*, 371 U.S. 808 (1963).
37. *The New York Times*, April 9, 1964.
38. *Ibid.*, July 22, 1963.
39. *Ibid.*, August 19, 1963.

CHAPTER FOUR
1. For more detail about trends in agricultural policy, see The American Assembly, *United States Agriculture: Perspectives and Prospects* (New York: Columbia University Press, 1955), and Claude T. Coffman, "Federal Aid in the Development of Agriculture," *Federal Bar Journal*, 21 (Fall 1961), 399–416.

2. *The New York Times,* December 12, 1963.

3. *United States* v. *Butler,* 297 U.S. 1 (1936).

4. *Mulford* v. *Smith,* 307 U.S. 38 (1939).

5. Lauren Soth, "Farm Policy: A Look Backward and Forward," *Social Research,* 27 (Summer 1960), 136.

6. Dale E. Hathaway, *Problems of Progress in the Agricultural Economy* (Chicago: Scott, Foresman & Co., 1964), p. 37.

7. *Hammer* v. *Dagenhart,* 247 U.S. 251 (1918), and *Bailey* v. *Drexel Furniture Co.,* 259 U.S. 20 (1922).

8. *United States* v. *Darby Lumber Co.,* 312 U.S. 100 (1941).

9. *Muller* v. *Oregon,* 208 U.S. 412 (1908).

10. *Adkins* v. *Children's Hospital,* 261 U.S. 525 (1923).

11. *Morehead* v. *New York ex rel. Tipaldo,* 298 U.S. 587 (1936).

12. *West Coast Hotel Co.* v. *Parrish,* 300 U.S. 379 (1937).

13. *Loewe* v. *Lawlor,* 208 U.S. 274 (1908).

14. *National Labor Relations Board* v. *Jones & Laughlin Steel Corp.,* 301 U.S. 1 (1937).

15. *Retail Clerks International Association* v. *Alberta Schermerhorn,* 11 L. ed. 2d 179 (1963).

16. *NLRB* v. *General Motors Corp.,* 373 U.S. 734 (1963).

17. A. H. Raskin, "The Government's Role When Bargaining Breaks Down," *The Reporter,* 28 (January 31, 1963), 30.

18. *Youngstown Sheet & Tube Co.* v. *Sawyer,* 343 U.S. 579 (1952). See also Grant McConnell, *The Steel Seizure of 1952* (University, Ala.: University of Alabama Press, 1960).

19. Lawrence Stessin, "A New Look at Arbitration," *The New York Times, Western Edition,* November 18, 1963 (reprinted from *The New York Times Magazine*).

20. *In the Matter of American Dietaids Co., Inc.,* 44 *FTC Decisions* 667, 706–707 (1948).

21. U.S. Department of Health, Education, and Welfare, *Food and Drug Administration: Its Programs — Problems — Resources,* Committee Print prepared for the House Committee on Interstate and Foreign Commerce (Washington, D.C.: 1963).

22. Morton Mintz, "New Drugs: Is Government Supervision Adequate?" *The Reporter,* 28 (March 28, 1963), 47.

23. Lawrence Lessing, "Laws Alone Can't Make Drugs Safe," *Fortune,* 67 (March 1963), 123.

24. *Ibid.,* p. 156.

25. *The New York Times,* July 16, 1963.

26. U.S. Department of Health, Education, and Welfare, *Smoking and Health,* Report of the Advisory Committee to the Surgeon General of the Public Health Service (Washington, D.C.: 1964), p. 33.

CHAPTER FIVE

1. *Helvering* v. *Davis,* 301 U.S. 619, 645 (1937).

2. Lucius Wilmerding, Jr., *The Spending Power* (New Haven, Conn.: Yale University Press, 1943), pp. 94–95.

3. U.S. Congress, Joint Committee on Reduction of Nonessential Federal Expenditures, *Additional Report on Federal Stockpile Inventories,* Senate Committee Print No. 46, 88th Cong., 1st Sess., 1963.

4. *The New York Times,* January 6, 1964.

5. Walter Lippmann, *Sacramento Bee,* December 21, 1963.

6. U.S. Congress, Senate, Committee on Government Operations, *Report to the President on Government Contracting for Research and Development,* Senate Document No. 94, 87th Cong., 2nd Sess., 1962, p. 2 (cited as *Bell Report*).

7. *The New York Times,* April 15, 1963.

8. *Sacramento Bee,* August 25, 1963.

9. On most of the foregoing statistics, see James L. Clayton, "Defense Spending: Key to California's Growth," *Western Political Quarterly,* 15 (June 1962), 280–281, and Charles E. Silberman and Sanford S. Parker, "The Economic Impact of Defense," *Fortune,* 57 (June 1958), 104.

10. House Subcommittee on Science, Research, and Development of the Committee on Science and Astronautics, *Geographic Distribution of Federal Research and Development Funds,* Committee Print, 88th Cong., 2nd Sess. (Washington, D.C.: 1964).

11. Clayton, "Defense Spending," p. 282.

12. *The New York Times*, August 16, 1963.

13. *Ibid.*, April 15, 1963.

14. *Ibid.*, April 17, 1963.

15. Paul F. Hannah, "Government Buying Erodes Management," *Harvard Business Review*, 42 (May-June 1964), 58.

16. *Time*, 82 (November 1, 1963), 104.

17. Donald F. Hornig, quoted in *The New York Times*, November 16, 1963. He assumed his position in January 1964.

18. Caryl P. Haskins, quoted in *The New York Times*, December 9, 1963.

19. Clark Kerr, *The Uses of the University* (Cambridge, Mass.: Harvard University Press, 1963), Chapter 2.

20. *Bell Report*, p. 45.

21. Kerr, *The Uses of the University*, p. 53.

22. Edward W. Weidner, *The World Role of Universities* (New York: McGraw-Hill Book Co., 1962), p. 9.

23. Meg Greenfield, "Science Goes to Washington," *The Reporter*, 29 (September 26, 1963), 22.

24. According to a study made by the Department of Justice, reported in *The New York Times*, August 23, 1963.

25. Paul Shnitzer, "Changing Concepts in Government Procurement—The Role and Influence of the Comptroller General on Contracting Officer's Operations," *Federal Bar Journal*, 23 (Winter 1963), 90.

26. Comptroller General of the United States, *Annual Report* (Washington, D.C.: 1964), p. 79.

27. Quoted in J. Stefan Dupré and W. Eric Gustafson, "Contracting for Defense: Private Firms and the Public Interest," *Political Science Quarterly*, 77 (June 1962), 163.

28. For examples of negotiated contracting, see *ibid.*, pp. 166–168.

29. Comptroller General, *Annual Report* (1964), p. 80.

30. *Loc. cit.*

31. Dupré and Gustafson, "Contracting for Defense," p. 170.

32. Admiral Hyman G. Rickover, atomic submarine builder, quoted in *The New York Times*, December 31, 1963.

33. Julius Duscha, "The Costly Mysteries of Defense Spending," *Harper's Magazine*, 228 (April 1964), 64.

34. Department of Defense announce-
ment, quoted in *The New York Times*, August 9, 1963.

35. *Ibid.*, and *Time*, 82 (October 25, 1963), 95.

36. *The New York Times*, October 7 and 4, 1963, respectively.

37. *Identical Bidding in Public Procurement*, Report of the Attorney General under Executive Order 10936, July 1962 (Washington, D.C.: 1962), p. 28.

38. *Identical Bidding in Public Procurement*, Second Report of the Attorney General under Executive Order 10936, July 1964 (Washington, D.C.: 1964), p. 24.

39. *The New York Times*, April 10, 1962.

40. *Bell Report*, p. 4.

41. *Ibid.*, pp. 12–14.

42. *The New York Times*, February 7, 1964.

43. *Ibid.*, June 29, 1963.

44. *Bell Report*, p. 13.

45. *Loc. cit.*

46. *Loc. cit.*

47. *The New York Times*, September 18, 1962.

48. *Loc. cit.*

49. Dupré and Gustafson, "Contracting for Defense," pp. 173–174.

50. *The New York Times*, September 28, 1964.

51. Samuel W. Bryant, "The Patent Mess," *Fortune*, 66 (September 1962), 112.

52. Overton Brooks, "Ownership and Use of Space Age Ideas—A Legislative Approach," *Federal Bar Journal*, 21 (Winter 1961), 36.

53. Quoted in Russell B. Long, "Federal Contract Patent Policy and the Public Interest," *Federal Bar Journal*, 21 (Winter 1961), 21.

54. Brooks, "Ownership and Use of Space Age Ideas," p. 29.

55. Long, "Federal Contract Patent Policy," p. 21.

56. Brooks, "Ownership and Use of Space Age Ideas," p. 26.

57. Long, "Federal Contract Patent Policy," p. 16.

58. See *Congressional Record*, October 10, 1963, pp. 18320–18321.

59. *The New York Times*, September 28, 1964.

60. *Sacramento Bee*, December 28, 1964.

61. *The New York Times*, April 20, 1964.

62. See, e.g., Senator George McGovern's testimony before the Senate Committee on Commerce, May 25, 1964, reprinted in *Congressional Record*, May 25, 1964, pp. 11484–11486.

CHAPTER SIX

1. The discussion in this paragraph relies largely on George R. Hall, "Conservation as a Public Policy Goal," *The Yale Review*, 51 (March 1962), 409–410.

2. *Ibid.*, pp. 401–407. Other commentators have used different labels.

3. Norman Wengert, *Natural Resources and the Political Struggle* (New York: Doubleday & Co., Inc., 1955), pp. 6–7.

4. The Council of State Governments, *Directory of Interstate Agencies* (Chicago, 1964, mimeographed).

5. Hearings before the subcommittee of the Senate Committee on Appropriations, 88th Cong., 1st Sess., *Public Works Appropriations, 1964* (Washington, D.C.: 1963), pp. 1416–1429.

6. Commission on Organization of the Executive Branch of the Government, *Water Resources and Power*, 2 vols. (Washington, D.C.: June 1955), I, 12–15.

7. Irving K. Fox, "National Water Resources Policy Issues," *Law and Contemporary Problems*, 22 (Summer 1957), 476–477.

8. See, e.g., Charles A. Reich, "The Public and the Nation's Forests," *California Law Review*, 50 (August 1962), 381–407.

9. *Water Resources and Power*, I, 5.

10. See, e.g., Paul S. Taylor, "Excess Land Law on the Kern?" *California Law Review*, 46 (May 1958), 153–184.

11. Arthur A. Maass, "The Kings River Project," in Harold Stein, ed., *Public Administration and Policy Development: A Casebook* (New York: Harcourt, Brace & World, Inc., 1952), pp. 533–572.

12. *The New York Times*, April 5, 1962.

13. William L. Rivers, "The Politics of Pollution," *The Reporter*, 24 (March 30, 1961), 36.

14. *Ibid.*, p. 34.

15. Surgeon General Dr. Luther L. Terry, quoted in *The New York Times*, April 2, 1964.

16. See U.S. Congress, Senate, Committee on Government Operations, *Government Competition with Private Enterprise*, Committee Print, 88th Cong., 1st Sess., June 21, 1963 (Washington, D.C.: 1963).

17. *The New York Times*, April 23, 1964.

18. *Ibid.*, April 21, 1964.

19. *Government Competition with Private Enterprise*, pp. 47–51.

20. *Ibid.*, p. 9.

21. *Sacramento Bee*, July 1, 1964.

22. For fuller descriptions, see the *Government Organization Manual*, issued annually by the Government Printing Office, Washington, D.C.

23. There is one other corporation, not quasi-commercial: the Smithsonian Institution.

24. Harold Seidman, "The Government Corporation in the United States," *Public Administration*, 37 (Summer 1959), 103–114.

25. *The New York Times*, September 14, 1963.

26. *Sacramento Bee*, March 12, 1964.

27. U.S. Department of Health, Education, and Welfare, Social Security Administration, *Social Security in the United States* (Washington, D.C.: 1959), p. 30.

28. Congressional Quarterly Service, *Current American Government* (Washington, D.C.: 1964), pp. 69–70.

29. U.S. Department of Health, Education, and Welfare, *Grants-in-Aid and Other Financial Assistance Programs Administered by the U.S. Department of Health, Education, and Welfare, 1963 Edition* (Washington, D.C.: 1963), pp. 153–247.

30. Charles I. Schottland, *The Social Security Program in the United States* (New York: Appleton-Century-Crofts, Inc., 1963), and Schottland, "Where Are We in This Business of Social Security?" *California Law Review*, 46 (August 1958), 315–330.

31. The Advisory Council on Social Security, *The Status of the Social Security Program and Recommendations for Its Improvement* (Washington, D.C.: 1965), p. 7.

32. *Ibid.*, p. 22.

33. Joseph M. Becker, "Twenty-Five Years of Unemployment Insurance: An Experiment in Competitive Collectivism," *Political Science Quarterly*, 75 (December 1960), 481–499.

34. U.S. Department of Labor, Bureau of Employment Security, *Unemployment Insurance: State Laws and Experience* (Washington, D.C.: 1963).

35. Schottland, *The Social Security Program in the United States,* p. 86.

36. Becker, "Twenty-Five Years of Unemployment Insurance," p. 492.

37. Two of his better-known works during this period were *A Treatise on Money,* 2 vols. (London: Harcourt, Brace & Co., Inc., 1930) and *The General Theory of Employment, Interest, and Money* (London: Harcourt, Brace & Co., Inc., 1936).

CHAPTER SEVEN

1. *The New York Times,* July 17, 1963.

2. *Ibid.,* September 23, 1962.

3. Daniel Marx, Jr., "The United States Eaters Export Credit Guarantee Competition," *Political Science Quarterly,* 78 (June 1963), 245–272.

4. *The New York Times,* July 4, 1964.

5. "The Global Stake of U.S. Business," *Fortune,* 68 (December 1963), 129.

6. *Ibid.,* and *Lansing State Journal,* October 11, 1962.

7. Andreas G. Papandreou and John T. Wheeler, *Competition and Its Regulation* (New York: Prentice-Hall, Inc., 1954), p. 489.

8. *The New York Times,* July 16, 1964.

9. Hearing before the House Committee on Banking and Currency on H.R. 12267 and H.R. 12268, 88th Cong., 2nd Sess., August 12, 1964 (Washington, D.C.: 1964), p. 37.

10. See, e.g., David G. Wood, "How Businessmen Can Fight 'Big Government'—and Win," *Harper's Magazine,* 227 (November 1963), 78–81.

11. "Public Opinion: New Sovereign Power," speech by Harold Brayman, Director of Public Relations, E. I. du Pont de Nemours & Company, at the opening session of the Sixteenth National Conference, Public Relations Society of America, San Francisco, California, November 18, 1963.

12. For some implications, see Dow Votaw, "The Politics of a Changing Corporate Society," *California Management Review,* 3 (Spring 1961), 105–118.

13. The President's Commission on National Goals, *Goals for Americans* (Englewood Cliffs, N.J.: Prentice-Hall, Inc., 1960), p. 9.

14. Arthur M. Schlesinger, Sr., "Tides of American Politics," *The Yale Review,* 29 (December 1939), 217–230.

15. Speech in the U.S. Senate, August 1919, excerpted in Thomas G. Manning, David M. Potter, and Wallace E. Davies, *Government and the American Economy, 1870–Present* (New York: Henry Holt & Company, 1950), p. 12.

16. From Louis D. Brandeis *Business—A Profession* (Boston: Small, Maynard & Co., 1914) and reprinted *ibid.,* p. 20.

17. Editorial in the *American Federationist,* reprinted *ibid.,* p. 23.

18. Editorial, *The New York Times,* August 7, 1964.

19. *Sacramento Bee,* August 8, 1963.

20. Douglass Cater, "The Politics of Poverty," *The Reporter,* 30 (February 13, 1964), 17.

21. John Davenport, "In the Midst of Plenty," *Fortune,* 64 (March 1961), 107.

22. The former was published in New York by The Macmillan Co. in 1962, the latter in Boston by Little, Brown & Co. in 1963.

23. Irving Kristol, "Is the Welfare State Obsolete?" *Harper's Magazine,* 226 (June 1963), 39–43.

24. Andrew Hacker, "Again the Issue of 'The Welfare State,' " *The New York Times Magazine,* March 22, 1964, pp. 9ff.

25. Gunnar Myrdal, *Challenge to Affluence* (New York: Random House, 1963).

BIBLIOGRAPHICAL ESSAY

The subject matter dealt with in this volume is too broad in scope to permit more than the listing of a comparative handful of sources in this brief space. The essay names only books dating from the mid-1940's; it omits books referred to in the footnotes, as well as government documents and periodical articles.

Those readers who seek an overview of changing attitudes toward promoting the general welfare may find Sidney Fine's *Laissez Faire and the General Welfare State* (Ann Arbor: University of Michigan Press, 1956) of considerable interest, especially since it contains an extensive bibliography. The intellectual ferment that resulted from the challenge of industrialism is depicted in a great variety of works dealing with American economic and intellectual history since about 1880. A few examples are Henry Steele Commager, *The American Mind* (New Haven: Yale University Press, 1950); Harold Underwood Faulkner, *The Quest for Social Justice, 1898–1914* (New York: The Macmillan Co., 1931) and *The Decline of Laissez Faire, 1897–1917* (New York: Rinehart & Company, 1951); Richard Hofstadter, *Social Darwinism in American Thought, 1860–1915* (Philadelphia: University of Pennsylvania Press, 1944); and Samuel P. Hays, *The Response to Industrialism: 1885–1914* (Chicago: University of Chicago Press, 1957). A factual study of the federal government's expansion is Solomon Fabricant, *The Trend of Government Activity Since 1900* (New York: National Bureau of Economic Research, 1953). Books dealing with the implications for our democracy of industrialism and governmental responses to it are abundant. Still the best known may be Friedrich A. Hayek, *The Road to Serfdom* (Chicago: University of Chicago Press, 1944); an angry answer is given by Herman Finer in *The Road to Reaction* (Boston: Little, Brown & Co., 1945) and a reasoned one in John M. Clark, *Alternative to Serfdom* (New York: Alfred A. Knopf, Inc., 1948). Clark's collection of essays, *Economic Institutions and Human Welfare* (New York: Alfred A. Knopf, Inc., 1957), is thought provoking. In *The Constitution of Liberty* (Chicago: University of Chicago Press, 1960), Hayek argues that the ideal of freedom is imperiled by the search for "distributive" justice. That attitudes toward the propriety of governmental action often depend upon whose ox is being gored is emphasized by Walter Gellhorn, *Individual Freedom and Governmental Restraints* (Baton Rouge: Louisiana State University Press, 1956). An argument for closer coordination between government and the economy in policy-making is contained in *The New American Political Economy: A Synthesis of Politics and Economics* (New York: Harper & Row, 1962) by Marshall E. Dimock.

The evolving nature of American capitalism is the theme of such works as Peter Drucker, *The New Society* (New York: Harper & Brothers, 1950); Adolf A. Berle, *The 20th Century Capitalist Revolution* (New York: Harcourt, Brace & World, Inc., 1954) and *Power Without Property* (New York: Harcourt, Brace & World, Inc., 1959); Gardiner C. Means, *The Corporate Revolution in America: Economic Reality vs. Economic Theory* (Cambridge, Mass.: Harvard University Press, 1960); Thomas C. Cochran, *The American Business System: A Historical Perspective, 1900–1955* (Cambridge, Mass.: Harvard University Press, 1957); and F. X. Sutton, et al., *The American Business Creed* (Cambridge, Mass.: Harvard University Press, 1956). John K. Galbraith's idea that corporate strength is offset by "countervailing power," elaborated in his *American Capitalism: The Concept of Countervailing Power* (Boston: Houghton Mifflin Co., 1956), is critically discussed in various books, two recent examples being Michael D. Reagan, *The Managed Economy* (New York: Oxford University Press, 1963) and Bernard K. Nossiter, *The Mythmakers* (Boston: Houghton Mifflin Co., 1964). Galbraith's thesis that the public sector of the economy has been neglected in favor of the private sphere is set forth in *The Affluent Society* (Boston: Houghton Mifflin Co., 1958). Public subsidies to the private sphere and the utilization of public controls by business and labor groups for their own self-advancement are cited by Paul K. Crosser as evidence of *State Capitalism in the Economy of the United States* (New York: Bookman Associates, Inc., 1960).

The thesis that regulated groups are adept at turning controls into sanctions for their own benefit is well presented in Walton Hamilton, *The Politics of Industry* (Ann Arbor: University of Michigan Press, 1957). This "guild effect" is related to a life cycle for regulatory commissions in Marver H. Bernstein, *Regulating Business by Independent Commissions* (Princeton, N.J.: Princeton University Press, 1955). Emmette S. Redford has presented the broad structural outlines of government regulation in *Administration of National Economic Control* (New York: The Macmillan Co., 1952). Constitutional struggles over governmental authority to deal with economic problems are described in Carl Brent Swisher, *American Constitutional Development*, 2nd ed. (Boston: Houghton Mifflin Co., 1954). Henry J. Friendly in *The Federal Administrative Agencies: The Need for Better Definition of Standards* (Cambridge, Mass.: Harvard University Press, 1962) has revealed something of the procedural complexities of regulation.

Specific areas of the economy and their relationship to the federal government are dealt with in a variety of volumes, although some areas have been covered much more extensively than others. Business competition and its regulation are the source of an endless stream of volumes. Much of the ferment has turned on the implications of bigness in industry, and on this point there have been some surprises in the sources of views. Thus, David Lilienthal, the former head of TVA, endorsed bigness in his *Big Business: A New Era* (New York: Harper & Brothers, 1953), while T. K. Quinn, a former executive for General Electric, wrote *Giant Business: A Threat to Democracy* (New York: The Exposition Press, Inc., 1953). Contrasting approaches are also found in A. D. H. Kaplan, *Big Enterprise in a Competitive Economy* (Washington, D.C.: The Brookings Institution, 1954)

and Walter Adams and Horace M. Gray, *Monopoly in America* (New York: The Macmillan Co., 1955). Examples of broad-gauged discussions of antitrust problems are Carl Kaysen and Donald F. Turner, *Antitrust Policy: An Economic and Legal Analysis* (Cambridge, Mass.: Harvard University Press, 1959) and Edward S. Mason, *Economic Concentration and the Monopoly Problem* (Cambridge, Mass.: Harvard University Press, 1959). The view that government should take over and operate all industries in which it is impossible to effectively maintain competitive conditions was put forth by Henry C. Simons in *Economic Policy for a Free Society* (Chicago: University of Chicago Press, 1948) as the logical position of an economist who dislikes governmental activity in the economic sphere but is loyal to the tenets of classical economic liberalism. Two books that discuss and evaluate the Robinson-Patman Act are Corwin D. Edwards, *The Price Discrimination Law: A Review of Experience* (Washington, D.C.: The Brookings Institution, 1959) and Joseph C. Palamountain, Jr., *The Politics of Distribution* (Cambridge, Mass.: Harvard University Press, 1955); the latter also deals with related statutes.

Dilemmas in the regulation of public utilities are well documented in Martin G. Glaeser, *Public Utilities in American Capitalism* (New York: The Macmillan Co., 1957) and G. Lloyd Wilson, *Transportation and Communication* (New York: Appleton-Century-Crofts, Inc., 1954). The intricacies of *The Regulation of Rail-Motor Rate Competition* (New York: Harper & Row, 1958) are dealt with by Ernest W. Williams, and *The Politics of Railroad Coordination, 1933-1936* (Cambridge, Mass.: Harvard University Press, 1959) by Earl Latham. Maritime regulations are reviewed in Carl E. McDowell and Helen M. Gibbs, *Ocean Transportation* (New York: McGraw-Hill Book Co., 1954). The battle between scheduled airlines and the "non-skeds" is detailed in Lucile S. Keyes, *Federal Control of Entry into Air Transportation* (Cambridge, Mass.: Harvard University Press, 1951). That domestic airlines should have less economic regulation is argued by Richard E. Caves in *Air*

Transporters and Its Regulators: An Industry Study (Cambridge, Mass.: Harvard University Press, 1962). Proposals for a *National Transportation Policy* (Washington, D.C.: The Brookings Institution, 1949) were set forth by Charles L. Dearing and Wilfred Owen. Jacob M. Edelman has written of the complicated background of *The Licensing of Radio Services in the United States, 1927 to 1947* (Urbana: University of Illinois Press, 1950). A more recent reference, bringing in the subject of television regulation, is *Broadcasting and Government: Responsibilities and Regulations* (East Lansing: Michigan State University, 1961) by Walter B. Emery. Recent books dealing with government and the investor are limited in number. A relatively recent survey of the topic is *The Watchdogs of Wall Street* (New York: William Morrow & Company, Inc., 1962) by Hillel Black. A three-volume work by Louis Loss, *Securities Regulation*, 2nd ed. (Boston: Little, Brown & Co., 1961) contains a systematic treatment of a technical subject.

A long perspective on agricultural programs is provided by Murray R. Benedict's *Farm Policies of the United States, 1790–1950* (New York: Twentieth Century Fund, 1953). Don Paarlberg has described more recent farm programs in simplified terms in *American Farm Policy: A Case Study of Centralized Decision-Making* (New York: John Wiley & Sons, Inc., 1964). Books that have stimulated much postwar thinking about agricultural policy include David G. Johnson, *Forward Prices for Agriculture* (Chicago: University of Chicago Press, 1947); Theodore W. Shultz, *Production and Welfare of Agriculture* (New York: The Macmillan Co., 1949); and Willard W. Cochrane, *Farm Prices: Myth and Reality* (Minneapolis: University of Minnesota Press, 1958). The subtleties of farm surpluses are discussed in Lauren Soth, *Farm Trouble* (Princeton, N.J.: Princeton University Press, 1957) and William H. Peterson, *The Great Farm Problem* (Chicago: Henry Regnery Co., 1959). Good insights into the policy-making process may be found in Charles M. Hardin, *The Politics of Agriculture: Soil Conservation and the Struggle for Power in Rural America* (Glencoe, Ill.: The Free Press, 1952) and Wesley McCune, *Who's Behind Our Farm Policy* (New York: Frederick A. Praeger, Inc., 1956). Two works dealing with agriculture's place in the economy are Grant McConnell, *The Decline of Agrarian Democracy* (Berkeley: University of California Press, 1953) and Walter W. Wilcox, *Social Responsibility in Farm Leadership* (New York: Harper & Row, 1956).

Works giving some background for governmental activity in the fields of labor, agriculture, and consumer protection are numerous. A comprehensive discussion of industrial relations policies and practices in their stormiest period is provided by Harry A. Millis and Emily Brown in *From the Wagner Act to Taft-Hartley* (Chicago: University of Chicago Press, 1950). How the Landrum-Griffin Act of 1959 came to be enacted is told by Alan K. McAdams in *Power and Politics in Labor Legislation* (New York: Columbia University Press, 1964). Specific policy and problem areas are dealt with in Herman M. Somers' *Workmen's Compensation* (New York: John Wiley & Sons, Inc., 1954) and in Joseph M. Becker's *The Problem of Abuse in Unemployment* (New York: Columbia University Press, 1953). The place of organized labor in the American scheme has been dealt with from a variety of points of view: Charles Lindblom, *Unions and Capitalism* (New Haven, Conn.: Yale University Press, 1949); Frank Tannenbaum, *A Philosophy of Labor* (New York: Alfred A. Knopf, Inc., 1951); John A. Fitch, *Social Responsibilities of Organized Labor* (New York: Harper & Row, 1957); Carroll R. Daugherty, *The Labor Problems of American Society* (Boston: Houghton Mifflin Co., 1952); Edward H. Chamberlain, *et al.*, *Labor Unions and Public Policy* (Washington, D.C.: The Brookings Institution, 1958); and Michael Harrington and Paul Jacobs, eds., *Labor in a Free Society* (Berkeley: University of California Press, 1959).

Books on the subject of government buying are scarce, unlike congressional and executive reports. Two good basic sources are Dickson Reck, *Government Purchasing and Competition* (Berkeley: University of California Press, 1954) and John Perry Miller, *Pricing of Military Procurements* (New Haven, Conn.: Yale University Press, 1949). The important subject of *Government Contracting in Atomic Energy* (Ann Arbor: University of Michigan Press, 1956) was dealt with well by Richard Tybout. A place to start in understanding procurement for the space program is *The National Aeronautics and Space Act* (Washington, D.C.: Public Affairs Press, 1962) by Alison Griffith. There have been a number of books on the new importance of scientists in governmental circles; two relatively recent ones are Robert Gilpin and Christopher Wright, eds., *Scientists and National Policy-Making* (New York: Columbia University Press, 1964) and Robert Gilpin, *American Scientists and Nuclear Weapons Policy* (Princeton, N.J.: Princeton University Press, 1962).

Consumer protection is dealt with systematically in consumer economics textbooks, but the selection of other volumes is spotty. Jessie V. Coles has argued well the case for *Standards and Labels for Consumer Goods* (New York: The Ronald Press Company, 1949). The background of food and drug regulation is detailed in *The Impact of the Food and Drug Administration on Our Society* (New York: MD Publications, 1956) by Henry Welch and Felix Martí-Ibáñez and in *The Health of a Nation* (Chicago: University of Chicago Press, 1958) by Oscar E. Anderson, Jr. A book indignantly reporting the difficulties encountered in enacting a drug control law until the thalidomide scare changed the political climate is Richard Harris, *The Real Voice* (New York: The Macmillan Co., 1964). An interesting historical study of American attitudes is *People of Plenty: Economic Abundance and the American Character* (Chicago: University of Chicago Press, 1954) by David M. Potter.

A thorough study of one aspect of government's early role as promoter is Carter Goodrich's *Government Promotion of American Canals and Railroads, 1800–1890* (New York: Columbia University Press, 1960). The influence of governmental grants upon the economy is set forth in James A.

Maxwell, *Federal Grants and the Business Cycle* (Princeton, N.J.: Princeton University Press, 1952).

Government's role as manager has been better documented in some areas than in others. Natural resources policy has been the preoccupation of many writers. The struggle to establish conservation policies has been graphically described in David C. Coyle, *Conservation: An American Story of Conflict and Accomplishment* (New Brunswick, N.J.: Rutgers University Press, 1957). Wallace Stegner has chronicled the efforts of a pioneer conservationist in *Beyond the Hundredth Meridian: John Wesley Powell and the Second Opening of the West* (Boston: Houghton Mifflin Co., 1954). The conflict over public lands and forests is set forth in such books as Marion Clawson, *Uncle Sam's Acres* (New York: Dodd, Mead & Co., Inc., 1951); E. Louise Peffer, *The Closing of the Public Domain* (Stanford: Stanford University Press, 1951); and two books about Gifford Pinchot, his autobiography, *Breaking New Ground* (New York: Harcourt, Brace & World, Inc., 1947) and *Gifford Pinchot: Forester-Politician* (Princeton, N.J.: Princeton University Press, 1960) by M. Nelson McGeary. Public policies for public lands and forests are reviewed in Marion Clawson and Burnell Held, *The Federal Lands: Their Use and Management* (Baltimore: Johns Hopkins Press, 1957) and Luther H. Gulick, *American Forest Policy* (New York: Duell, Sloan & Pearce, Inc., 1951). Some interesting administrative studies in these areas are Herbert Kaufman, *The Forest Ranger* (Baltimore: Johns Hopkins Press, 1960); Philip O. Foss, *Politics and Grass* (Seattle: University of Washington Press, 1960); and Ashley L. Schiff, *Fire and Water: Scientific Heresy in the Forest Service* (Cambridge, Mass.: Harvard University Press, 1962). A critical case study of conservation policy in action is *Politics and Conservation: The Decline of the Alaska Salmon* (New York: Harper & Row, 1963) by Richard A. Cooley. Books on water resources development are plentiful, especially for the Tennessee Valley Authority. *Irrigation Development and Public Water Policy* (New York: The Ronald

Press Company, 1953) by Roy E. Huffman covers one important area. A quick introduction to the rivalry of two leading water agencies is provided by Arthur Maass in *Muddy Waters* (Cambridge, Mass.: Harvard University Press, 1951). Vincent Ostrom's *Water and Politics* (Los Angeles: Haynes Foundation, 1953) is a systematic study of water resources policy and administration. Interesting studies of the struggle over river basins are Roscoe C. Martin, *et al., River Basin Administration and the Delaware* (Syracuse, N.Y.: Syracuse University Press, 1960); William E. Leuchtenberg, *Flood Control Politics: The Connecticut River Valley Problem* (Cambridge, Mass.: Harvard University Press, 1953); and Henry C. Hart, *The Dark Missouri* (Madison: University of Wisconsin Press, 1957). A collection of essays entitled *TVA: The First Twenty Years* (University, Ala.: University of Alabama Press, 1956), edited by Roscoe C. Martin, gives some idea of the various activities of the best-known federal water development and can serve as an introduction to other volumes. A highly controversial incident involving an aspect of policy for the TVA is explained in Jason L. Finkle, *The President Makes a Decision: A Study of Dixon-Yates* (Ann Arbor: University of Michigan Press, 1960) and in Aaron Wildavsky, *Dixon-Yates: A Study in Power Politics* (New Haven, Conn.: Yale University Press, 1962).

Book-length public ownership studies, plentiful in the 1930's, are now almost nonexistent. R. J. Saulnier, *et al., Federal Lending and Loan Insurance* (Princeton, N.J.: Princeton University Press, 1957) deals with an important federal activity conducted in part by public corporations. The development of public housing policy in a large metropolis is explained well in *Politics, Planning and the Public Interest* (New York: The Free Press of Glencoe, 1955) by Martin Meyerson and Edward C. Banfield. Another level of governmental jurisdiction figures in Robert E. Firth's *Public Power in Nebraska: A Report on State Ownership* (Lincoln: University of Nebraska Press, 1962).

Social welfare management is another area in which books are plentiful. Margaret S. Gordon in *The Economics of Welfare Politics* (New York: Columbia University Press, 1963) has traced the growth of governmental expenditures for public welfare and compared and related them to private programs in the United States and to programs in other countries. An argument for concerning public welfare statutes and regulations more in enabling than restraining terms is found in Elizabeth Wickendon and Winifred Bell, *Public Welfare: Time for a Change* (New York: The New York School of Social Work, 1961). Somewhat dated descriptions of social insurance in the United States are provided by Eveline M. Burns, *The American Social Security System* (Boston: Houghton Mifflin Co., 1959) and by Domenico Gagliardo, *American Social Insurance* (New York: Harper & Brothers, 1949). A posthumous publication by the "father" of the Social Security Act, Edwin E. Witte, *The Development of the Social Security Act* (Madison: University of Wisconsin Press, 1962), is of historical interest. The controversy over government health plans is presented from various points of view by Herman M. Somers and Anne R. Somers, *Doctors, Patients and Health Insurance* (Washington, D.C.: The Brookings Institution, 1961); Seymour E. Harris, *National Health Insurance and Alternative Plans for Financing Health* (New York: League for Industrial Democracy, 1953); O. D. Dickerson, Jr., *Health Insurance* (Homewood, Ill.: Richard D. Irwin, Inc., 1959); Freddy Homburger, *Medical Care for the Aged and Chronically Ill* (Boston: Little, Brown & Co., 1955); and J. H. Means, *Doctors, People and Government* (Boston: Little, Brown & Co., 1953).

Government policy for economic stabilization and growth has come in for an increasing amount of discussion, though its extent can be only briefly indicated here. Useful studies of the management of money and credit are G. L. Bach, *Federal Reserve Policy-Making: A Study in Government Economic Policy Formation* (New York: Alfred A. Knopf, Inc., 1950); A. E. Holmans, *United States Fiscal Policy, 1945–1959* (New York: Oxford University Press, 1961); Paul J. Strayer, *Fiscal Policy and*

Politics (New York: Harper & Row, 1958); and James A. Maxwell, *Fiscal Policy: Its Techniques and Institutional Setting* (New York: Henry Holt & Company, 1955). The early operations of the President's Council of Economic Advisers were reviewed by its first chairman, Edwin G. Nourse, in *Economics in the Public Service: Administrative Aspects of the Employment Act* (New York: Harcourt, Brace & World, Inc., 1953). How this statute evolved is interestingly told in Stephen K. Bailey, *Congress Makes a Law: The Story Behind the Employment Act of 1946* (New York: Columbia University Press, 1950). Gunnar Myrdal in *Challenge to Affluence* (New York: Pantheon Books, Inc., 1963) has offered a strong challenge to the notion of the adequacy of recent economic policy in meeting today's needs for economic growth and for the eradication of poverty. Hobart Rowen in *The Free Enterprisers: Kennedy, Johnson and the Business Establishment* (New York: G. P. Putnam's Sons, 1964) has argued that government measures for economic stabilization should include increased government spending as well as a tax cut.